Mrs. C.M Day

History of the Eastern Townships

Province of Quebec, Dominion of Canada, civil and descriptive

Mrs. C.M Day

History of the Eastern Townships
Province of Quebec, Dominion of Canada, civil and descriptive

ISBN/EAN: 9783337186685

Printed in Europe, USA, Canada, Australia, Japan

Cover: Foto ©ninafisch / pixelio.de

More available books at **www.hansebooks.com**

HISTORY

OF THE

EASTERN TOWNSHIPS,

PROVINCE OF QUEBEC, DOMINION OF CANADA,

Civil and Descriptive.

IN THREE PARTS.

By MRS. C. M. DAY.

Montreal:
PRINTED BY JOHN LOVELL, ST. NICHOLAS STREET.
1869.

PREFACE.

An apology is due for the non-appearance of the following work at the time expected. Suffice it to say that the delay in its preparation and issue, has been the result of unforeseen and unavoidable circumstances.

Part First of the book contains a brief sketch of the discovery of America; the colonization of Canada by the French; its state up to the conquest; a short account of that event, and a reference to important changes that have transpired from time to time. Also, a synopsis of the civil history of Canada, including notice of the several organic changes occurring in the Government of the country. This has been drawn from the histories extant; from public records; and from such authenticated documents as have been issued at various times; and may therefore be considered a condensed compilation rather than an original production.

Part Second contains a series of miscellaneous chapters, very small portions of which have before been published. They relate principally to the aborigines of our own section; the earliest explorations and general opening up of the country for settlement; the conditions on which lands were granted; the method of erecting townships; and finally, the difficulties, perils, and privations, encountered by the early settlers. It also includes some account of the north-eastern extension of territory attached to the Eastern Townships; presents some of the advantages offered by Canada to the intending emigrant; and also gives a summary of the mineral wealth found in the region.

Part Third gives short Historical Sketches of each Township within the Districts of Bedford and St. Francis, with brief notices of many individuals who have been prominently interested in their early settlement. Such incidents and adventures as are proper to embody in a work of this nature are also given.

These pages are designed to supply a want that has been felt and regretted by many among our people, as in much that has been written on Canada, our own section, if considered at all worthy of mention, has been brought into notice in a very equivocal and unsatisfactory manner. Little doubt is therefore felt that any well-directed effort to fill that want, will meet with approval.

Circumstances have seemed to require a departure from the original plan of giving separate and detailed accounts of the erection and settlement of each township in succession; for it will be observed that in all the general business relating to this, what is true of the one seems nearly or quite applicable to the many, and to avoid tiresome and uninteresting repetition, a general and comprehensive account has been given of the usual methods of procedure.

In the compilation of Part First, the language as well as facts of other authors have been freely used without formal acknowledgment by quotation marks. The author's ambition has been the preparation and presentation of a work that shall prove acceptable to our own people, and a source of reliable information to strangers coming among us; and if these humble efforts shall meet with an approval at all commensurate with the interest that has prompted and directed them, it will prove a source of unfeigned satisfaction.

Waterloo, Nov. 10th, 1868.

INTRODUCTION.

It is well understood that Canadian authors have very generally failed to enlist the sympathy and encouragement of the reading public of our country; but the reason of this indifference may not be so apparent to the casual observer. Yet it is but too certain that the direct effect of this has been to chill and repress the growth of native talent, and to retard the much-to-be desired period, when party and sectional feelings and jealousies shall be merged in a broad and comprehensive Canadian nationality.

An "Introductory Essay," prefixed to a volume of "Poems from Canadian Authors," which was published in Montreal some few years since, contains so much that is sensible and just, and withal so relevant to the subject under consideration, that it has been largely drawn from in the preparation of a short introductory chapter.

The importance of encouraging and building up a literature decidedly Canadian, commends itself to the intelligent and patriotic, with all the strength of conviction. A national literature is an essential element in the formation of a national character; a fact confirmed by all history; for among the nations of antiquity, the fame of poet, philosopher, hero or statesman, belonged to the people : was celebrated by them in story and in song; was incorporated into the national heart, and became a strong bond of national unity. So also has it been in later ages of the world.

Foremost in the array of antagonistic influences which have operated to discourage efforts at forming a Canadian literature, are those arising from national prejudices and religious animosities. That so many elements are combined in our population, has been considered Canada's greatest weakness; as it is thought thus to contain within itself the germs of disintegration and disunion. Hence the necessity of a strong counteracting influence in a literature freed from the trammels of partisan bigotry.

It is perfectly reasonable and natural that those who come to our shores from the old world, should look back with lingering affection and veneration to the land of their fathers, or dwell with tender and regretful emotion on the endearing name and memories of "Home," or yet, that they should feel a pardonable pride in its time-honored institutions and associations; but that an intense national prejudice amounting to bitterness and leading to discord and strife, should usurp the place of those holier feelings, is greatly to be deplored.

And yet such is often the case. These people seem to think their only duty in the land of their adoption, is to point out defects, and appear not to think of having assumed any obligations, or that they are at all identified with its interests.

Another reason of the coldness and indifference with which literary effort is regarded by many among us, is that the greater number of our people are necessarily engaged in either commercial, mechanical, or agricultural pursuits, and are so absorbed in business cares as to possess little leisure to cultivate a taste for reading. There is no question that this operates unfavorably; yet back of it lie other and still more untoward influences, originating in the narrow and superficial views that prevail, to a great extent, respecting our intellectual wants. People think that because so many books are already written, further literary effort is unnecessary, and to encourage it is but a waste of time and money. This idea—as mistaken as it is common—completely ignores the fact that in all progress and improvement, books are the circulating medium through which mind communicates with mind, and are not only essential as records of all scientific discoveries, but of all progress in the arts; of all historical events; and, in short, of all permanent expression of thought. And as regards the superfluity of books complained of, those which are really unnecessary and unprofitable, would soon find the proper level, were an understanding and judicious discrimination cultivated and practiced among those who purchase and read.

The equally erroneous and wide-spread impression,

that because we may be fully supplied with books and periodicals, from other countries, it is useless and absurd to attempt establishing a literature of our own, may be considered as already disposed of in our reference to the necessity there exists for that union which gives strength, and the importance of harmonizing the discordant elements among us.

The truth is but little realized in this world of hurry and encroachment, that true merit is often far removed from obtrusiveness and self-seeking; and that real talent is usually, if not always, allied with a delicacy and refinement of feeling that instinctively shrinks from contact with coldness and distrust, while it seeks in other walks the reward to which it is legitimately entitled, leaving the field to less gifted and, perhaps, less susceptible minds.

These are some of the more prominent causes which have prevented the due appreciation and encouragement of native talent; and repressed the ardor of Canadian Authors. But if we rightly interpret the signs of the times, there is a growing conviction in the minds of the observing and clear-thinking of our people, that the evils to which we are unavoidably subjected, should find counteraction in a patriotic literature based on loyal sentiment and intelligent appreciation. Were the truth properly kept before the minds of our people, accepted and adopted by them, that Canadians of all origins and creeds, should merge minor differences in a nationality where all might meet on common ground ; and were the pulpit, press and schoolroom rightly enlisted in forming correct standards of thought and action on this subject, we should soon witness improvement in a matter that vitally concerns us as a people.

An affection amounting even to enthusiasm for the government and institutions of our country, is not only excusable but worthy of approval. Patriotism is a sort of political piety : something more than a careless assent or a passive obedience to the laws of the land. It has its seat in the heart rather than the head, and is an elevating and ennobling principle. The real lover of his country will never seek to evade his responsibilities as a citizen: no considerations of personal advantage or private interest will induce him to compromise his allegiance. He feels that in claiming the protection of laws, he binds himself to a ready and willing submission to them, and an acquiescence in whatever measures the authorities may find it necessary to enforce. It may not be possible always to approve legislation, and the rights of opinion are assured; yet the object we should all hold sacred, is the consolidation and perpetuation of our nationality, and this is high above all the means used to effect it.

Part First.

CHAPTER I.

AN ATALANTIS.—PORTUGAL.—COLUMBUS.—SPAIN.—SUCCESSFUL VOYAGE OF COLUMBUS.—SUBSEQUENT HUMILIATIONS, DEATH AND BURIAL.—MISTAKES OF THE AGE.—SPANISH AND PORTUGUESE CONQUESTS.—DISCOVERIES UNDER THE AUSPICES OF THE FRENCH.—CARTIER'S EXPEDITIONS.—ABANDONMENT OF CANADA.—DEATH OF THE FRENCH KING.

THERE is evidence that before the discovery of the New World by Columbus, the ancients and early navigators suspected the existence of land intervening between the western coast of Spain and the rich eastern country with which the civilized nations of Europe then held commercial intercourse; but they could have had no properly conceived ideas of its location, size or importance. The traditions of the Egyptians, Carthagenians, and some of the nations of northern Europe, all point to the fact that a numerous and powerful people inhabited a vast island to the west of the " Pillars of Hercules," as the Straits of Gibraltar were then called.*

Portugal, though one of the smaller Kingdoms of Europe, then held a prominent position and was a leading power in the cause of discovery and exploration. The success of their mariners had drawn the attention of other nations, and numerous adventurers repaired thither; among whom was Christopher Columbus who reached Lisbon in 1470.

This remarkable man, whose name is for all time connected with the annals of the New World, was born at Genoa, Italy, in 1435. At an early age he showed a preference for a sea-faring life, and an aptitude for acquiring geographical knowledge. Being in humble circumstances his father could do little for him, and at the age of fourteen we hear of young Christopher as a boy mariner. Little is known of his experiences as such, but that little is favorable. On his arrival in Lisbon, he took service with the Portuguese King, and was thus thrown into frequent and intimate relations with several of the most eminent scientific men of the age, and with those navigators who had taken part in the voyages and discoveries which had already made Portugal famous. Living thus in the society of enterprizing and aspiring spirits, and fully understanding the general anxiety for a more

---

* These traditions assume a semblance of reality when taken in connection with the accounts of discoveries made in later times, by explorers in Central and Southern America.

direct access to India or Cathay, he had become ambitious of discovering a western route.

His first application for assistance was made to the Portuguese King, who unwisely refused the necessary help. He next turned his longing eyes on•Spain; and in 1484, set out for Madrid to make Ferdinand and Isabella, then on the united throne of Castile and Arragon, the same proposals. He was for a long time unsuccessful; but during eight years of fruitless solicitations, though regarded as an impracticable visionary, he retained a firm confidence in the soundness of his own views, and the feasibility of his plans.

Their Spanish Majesties finally gave in to the project, and placed a flotilla of three small vessels at his disposal, with which he sailed from Spain in August, 1492; and on the 70th day, came in sight of land. This proved to be one of the group now known as the Bahamas, then called Guanahani by the natives, but named San Salvador by Columbus. He took possession of this and others, including St. Domingo and Cuba, in the name of the Spanish monarchs. On his return, the King and Queen received him at a Royal Sitting, and for a time both rulers and people delighted to do him honor. A patent of Nobility was at once made out for him and his posterity.

News of this discovery created an immense sensation throughout Europe, and roused the emulation of other nations. Columbus afterward made three voyages to the New World, each time adding to his discoveries;

but bitter disappointment and grievous humiliation awaited him, when on one of them he was made a prisoner and *sent back to Spain in fetters;* and thus instead of the rewards and honors which were his just due, he was allowed to be victimized and ruined through the envy and machinations of enemies. After some years of suffering through courtly neglect, poverty and bodily pain, he died at Valladolid in Spain, May 20th, 1506. His body was first taken to Seville, then across the Atlantic to St. Domingo, and finally to Cuba, where it reposes under a monumental tomb in the cathedral at Havanna.

At this period of time the idea was universal that the new discoveries were but parts or were partaining to the continent of Asia, and hence the name West Indies; an error which was not corrected till the isthmus of Panama was crossed and the Pacific ocean discovered in 1513. By another grave mistake never likely to be corrected, the name America was given to the New World, from Amerigo Vespucci, who was sent by the Portuguese King to examine the new countries. He took a plausible and extensive, but superficial view of the whole, with a chart of the Brazilian coast; and thus through the presumption, skill and address, of an obscure drawer of charts, the New World missed taking its rightful name of Columbia.

While Columbus had been busied in prosecuting his researches in the vicinity of the Mexican Gulf, other Spanish and Portuguese navigators were making discoveries farther South. The attention of Spain was greatly given to the colonization of the West Indies, and to looking out these parts which promised the most ready returns in gold and silver. England was also in the field, and had sent out the Cabots in search of a north-west passage. As early as 1504, French subjects had discovered the bank and island of Newfoundland, but the French government claimed no interest in the New World before 1523.

At this period King Francis I, gave command of four vessels to Verrazani, a Florentine navigator in the French service, who made three voyages; on the last of which, vessels and crews were lost.

In 1534, the attention of the French King was again drawn to the subject of seeking to share with his brother monarchs in their golden and territorial acquisitions ; and to obtain a firm footing upon the main land of America, an armament was equipped and placed under the direction of Jacques Cartier, a skilful and experienced navigator.

Cartier sailed from St. Malo in 1534, and in 20 days reached the coast of Newfoundland, whence passing into the Gulf, he touched at some points and took possession in the name of the King. He also held some intercourse with the aborigines, two of whom embarked and returned with him to France. From these, he first learned of the great river, and in May, 1535, he made a second voyage, and guided by these Indians, entered the river which he named the St. Lawrence, and ascended to Stadaconé, an Indian village then occupying the site of Quebec. Resolving to winter in the country, he moored his vessels at the mouth of the stream now known as the St. Charles, when with canoes and several men he ascended the river to Hochelaga, where he found a considerable Indian town. He was kindly received and hospitably entertained by the natives, several of whom conducted him to the top of an eminence near, which he named Mount Royal; words which time and use have combined and modified into Montreal.

The party returned to their vessels at Stadaconé to pass the winter. In December, scurvy of a violent kind broke out among the men, twenty-five of whom died before April; the remainder being much reduced and debilitated. When too late to save the many lives so valuable to him, Cartier learned of a native remedy which speedily cured the survivors.* When spring opened they all returned to France, taking several natives with them, among whom was the Indian chief Donaconé.

On his arrival in France, Cartier found his native land plunged in war and distracted with both civil and religious dissensions; amid which troubles his presence was unheeded and his projects were disregarded; and thus for a period of years, no attention was given to French interests in America.

---

* A decoction of the spruce fir, which yields the well-known Canada Balsam.

About the year 1540, another attempt was made to revive them by a person high in position and influence named LaRoque, who asked and obtained the right and title to govern all the newly discovered countries in the King's name; when another expedition was sent out under Cartier. He was again obliged to winter in the country, but returned in the spring, taking his colonists with him. On his way out to sea, he met his superior with reinforcements and supplies, but nothing could induce his return to Canada.

It appears that on this arrival of colonists, the Indians, though not openly hostile, were yet averse to further intercourse with the strangers, and opposed to their settlement in the country. This was no doubt owing to a just resentment against the French for having carried off their countrymen and chief; which act on the part of Cartier and his associates, was both untimely and unwise, though in accordance with the spirit of the age. This feeling against the French was increased by the fact that, of the captives taken away, all had pined and died in the stranger's land, except one little girl; though accounts agree in saying that they were humanely treated. Roberval, who had been associated with LaRoque in the establishment and governorship of the colony, reached his destination safely, but failed in his attempts to found a permanent settlement, and on the breaking out of a war in Europe, was recalled with his colonists to France. King Francis I, died in March 1547.

CHAPTER II.

THE ABORIGINES OF NORTH AMERICA.—DIVISIONS INTO NATIONS AND TRIBES.—PERSONAL CHARACTERISTICS.—HABITS OF LIFE. —INTELLECTUAL CAPABILITIES.—PROBABLE ORIGIN.—INFLUENCE OF CLIMATE ON THE PHYSICAL NATURE OF MAN.— ABORIGINES OF CANADA.

WHEN European settlements were first commenced in America, the expanse of country between the Atlantic ocean and the Mississippi river, was occupied by tribes belonging to the eight great families or divisions of the Indian race, viz., the Algonquins, Hurons, Sioux, Cherokees, Catawbas, Uchées, Natchez, and Mobiles. These were considered substantive nations, because each spoke a language not understood by the others; whereas, individuals of the different tribes belonging to a nation, could understand the language of any other tribe of that nation.

In person the Indians are rather tall and slender, with frames indicating agility rather than strength; their faces wearing that stern expression natural to such as are dependent on the chase for a subsistence, and exposed to the vicissitudes of war. Their visages are rather round than oval; with high cheek bones; small but lustrous and deeply-set hazel eyes; narrow forehead; flattish nose; thick lips: black, straight, long, coarse hair; and beard wanting, owing to a custom of depilation, which is begun at an early age and continued through life, by the males. Such are the physical characteristics of the red men; to which it may be added that their bodily senses while denizens of the forest, are exquisitely keen. Their complexion is a reddish brown. When first known to Europeans they went almost naked in summer, but in winter were clothed in skins and furs. The chiefs and warriors were often grotesquely arrayed in such guise as was intended to give indication of their exploits in war or the chase. They were fond of painting or staining their bodies with real or imagined resemblances, in lively and varied colors; being extremely partial to a bright red. The hair was worn differently, many of them having head tufts of colored feathers or animal's hair arranged in the most fantastic ways. A pair of moccasins variously ornamented, composed the feet covering. The ears and septum of the nostrils were often pierced for affixing pendant objects, and bracelets of serpent's skin or wampum were worn on the h nation and tribe had their distinguishing symbols, and even families had their armorials or distinctive marks.

The only offensive weapons in use among them before the advent of Europeans, were the arrow and tomahawk. Their defensive armour was a sort of cuirass of light wood, or a buckler of cedar wood. In times of peace, the occupations of the men were chiefly hunting and fishing; and even the labor involved in these was put off, till hunger forced them to take to the woods for game, or the water for fish.

The ative *bourgades* or settlements were being constantly broken up, as they were obliged to move from place to place, as the game in the woods or the fish in the streams were either killed or driven away, and those parts of the wilderness had to be left to recover.

Without fixity of habitation there could, of course, be no governmental institutions worthy of the name, and none of the stability in their communities, requisite to security of life and property.

It was the unanimous opinion of those Europeans who first had intercourse with these Indians, that they had no religion as we understand that term; but though no religious worship existed among them, they made habitual offerings to departed or unseen existences, and were great believers in supernatural agencies.

Their *medicine* men pretended and were believed to be able to permit or prevent rain at will; to turn aside thunderbolts; predict events; ensure success in any undertaking; and were held in high estimation accordingly. They also undertook to heal wounds and cure diseases by the use of herbs, administered with superstitious ceremonies to enhance the curative virtues.

Their funeral observances were of a touching character. If a person of distinction had died, he was mourned over for days, and when the time of sepulture came, with peculiar and significant ceremonies the body was lowered into a deep grave lined with furs, covered over tenderly, and a memorial stone or other mark set up, to which were affixed divers votive articles as signs of esteem for the departed.

Females among the Indians, were the men's born slaves ; and as such did all the drudgery and servile work, outdoor labor included. To put hand to the latter, was beneath the dignity of a savage, and not only lowered his self-esteem, but degraded him in the eyes of his fellows.

Although reasonable causes for going to war could not often exist, hostilities among the tribes were very frequent. The very mention of a coming war, raised in the bosoms of the younger savages, an uncontrollable feeling of joy. Imaginary enemies palpitating and bleeding at their feet, caused a kind of sanguinary intoxication.

Questions respecting the mental capabilities of the red man have often been raised. Some reasoners draw explanatory and unfavorable inferences from the make of their skulls, the cast of their features, and even their complexion; but such suggestions are hypothetical, absurd, and unworthy of acceptance. How many generations had to pass away before the barbarians who inundated the Roman empire, were civilized and christianized ? and yet they settled among numerous and well policied populations, and were every where surrounded with monuments of art, scientific inventions, and all the products of genius and skill that had then existed. If, instead of this, they had found a wilderness to rove in, inhabited by wild animals only, how soon would they have raised themselves from the abyss of their degradation?

We know that central America was once the seat of civilization: the relics of cities that once stood proudly on the table lands of Mexico, reveal this fact; but when and by whom they were built, and how long they existed, are questions still unanswered. But taking into account the evidence and probabilities in the case, we must believe that the aborigines of the New World had their origin in the Old; that those of North America coming from the deserts of Tartary, were a people distinct from those who had reared the monuments and cities on the plains of Mexico ; and that the latter had been subjugated by the former, and if not exterminated, by becoming assimilated with them, had relapsed into barbarism. It would be impossible to conceive in reality, of a greater similitude between two peoples, separated so long in time and so far removed in space, than we find between the American savages and Asiatic Tartars.

At the present day, we are made aware of the influence of climate upon the physical nature of man ; how it modifies his manners, his morals, and even the tendencies of his mind. For instance, the British races in America retain little of the outward aspect that would conclusively identify them as being in flesh, blood, and bone, the same human stock that emigrated there during the seventeenth and eighteenth centuries.

It appears that when Canada was first visited by the French, the expanse of territory was divided between three principal nations, viz. the Algonquins who occupied the banks of the St. Lawrence and Ottawa rivers; the Hurons or Wyandots who dwelt in the section since known as Upper Canada; and the Iroquois or *Five Nations*, comprising the lesser tribes of Mohawks, Oneidas, Onondagas, Senecas, and Cayugas, who mostly occupied the territory now known as the State of New York.

The Algonquins are said to have been somewhat superior in mien and manner, to the other nations. They lived entirely by the chase, and considered all industrious pursuits as beneath their dignity; looking with contempt on those who drew any part of their subsistence from the earth.

The Hurons were more given to agricultural pursuits, but were indolent and effeminate, having "less of the proud independence of savage life," than their haughty neighbors.

The Iroquois were a powerful and warlike people, said to be mentally superior to the others, and to have had more knowledge of the few simple arts in use among the aborigines.

Though not inhabiting the country immediately adjacent to the early French settlements, they were unquestionably the fiercest, most determined and vindictive enemies encountered by the early colonists of Canada. By repeated encroachments this proud nation had succeeded in acquiring the domination of a vast territory; but the French by resisting them and protecting their adversaries, suddenly stopped the former in their career of conquest, and temporarily exalted the latter. Both were obliged finally to succumb before the over mastering power of civilization, to which their brute force and cautelous strategy were occasionally made subservient.*

---

* The foregoing account of the aborigines of North America, has been mostly drawn from Bell's translation of Garneau's History of Canada.

EASTERN TOWNSHIPS. 25

CHAPTER III.

RENEWED EFFORTS AT COLONIZATION.—LOSS OF THE BROTHERS ROBERVAL.—INDIVIDUAL ENTERPRIZES.—HENRY IV.—CHAMPLAIN'S EXPEDITION.—THE SIEUR DE MONTS.—ACADIA.—CANADA.—CHAMPLAIN'S CHOICE OF LOCATION.—SUMMARY OF EVENTS TILL 1663.

Two years after the death of King Francis, Roberval organized another expedition to Canada, but on the voyage out, himself and brother, with all their followers, perished at sea ; an event which caused all projects of the kind to be looked on unfavorably.

Religious dissensions were then rife in France, and Admiral Coligny, who was himself a chief of the Huguenots as well as a patriotic man, resolved on founding an asylum in America for his co-religionists, upon whom pressed the rigors of a cruel persecution. Attempts of the kind were made in different sections of the New World, but through mismanagement or other cause, they failed of becoming permanent settlements. An establishment of the kind had existed in Florida for three years, when the Spanish King sent a fleet to " fight the heretics and prevent them from establishing their worship in America ;" and accordingly the

French protestant colony was mercilessly destroyed. This act being a direct violation of treaties existing between the nations, caused great indignation in France; catholics as well as protestants regarding it an insult to the national honor. Under the enthusiasm born of that feeling, a private expedition was fitted out to wreak a summary vengeance on the murderers. The command of this was given to the chevalier Dominique de Guorgues, himself a good catholic and an officer of merit. The purpose was successfully carried out, but Catherine de Medicis, who was then the *real* sovereign of France (as the young King was but fifteen years of age), would have sacrificed De Guorgues to the resentment of the Spanish King, but for the intervention of friends high in authority. In effort to palliate the act, the Spaniards insinuated that an understanding had been arrived at, that the *Huguenots of Florida should be exterminated;* but the young King was too immature in years to be held personally responsible for the policy carried out in his name, and the connivance of the Queen-mother, though quite probable, was never clearly established.

At length the storms that had long convulsed the country subsided; Henry IV was established on the throne, and brought his kingdom into order. Its internal affairs were regulated, commerce encouraged, manufactures established, and a general state of prosperity pervaded the kingdom, opening up new resources, and requiring some new career for its disposable energies.

America was now more than ever before, fixing the attention of Europeans : Spain and Portugal had appropriated much of her territory ; England and Holland were in the field, and France could no longer remain a spectator while her enemies and rivals were actively at work in the New World.

A trading society was formed of men of rank and leading merchants, and an expedition fitted out for the purposes of trade and colonization combined ; the command of which was given to Captain Samuel Champlain, a naval officer who had seen service and was in good repute at Court.

He set sail in 1603, and on arriving in Canadian waters, ascended the St. Lawrence as far as the Sault St. Louis (Lachine rapids). On his return he gave an account of his adventures, with a chart of his voyage which so pleased His Majesty that he promised him patronage and encouragement. A new expedition was planned under the superintendence of the Sieur de Monts, comprising a mixed number of catholics and protestants, gentlemen volunteers, soldiers, and skilled artizans. They sailed from Havre de Grâce in March, 1604, bound for Acadia (Nova Scotia), which M. de Monts preferred on account of its milder climate.

Acadia was at that time the chief place of resort for French traffic, and was considered the finest section of French America. It certainly had good ports, a temperate climate, and in parts, a fertile soil. The coasts were frequented by different species of marine animals, and the numerous bays and rivers abounded with a variety of fish. A still greater advantage was, that its harbors were accessible at all seasons of the year.

The choice of a location being made, a settlement was commenced, named Port Royal (now Annapolis) ; but notwithstanding its auspicious beginning, the expectations of its patrons and friends were not realized in at once rearing a flourishing establishment : indeed, for many years it had but a languishing existence, as influences were at work unfavorable to its interests.

The Sieur de Monts now turned his whole attention to Canada, in hope of extending the French possessions in America, and of finding the long sought passage to India ; which dream was still cherished. An expedition was now fitted out, one vessel of which was to traffic at Tadousac ; while the other under command of Champlain, was to land colonists and form a settlement at some point on the St. Lawrence. It arrived at Stadaconé early in July, and landed at what is now known as the " Lower Town " in Quebec, when the men at once commenced the erection of cabins for temporary accommodation. While some were engaged in this work, others were building a fort, and others still, in clearing land ; and thus the foundation of a town was laid in the presence of wondering savages. *

---

* The derivation of the name Quebec, has been the subject of discussion and dispute, but Champlain distinctly says: " We landed at a place which the Indians called *Kébec*, in their language signifying a *strait* " ; and we have other authority for believing the name to be of native origin.

Champlain found that time had wrought great changes among the aborigines since Cartier's day. Their chief towns of Stadaconé and Hochelaga had passed away, and the section was in possession of another people, more barbarous still, than those encountered by the first explorers of the region. They eagerly sought alliance with the French against their oppressors the Iroquois, who occupied the wilderness to the south of Lake Ontario. Actuated by a very natural desire to stand well with his nearest native neighbors, and expecting by securing the people of one nation as allies, to subdue or awe into neutrality all others disposed to be troublesome, Champlain consented,—perhaps unwisely—and thus the colonists became involved in troubles that lasted more than a century.

In 1609, he first took part with his native allies against their enemies, and as these savages were then entirely unacquainted with the use of fire-arms, when the Iroquois saw their chiefs and warriors fall dead or mortally wounded in such a mysterious manner, they the woods in terror. On this as on several successive occasis , volleys of musketry decided the contest in favor of Champlain's allies.

He now for the first, witnessed their method of treating their prisoners; and shocked at their barbarity, sought leave to put an end to the wretches' tortures; but this could not be allowed till the tormentors had exhausted every device of savage cruelty.

Tidings of the death of Henry IV by foul assassination, were received with sorrow and consternation at Quebec, and Champlain hastened home to attend personally to the interests of the colony, which he feared might be jeoparded by that deplorable event.

Jealousies had risen respecting competition in traffic, the old Society giving up their projects entirely. Champlain now sought to form a new Company, and place the colony under the protectibn of some high personage capable of assuring the favorable dispositions of the Court. The Count de Soissons succeeded M. de Monts as Lieutenant-general of Canada, retaining Champlain as his deputy; when armed with a new commission and invested with extraordinary powers, he returned to America. Here he was occupied in attending to the general interests of the colony, and on a visit into the interior in 1613, discovered lake Ontario.

Business relative to the colony of which he was acting governor and agent, called him again to France. Having succeeded in averting the threatened dissolution of the association, and being confirmed in his office, he again returned to Canada.

The Lieutenant-generalship of New France * had

---

* Early in the 17th century, the appellation " New France " was given to a vast region which now comprises the Hudson's Bay territory, Labrador, the provinces of Nova Scotia, New Brunswick, Quebec, Ontario, and a great part of the United States.

About the same time the eastern peninsula (Nova Scotia) be-now devolved upon the Duke de Montmorency, who took a much warmer interest in the affairs of the colony than his predecessor had done.

As early as |1614, members of the order of Franciscan Friars called Recollets, had been invited to Canada, and four of their number arrived in 1615. They began to erect a convent on the bank of the St. Charles, while yet the population of Quebec did not exceed fifty souls.

About the year 1621, many of the colonists began first to live on the product of their land, having subsisted hitherto mostly upon the profits of the peltry trafffic. The four principal fur factories were at Tadousac, Quebec, Three-Rivers, and at the Sault St. Louis.

In 1622, a solemn treaty of peace was ratified among the Indian tribes, who according to their own accounts had waged war for fifty years. But though the savages of Canada were at peace, the Society that through its agents trafficked with them, was divided and distracted by conflicting views and interests among its directors and shareholders. Wearied with the cares and vexations of his titular governorship, M. de Montmorency ceded his functions to the Duke de Ventadour, in 1625.

The new Governor, who was an enthusiastic religion-

---

gan to take the name Acadia. The territorial term Canada, from the native word *Kanata*, was already not only the appellation of the country we now inhabit, but a name that covered a much larger region than the united provinces which have since borne it. — *Garneau.*

ist, sought to make his office helpful to the conversion of the heathen of Canada, rather than the advancement of the material interests of the colony.

Impatient and dissatisfied at the delays and indifference of the association, Champlain entered a formal protest against them, and addressed a letter to the new Lieutenant-general, in which he represented in lively and forcible terms, the consequences of neglecting the colony. These complaints reached the ears of the Cardinal Duke de Richelieu, prime minister of France, who lent his attention the more readily to the patriotic representations of Champlain, that the one leading idea of his powerful mind was the aggrandizement and glory of France. He therefore took upon himself the title of " Head superintendent of all the French possessions beyond the sea ; " but the state of the country left him little leisure to carry out his plans. He however, projected a renovated association which was organized in 1628, under the name of the " Company of the hundred partners," to which was granted powers and privileges amounting to an exclusive monopoly of the colonial trade. The King made the Society a present of two new stout ships, and conferred patents of nobility on twelve of his chief members. They engaged to send out during the first year, a large number of artizans of the more useful callings, and to reinforce the colony largely, providing temporarily for the wants of the settlers. The Cardinal Minister and others of the nobility were members of the Company, and among the colonists were nobles, chief merchants, and men of substance, from the cities of France.

Hostilities begun between European powers, soon extended to their American colonies, and an English fleet was sent to cruise in these waters. Quebec being then in a most defenceless state, fell into the hands of the British, but was restored after three years' possession.

Champlain was then re-appointed governor and again assumed charge of the colony under the auspices of the " Company of the hundred partners." For a time the population increased rapidly, many seeking in New France the tranquillity denied them at home.

In 1635, the foundation stone was laid for the college at Quebec. This was altogether a year of great promise for the colony ; but before its close, Canada suffered a heavy loss in the person of its governor and best friend, who died on Christmas day.

Samuel Champlain was a native of Brouage in Saintonge. He had distinguished himself in the marine service, and was chosen as a fit person to conduct those colonizing expeditions which have made his name a household word in Canada.

Thirty years of his life were devoted to his great task of establishing and extending the French possessions in America. He crossed the Atlantic fully a score of times to defend the colony's interests at Paris, and has left a relation of his voyages and expeditions, which prove him to have been a judicious observer and just narrator,

In person he is said to have had a comely visage, a noble and soldierly bearing, and a vigorous constitution which enabled him to endure the wear and tear of body and mind he underwent in the accomplishment of the work which was chiefly effected through his native strength of character.

The immediate successor of Champlain in office, was M. de Châuteaufort, of whom little is known more than the name, as he was soon replaced by M. de Montmagny. This nobleman purposed to carry out the views of Champlain, but he took the reins of government at a very critical time, as the Indians of Canada were then engaged in a bloody and destructive war. His situation was humiliating and disquieting, as with small garrison and scanty stores, he could only witness contending struggles.

In 1642, a foundation was laid for the settlement of Montreal, by M. de Maisonneuve in his capacity as agent for a company of rich and influential persons. The Iroquois had now obtained fire-arms and ammunition and learned their use from the Dutch at Manhattan (New York), and were becoming more insolent and encroaching than ever, as the French were obliged to confine themselves to defensive action.

The next governor was M. d'Aillebout, who however, was constrained by circumstances to remain, to a great extent, a passive spectator of the tragic events going on around him.

In 1651, M. de Lauzon arrived to fill the office of

governor. The short period of his administration was marked by continued troubles with the Indians. The population of the colony was sensibly diminishing through the numbers who were killed or captured by the Iroquois, till at length the critical state of the country was brought to the notice of the friends of colonization in France, by M. de Maisonneuve. He obtained a reinforcement of colonists, who arrived at Montreal in 1653. They were picked men, alike fit for the needs of war or peace. Events were proving that the governor was too inefficient in action, and in 1658 he was superseded by the Viscount Voyer d'Argenson.

At this crisis, Canada was everywhere overrun by armed barbarians : in addition to which, civil and religious quarrels involving questions of right and precedence, broke out between the clergy and chief laity.*

In 1659, a royal edict was issued for harmonizing the action of the civil government of the colony ; defining the jurisdiction of the courts ; and reserving certain appointments to be made by the King in council.

M. d'Argenson had solicited his recall before his term of service had expired. Troubles with the In-

---

* In 1657, the Pope had constituted Canada a Vicariat-apostolical, with M. de Laval as its first head. He was consecrated titular bishop before coming to Canada, and when in 1674, Quebec was constituted a Diocese, was nominated its first bishop.—*Garneau.*

dians, and angry discussions with the clergy, had filled up his short administration.

In 1661, the government passed into the hands of the Baron d'Avougour, a man of resolute temperament and unbending character. Through his efforts, an interest in the country hitherto wanting, was roused, and reinforcements were sent to Quebec. A treaty of peace was also ratified with the Iroquois. Unfortunately however, differences rose between the governor and bishop, which finally culminated in open quarrel. The bishop was a man of inflexible temper and lofty bearing; the governor was equally unyielding and stood upon his official dignity, contending that the civil power should be independent of the sacerdotal. The dispute was referred to France; the bishop went there to justify himself, and succeeded in obtaining the recall of M. d'Avougour, and the appointment of M. de Mésy in his place.

CHAPTER IV.

THE NEW GOVERNOR.—THE FEUDAL TENURE.—REFORMS.—AN IN-
TENDENCY.—CHURCH AND STATE.—DIVISIONS.—QUARRELS.
—COMPLAINTS CARRIED TO FRANCE.—REMOVAL AND DEATH
OF M. DE MESY.—A VICEROY.—SUMMARY OF EVENTS TILL
1685.

The Chevalier de Saffray Mésy having been appointed to succeed Baron d'Avougour, arrived at Quebec in the spring of 1663. He had been the choice of M. de Laval and the Jesuits concurrently, and was charged with orders to institute several important reforms. He came to Canada with his episcopal patron.

The Iroquois still maintained a threatening attitude, the colonists being kept in a state of perpetual inquietude. The governor showed firmness and tact in negotiating with these savages, and gave them to understand that it was his determination to punish enemies with whom no lasting peace could be kept. At this period the population of Canada did not exceed 2,500 souls, sparsely distributed between Tadousac and Montreal, 800 of whom were in Quebec.

The introduction of the feudal tenures into Canada,

conformable to those of olden France, dates from the last years of the 16th century; and when Richelieu re-constituted the Company of a hundred partners, he invested it with such powers, rights, privileges, and faculties, as should be judged fitting; all its erections and creations however, being subject to royal confirmation. Parts of their territory were divided into simple seigniories which were accorded to merchants, military officers, religious corporations, &c., and were apportioned into farms burdened with a yearly ground rent. Territorial jurisdiction over Canada having been now resumed by the King, a new system seemed called for by the growing wants of the country. A royal commissary had been sent out with the governor, whose business was to examine into the internal affairs of the country and ascertain the needs and wishes of its inhabitants. His reports were by no means favorable, and a sweeping reform was determined on.

The first step was the establishment of a supreme tribunal in April, 1663. It was composed of the governor, bishop, five councillors and an attorney-general the six latter being appointed every year by the two chief dignitaries conjointly. On the arrival of an Intendant, that functionary also took his seat at the council board. As a law court, this council sat only as a court of appeal. The Royal Intendant as chief of justice and police, had also his tribunal for criminal and civil affairs.

Difficulties soon rose in the council, which were

followed by an entire estrangement between the governor and bishop. Their actions at length became invariably antagonistic: the bishop was supported by the Jesuits and clergy, but the sympathies of the people were with the governor and his minority. In this exigency, M. de Mésy very imprudently resorted to extreme measures which gave his enemies an advantage; complaints were carried to France; the King was highly incensed, and resolved to make an example of this rash governor as a warning to all others.

A new viceroy was appointed for New France; M. de Courcelles was to replace De Mésy, as provincial governor of Canada, and a new intendant was also sent out. These were commissioned to collect evidence and bring the offending functionary to trial; but this was not needed, for he sickened and died before their arrival. He however, dictated a letter to M. de Tracy, the new viceroy, in which he protested that in all he had done he had ever in view the interests of his king and the prosperity of the colony; and confided to him as his successor, the clearing up of the whole business.

In the eyes of the people of the colony, De Mésy passed for a victim of the twice triumphant bishop; his disgrace being yet more signal than that of his predecessor.

The Marquis de Tracy reached Quebec in June, 1665, accompanied by the Carignan regiment of troops. Energetic measures were taken now against the hostile Iroquois. An expedition conducted by the viceroy in person, penetrated the enemy's country, effectually humbled them, and obliged them to sue for a peace which lasted several years.

De Tracy returned to France in 1667, the functions of government devolving on M. de Courcelles, a prudent far-seeing man, who possessed in an eminent degree, the qualities valuable in an administrator. The intendant, M. Talon, was also a faithful and efficient public officer. According to the spirit of their instructions from the penetrating home minister Colbert, while showing all proper respect for the clergy, care was taken that they were not allowed to overstep the bounds that separate ecclesiastical from civil functions.

In 1772, the Count de Frontenac replaced M. de Courcelles as governor. His reputation for talents and energy had preceded him, and in addition, he was shrewd, fertile in mental resources, and had an ambitious mind ; but his manners were cold and haughty, and his tendencies altogether despotic. Unfortunately at the outset, he came in contact with prejudices as strong, and wills as unpliant as his own, and excited an implacable enmity against himself. Questions of precedence were allowed to become a fruitful source of dispute between the governor and bishop ; and notwithstanding repeated and authoritative admonitions from court, the quarrel rose to such a height that it became necessary to recall De Frontenac.

It was during these successive administrations that those discoveries were made which tended so largely to increase the territorial possessions of New France. Between the years 1635 and 1647, the countries bordering on the western lakes, were visited by eighteen Jesuit missionaries. The American historian Bancroft pays a just compliment to these adventurous men, when on this subject he says : " The annals of missionary labor are inseparably connected with the origin of all the establishments of French America. Not a cape was doubled, not a stream discovered, that a Jesuit did not show the way." It was these men who first heard from the natives of the " Father of waters" as they called Mississippi river; and from the same source were derived ideas of the real boundaries of North America, which though vague and indistinct at first, gradually became clearer, and were in time, found correct.

M. de la Barre, sent to supersede De Frontenac, was a marine officer who had seen service in the West Indies, and arrived at Quebec in 1682. The Iroquois were again assuming a threatening attitude. The governor wrote home complaining that the people of the adjoining colonies were using unfair means to detach the Indians from the French interest, and constantly exciting the Iroquois against the colonists of Canada. He also urged the necessity of reinforcements of men and supplies. In response, the King sent out 200 regulars, and informed M. de la Barre that he had taken steps to prevent any future violation of existing treaties.

It would appear that a most astounding blindness pervaded the councils of the French nation at that period, as the repeated calls for extended emigration received no practical response, though thousands upon thousands of the King's protestant subjects were seeking leave to settle in French America, and promised to live peaceably under a flag they much preferred. The mystery involved in this, may find clear elucidation in the history of the religious persecutions then so rife in France.

The course of M. de la Barre in dealing with the Iroquois, showed him plainly unequal to the emergency; as the more timid and perplexed he allowed himself to appear, the more insolent and encroaching they became.

While matters were in this critical state, the governor was superseded in office, by the Marquis de Denonville, who arrived at Quebec in 1685. He was a Colonel of Dragoons and brought with him 600 regular troops; which significant act on the part of the home government, showed plainly its disapproval of the late governor's inaction.

The new governor had the reputation of being a brave and efficient officer, possessed of a lofty sense of honor, and of being cultivated and polished in manner.

CHAPTER V.

INDIAN TROUBLES.—MASSACRE AT LACHINE.—INEFFICIENCY OF THE GOVERNOR.—RETURN OF DE FRONTENAC.—SPIRITED ACTION OF THAT NOBLEMAN.—IMPROVED STATE OF AFFAIRS.—SUMMARY OF EVENTS TILL THE TREATY OF UTRECHT.

TIME passed in preparations for war, and on the part of the Iroquois, in fraudful negotiations for peace. The governor was extremely averse to any attempt to act against them before other reinforcements arrived from France, and the perplexities of the situation were greatly aggravated by the trading relations of the hostile savages with the English colonists. The expected reinforcements at length arrived, yet even then, no very decisive action was taken; the dilatory conduct of the governor being very unsatisfactory to the country. Worse evils were in store for the later days of the administration; the most calamitous period known to the early colonists of Canada. An unwonted quiet had for a time prevailed among the tribes, which was all the more dangerous as it tended to slacken preparations for the coming storm.

During the night of the 5th of August, 1689, amid

a storm of rain and hail, 1400 Iroquois crossed lake St. Louis and silently disembarked near Lachine, and before daybreak, parties of them had surrounded every considerable dwelling in the vicinity. The inmates were buried in profound slumber, soon to become for many of them, the "Dreamless sleep that knows no waking." At a given signal, doors and windows were driven in and the victims dragged from their beds— men, women and children, struggling in the hands of their butchers. Such houses as could not be readily forced, were fired; and as the terrified inmates were driven forth by smoke and flame, they met certain death from beings who knew no mercy. Two hundred persons were burned alive, and numbers died under prolonged tortures. Houses and outbuildings were reduced to ashes, and crops were totally destroyed. After having ravaged the whole vicinity, they crossed the river, and on the opposite side continued their fearful work. Those who escaped the destruction were paralyzed by the brain-blow. The governor who was in Montreal, seemed to lose self-command altogether. It had been long evident that he exercised no proper influence; but the small use he made of the means at his disposal when this crisis arrived, was most surprising. His incapacity on every occasion where promptitude and energy were required, gave little room for doubt that had he not been soon recalled by royal order, the colonists themselves would have set him aside. The last season of his unfortunate administration was called the year of the massacre. In not one particular, had he justified his reputation for bravery and efficiency.

His successor was no other than the Count de Frontenac, who landed at Quebec in 1689. His return was hailed with joy by all, by none more than those who had labored to obtain his recall.

Despite the unpropitious aspect of affairs, Frontenac saw that if it were possible to raise the minds of the people from the apprehension and despondency into which they were sunken, matters might yet be retrieved. His presence and counsels were already beginning to operate favorably, and a feeling of restored confidence was extending to the friendly natives. They were encouraged to make raids into the English colonies, in which, true to their savage nature they practiced all the horrors of Indian warfare. About this period the town of Schenectady was destroyed by a party of French and Indians, said to have been done in reprisal for the massacre at Lachine. Presents were also distributed among such tribes as still appeared hesitating, which with the news of the successful raids, gave them assurance that the French were now on the winning side.

The European nations being now at war, an expedition was planned against Quebec, and a fleet under command of Sir William Phipps, appeared before that city ; but by assuming a bold and fearless attitude, and making the most of scanty resources, with no little manœuvring and *finesse*, and by the aid of concurrent circumstances, Frontenac succeeded in creating the impression that he was prepared for a formidable resistance; when after a few hostile demonstrations which were vigorously met, Sir William drew off his ships.

No assistance having been sent to help against the Iroquois, they had become more bold and encroaching than ever. Frontenac now determined to abase their pretensions and conquer a peace. He therefore assembled a corps at Lachine, moved thence to Cataraqui, then crossed into the enemy's country and destroyed two Indian cantons.

De Frontenac died November 28th, 1698, aged 77 years; preserving to the last, the talent, firmness and energy, that had characterized him through life. His character has been variously estimated. That he had great faults is certain; but Canada owed him much.

The Chevalier de Callières was appointed to succeed him. The new governor had occupied a subordinate position in the colony, and was well experienced in the affairs of the country; was also popular with the soldiers under his command, and possessed qualities which rendered him very acceptable to the people, and made the savages pliant to his will. The principal events of his administration were the ratification of a treaty of peace with the assembled deputies of the various tribes, and the formation of a settlement on the site of the city of Detroit. De Callières died in May, 1703, and was succeeded by the Marquis de Vaudreuil, some time governor of Montreal.

A war was now in progress in Europe, which soon extended to the American colonies, and a fleet was preparing to ascend the St. Lawrence, to capture Quebec; but the elements were now the best defenders of the country, and in consequence of the dispersion of the fleet by a storm, the enterprize was abandoned.

The Iroquois had now begun to waver in their fidelity to the English, and appeared anxious to sell their services to the highest bidder. One of their chiefs remarked that their independence was only maintained by the mutual jealousy of the rival nations, and that it would be impolitic to let either quite prevail over the other. The English had claimed them as British subjects; but this had roused their jealousy, and they loudly disclaimed all foreign supremacy, asserting an independence in which they gloried. Their trading interests inclined them to the English; but the religious sympathies of numbers among them were with the French, owing to the influence the missionaries had obtained over them. A favorite project with them had been the formation of a confederacy, of which they were to take the lead, powerful enough to resist the encroachments of Europeans, and avenge the wrongs done to their race.

A treaty of peace was signed at Utrecht in 1713.

CHAPTER VI.

INTERVAL OF PEACE.—FRONTIER LIMITS.—DE VAUDREUIL.—THE
MARQUIS DE BEAUHARNOIS.—DISCOVERY OF THE ROCKY MOUN-
TAINS.—TRADERS AND EXPLORERS.—SUMMARY OF EVENTS
TILL THE DECLARATION OF WAR.

THE treaty of Utrecht was followed by some of the most peaceful years Canada had ever known. Both French and English colonists, wearied of an exhausting war, were now able to turn their attention and energies to internal improvements. At the period of which we write, the colony was divided into three distinct governments, viz, Quebec, Three Rivers and Montreal; but no regular subdivisions, civil or parochial, had been properly fixed. In the years 1721-2, the whole was parceled into 82 parishes; 48 being on the north side, and 34 on the south side of the St. Lawrence. In the year 1721, the whole estimated population of Canada was only 25,000 souls, of which number 7000 were in Quebec, and 3000 in Montreal. There were 62,000 acres of land under tillage, and 12,000 acres in grass. The question of the frontier lines between the two countries was becoming every year more complicated and difficult to deal with. The former attempts to settle it, had always come to nothing. By a stipulation of the treaty of Utrecht, commissioners were appointed for this object, who met, conferred long, and parted, leaving the matter as they found it. Disputes concerning boundaries between national possessions are proverbially the most difficult to terminate by any other arbitrament than that of war.

De Vaudreuil died October 10th, 1725, after ruling Canada 21 years. He was much and deservedly esteemed in private, and his death was generally lamented. After having passed 53 years in the royal service, he received the cross of St. Louis as a distinguishing mark of his sovereign's favor. He was an energetic and successful public officer.

His successor in office was the Marquis de Beauharnois, who arrived at Quebec in 1726. Among the principal events that occurred during this administration, was the discovery of the Rocky Mountains by the Messrs. Vérandrye in 1743. For the purpose of continuing these explorations, an association was formed, comprising nearly all the chief functionaries of the colony, which company had its own trading projects in view. This speculation was carried on at the cost of the State, though the profits were divided among the partners.

In the year 1715, there had appeared two published memorials or reports, in which the management of colonial affairs was very freely discussed and exposed;

D

and the chief colonial functionaries were often compromised as being more or less directly engaged in the unscrupulous speculations so rife at that period; or at best, as being wholly indifferent to such proceedings. They were made to appear as if in having no permanent interest in the country, they only thought of enriching themselves while here, that they might pass hence to higher stations at home.

The legitimate trade of Canada was from time to time, through the monopolies of associations or the rivalries of other colonists, subjected to such burdens, restrictions, and consequent fluctuations, as greatly embarrassed and retarded it. Peltry was the main article of export, but was at most times a strict monopoly carried on under licenses granted to favored persons, who usually sold them to inland traders. Those who held them often strained every nerve to make the most they could—by fair means or foul—during the time for which they were given; and to beguile the Indians to accept insufficient values for their furs, it was not unusual to ply them with liquor. The natives at length became aware of the dishonesty often practiced upon them, through intercourse with rival traders. *

In 1721, posting first began in the colony; a monopoly of the posts between Montreal and Quebec having

---

* It is related that at a western post on one occasion, beaver skins were bought for four grains of pepper each, and that as much as 800 francs were realized by the sale of one pound of vermillion. No wonder at the Indian's want of faith in Europeans!

been granted to one person for twenty years ; the carriage of letters being charged by a table of fixed rates according to distance.

As early as 1689, it had been proposed to introduce negroes into the colony ; but though the institution of slavery might have been legally recognized at one period, it never prevailed to any great extent in Canada.

In 1755, Canadian exports were valued at 2½ million dollars ; its imports at 8 millions ; much of the latter being supplies and munitions of war during those years of hostility. Owing to systems of secret confederacy, favoritism and intrigue, which at that period operated to throw patronage into certain channels, all healthy action in trade was destroyed.

During the later years of French domination in Canada, there was great confusion in the monetary circulation of the country ; indeed, it seemed to have become almost destitute of a reliable circulating medium, and to be fast sinking into insolvency ; the miserable effect of purblind expedients, the legitimate fruit of unscrupulous mal-administration, and the inevitable precursor of revolution and change. France and England were again at war, and their respective American colonies were, of course, involved in the quarrel. Their frontier relations were every year becoming more difficult to adjust, and long before any European aid could reach them, they were engaged in hostilities.

The Marquis de la Jonquière who had been sent out to supersede M. de Beauharnois, was taken prisoner by the British, and the Count de la Gallisonière who had been nominated to fill his place, arrived at Quebec in September, 1748, bringing news of approaching peace. The treaty of Aix-la-Chapelle was signed October 7th, 1748, by which the territory either power had acquired during the war, was mutually restored. But this peace was only a truce as regarded the American colonies; hostilities scarcely ceasing, so determined were the rival parties to extend their frontiers to the utmost. A sharp correspondence was kept up between the governors; but this did not answer the end, each party taking forcible possession of disputed grounds. A general war was now imminent. Late in the year 1752 the Marquis Duquesne de Menville arrived as governor, and the next year, war was declared.

CHAPTER VII.

HOSTILITIES.—DE VAUDREUIL.—RELATIVE STRENGTH OF CONTESTANTS.—CANADIANS.—ANGLO-AMERICANS. — BRADDOCK'S DEFEAT AND DEATH.—DEFEAT OF THE FRENCH UNDER BARON DIESKAU.—ARRIVAL OF MONTCALM.—SUMMARY OF EVENTS ATTENDING THE DOWNFALL OF FRENCH POWER IN CANADA.

A BRITISH fleet left England in January 1755, for the purpose of cruising in American waters; and a French fleet sailed from Brest, in April, bearing reinforcements and warlike stores to Canada. Hostilities were now commencing in earnest. M. Duquesne had asked to be recalled, and transferred to the marine service. His departure caused no regret, although he had governed with success and been heedful of the colony's interests; but his haughty bearing made him unpopular, and the people looked for the appointment of another in his stead. He was succeeded in 1755, by the Marquis de Vaudreuil de Cavagnol, son of the Marquis de Vaudreuil, who had been governor from 1703 to his death in 1725. The new governor was joyously greeted by the Canadians on his arrival, as they regarded him the more for his being a compatriot, and had anxiously solicited the king to appoint him for their chief.

The state of France at this period was anything but favorable to a successful prosecution of the war in America. The king at all times too indolent and indifferent to act with energy, was at this period under the influence of a female favorite of most capricious temper; and there being neither unity nor accord in state councils, they underwent almost constant mutations. Ecclesiastical dissensions, new and startling innovations, the needs of war and troubles in the state councils, greatly occupied the public mind; in fine, all was commotion among both moral and political idealists; and the government itself moved with uncertain and hesitating step. France had allowed herself to be again led into a continental war, and the defence of Canada was thus left greatly to its own inhabitants.— The regular force in the country, never large, in 1755 was augmented to a total of 2,800, under the command of Baron Dieskau. The militia were armed, so that there was soon ready for action, in garrison and in field, an army 7000 strong, besides a force of 800 men employed as escorts.

On the other hand Great Britain was in a prosperous state. The English government habitually yielded to popular inspirations, and thus observant of the national instincts, might safely assure itself in advance, that success would attend any enterprize undertaken in obedience to the popular will. No preceding war had been so agreeable to the people as that about to commence; and warlike ardor was no less manifest among the people of the American colonies, who far out-numbered the inhabitants of Canada. The same difference extended to their pecuniary resources.

But though false and illiberal views prevailed in France, and caused indifference to the coming struggle, the Canadians were patriotic, and though mostly cultivators and traders, were inbued with a confident and self-reliant spirit. They had all the military ardor necessary to make them vigorous soldiers, especially now that their homes were menaced by aliens.

On the other hand, the English colonists of America had long looked for the interference of their mother country in putting an effectual end to those barbarous irruptions that had so frequently desolated their frontier settlements; and now that their hopes were about to be realized, they welcomed war, and seconded it with united energies and untiring zeal.

The British General Braddock, had been sent out in command of regular forces, with instructions which comprised a detailed plan of hostile operations; the first step in which was to drive the French from the Ohio valley. On his arrival, a concerted plan of action was agreed upon, by which four different points were to be attacked at once.

According to the arrangement, he advanced to the attack of Fort Duquesne, but an ambuscade was formed by the French and Indians, into which the British forces fell, when a desperate struggle ensued. Out of 86 British officers, 26 were slain, and 37 wounded; for they made heroic efforts to rally and inspirit their men who were all unused to the savage mode of warfare, and fell back panic-stricken upon a reserve of 1000 men left with the baggage, artillery, &c.; when the whole force retreated in disorder.

In the heat of action, Braddock had two horses killed under him, and mounted a third, only to receive a mortal wound. He was then carried to Fort Necessity where he died on the 13th of July. He was a brave and experienced officer, but an arrogant man; contemning his enemy; despising alike militia and savages; yet had the mortification of seeing his regulars madly flee, while the provincials stood their ground and fought bravely. Singularly enough, Col. Washington, then in command of the colonial militia, was the only mounted officer who escaped unhurt.

The news of this defeat spread dismay among the English, and the back settlements of Virginia, Pennsylvania, and Maryland, were forthwith abandoned.

Soon after this, a body of French, under Baron Dieskau posted near lake Georga, was attacked by the British under Col. Johnson, when after a series of spirited conflicts with varying success, a severe action was fought, in which the French were beaten and dispersed, and their leader, who was severely wounded, taken prisoner. Like the British General, Braddock, this commander owed his defeat, in a great measure, to an absurd reliance on European discipline, an under estimation of the colonial forces, and a contemptuous disregard of the advice of provincial officers.

The most urgent demands were now made for troops, supplies, &c., and it was also solicited that a chief of tried bravery and military experience, should be sent over to take the place of Baron Dieskau. In response to this appeal, the Marquis de Montcalm was sent as military chief, and with him came several officers of merit, beside reinforcements of men and munitions of war. At this time the whole force on foot for the defence of New France, from Cape Breton to Illinois, did not exceed 12,000 men; and many of these were cultivators, obliged to be absent in seed-time and harvest.

The preparations of Britain for the campaign of 1756, were far more considerable. America, as the chief field of military operations, drew to her colonies many officers of distinction. Two entire regiments of regulars were sent out, and a force raised which in all amounted to 25,000 men. Nothing of importance was effected, however, in this campaign.

Though still holding her own and able to keep her outward foes at bay, Canada was in a critical state from a scarcity of food among its inhabitants. Small-pox had also broken out and extended its ravages, to the native tribes. Thus threatened without, and reduced by pestilence and famine within, all joined in earnestly petitioning the home government to come to the rescue. Yet home politicians and favorites of the

King, who profited by courtly prodigality, called out in concert that Canada was an icy wilderness which cost more than it was worth. An unscrupulous intendant named Bigot, was guilty of peculations to an enormous extent at this period ; abusing his official power, and through secret agents playing an odiously dishonest part in order to enrich himself ; and it is said that his fraudful policy had its confederates even in France.

The governors of the Anglo-American colonies met at Boston in January, 1757, to concert action for the year's campaign, when an attack on Louisbourg in Cape Breton, was projected.

On the 9th of August, 1757, Fort William Henry near lake George, capitulated to the French and Indians; when a large number of prisoners,—men, women, and children,—were massacred by the merciless savages ; an event which inflicted an indelible stain upon the record of this military success. The Fort and its precincts were literally converted into a *place of blood*, and the works entirely destroyed. If the resentments of the Anglo-American colonists against the French and their native allies were strong before, the butchery that followed the surrender of this Fort, and others similar, rendered them more deep and fixed ; and a deadly determination took possession of the British mind and heart, to put an effectual end to these massacres.

It was therefore determined to attack concurrently, Louisbourg, Carillon (Ticonderoga), and Fort Duquesne. The first blow fell on Louisbourg ; the place was bravely defended, but step by step was gained by the besiegers, till the French were obliged to retire within the town, and its fall only became a question of time. In order to prevent or delay attack on Canada, the Fort was persistently defended, so long as the works were tenable ; but the siege was closely pressed by the invaders and the fortress capitulated July 20th, 1758.

The force sent against Fort Duquesne was equally successful, as the French commandant, hopeless of succor, retired with his men and munitions, and burned the works. The British took possession of the ruins and in compliment to their great minister, gave the name of Pittsburg to a locality which is now the site of a flourishing city.

The attack on Carillon was not as successful however, as the assailants met a spirited resistance. The season of repose was now come, and the invasion of Canada was again postponed ; yet, left a prey to famine and the sword, the consummation of its fall could not long be delayed. In vain the governor wrote that if no help came, they must succumb.

In April 1759, Montcalm wrote to the minister imparting his own inquietudes regarding the destiny of Canada ; plainly expressing his entire want of faith in both governor and intendant ; and also complaining, that the most unscrupulous corruption existed among all classes and grades of officials. He also solicited his recall from the King.

An unfortunate estrangement had grown up between the civil and military chiefs of the colony; owing in part to a natural dissimilarity of character, and in part to the evil machinations of others. The partisans of either, made mutual and grave accusations against the other; one of Montcalm's friends strongly advising that De Vaudreuil should be superseded by the military chief; the fact that the former was a *native born Canadian*, being alleged against him as a principal demerit. Such differences were particularly unfortunate at this juncture; and efforts were made by the real friends of both, to restore a good understanding between the parties, with partial success.

In the meantime, the British were making vigorous preparations for an attack on Canada. A corps had been assigned to General Wolfe, with which he was to ascend the St. Lawrence and invest Quebec. A fleet of ships of the line, frigates, smaller vessels and transports, were sent to convey them up the river. Amherst was to force a passage by Lake Champlain; a third corps was to take Niagara and descend Lake Ontario; while a fourth was to clear that whole section of every enemy to Britain. The savages foreseeing the fall of French domination, and anxious to secure favor in time, mostly allied themselves with the stronger power. The regular force in Canada now amounted to 5,300 men, and all the valid males in the colony between the ages of 16 and 60, were found to number 15,229. All being in readiness, the governor, Montcalm, and De Lévis, withdrew to Montreal to watch the movements of the enemy, and see in what direction the disposable forces were most needed. On the first appearance of the hostile fleet in the St. Lawrence, they returned to Quebec where all was soon in a state of activity.

On the 25th of June, 1759, the British fleet reached the island of Orleans ; and on the 30th, batteries were erected opposite Quebec, and fire opened on the city. An attempt was made on the position of Montcalm, which however, was spiritedly repulsed with loss to the assailants.

It was finally decided to operate from above rather than below the city as the surest means of striking a decisive blow; and while active demonstrations were kept up against Montcalm's position in order to mystify the French and cover the real design, part of the forces embarked and ascended the river to Cap Rouge : soldiers were landed on either bank of the flood, and with their officers were closely inspecting the shore from Quebec to that point.

Not being able to understand the enemy's movements and apprehensive that they threatened the magazines of the army, * Bougainville had been despatched to watch them in that quarter.

Threatening demonstrations were continued against

(*) Before the enemy's arrival, the garrison stores and government archives had been removed to Three Rivers, and the army magazines fixed at Montreal.

Beauport, while the vessels and troops at Cap Rouge neared other points to retain Bougainville in that quarter; and having learned from deserters that a convoy of provisions were to descend the river during the night of September 12th, and by the same means learning the watch-word that was to be given by the crews of the barges to the sentinels on shore, Wolfe resolved to profit by these fortuitous circumstances, land his troops at the Fuller's Cove, and carry the adjoining heights. Officers who were perfectly acquainted with the French language and customs were chosen to respond to the sentinel's challenges, and during the obscurity of the night, the barges with their hostile freight, were allowed to pass on.

Arrived at the goal, the vanguard landed without resistance; the light infantry, headed by Wolfe himself, forced the guard-house at the foot of the steep pathway leading up the cliff, scaled an escarpment partially covered with trees and brushwood, reached the table-land above, surprised and dispersed the men on guard, and as the day broke, an army was ranged in battle order on the Plains of Abraham. A battalion of Scots Highlanders took part in this enterprise and contributed very materially to its success. The only cannon in use had been dragged up the height with ropes.

Intelligence of these movements reached Montcalm, at six o'clock in the morning; but under the impression that it was some detachment of no account, he started for the scene with only part of his men ; yet when in sight of the enemy to his consternation and dismay, found them ready for his reception. Through a fatal precipitation, despite the advice and remonstrances of his brother officers, and in face of the positive commands of the governor who had sent him written orders to act on the defensive till all the forces could be got together, he resolved to commence the attack at once, formed the ranks and ordered his men to advance against the enemy.

Knowing that retreat would be impossible were he beaten, Wolfe passed along the ranks animating his men to fight well, but not to fire a gun till the enemy were within twenty paces. The French advanced boldly to the attack, but began firing too soon, and when near enough were assailed with so deadly a discharge that they fell into immediate confusion. Wolfe chose this moment to attack in turn, and though already wounded in the wrist, led on his grenadiers to the charge, but had not advanced many steps when he sunk to the earth mortally wounded. He was carried to the rear, and his troops, in ignorance of his fall, continued to press their enemies, part of whom were already giving way. Wolfe was dying ; but hearing the cry " They fly, they fly !" his eyes lighted with their wonted fire as he eagerly asked " Who ?" and when answered " The French," he exclaimed " What,

already? then I die content," and falling back, expired.*
General Monckton being also severely wounded, the
command fell on General Townshend.

The defeated French were pressed with bayonet and
broadsword. Montcalm though wounded, made every
effort to rally the fugitives and regularize their retreat,
but in the vain attempt, fell mortally wounded and
was carried into the city. He acknowledged his fault
when too late to retrieve it, and regret was unavailing;

---

*General Wolfe was born at Greenwich, England, in 1724, and was 35 years of age at his death. His father was an invalid general who had served with distinction. Being anxious to engage in active service, young Wolfe had renounced a considerable place on the Irish staff, and took his chance of obtaining promotion in the American war. His conduct at the siege of Louisbourg, where he was only subordinate in command, drew the attention of his superiors, and he was chosen to lead in the expedition against Quebec; a charge which required activity, daring, and prudence combined. His lieutenants, the Brigadiers Monckton, Townshend, and Murray, all three of whom were in the flower of manhood, were leaders who had studied the art of war, and gained experience in action.

The news of the capitulation of Quebec, created universal joy in England, chastened however, by an equally wide-spread sorrow for the death of the brave and talented young general, as its costly price. "Throughout broad England, were illuminations and songs of triumph: one country village alone was silent and still: there Wolfe's widowed mother mourned her only son." His remains were taken to England and laid beside those of his father in his native place; and a suitable monument was erected to his memory in Westminster Abbey. He is described as having been comely in person and pleasing in address; and was to have been married on his return to England.

but whatever his errors and mistakes had been, they were expiated in his death. After receiving the sacraments of the church, and dictating a letter commending the French prisoners to the generosity of their victors, he died on the morning of September 14th, and was buried by flambeau light the same evening, in the chapel of the Ursuline sisterhood; his grave being a trench along the wall of the edifice, made by the ploughing of a bomb shell.*

Such was the battle of the Plains of Abraham, so fatal in its final results to French domination in Canada. Quebec capitulated on the 18th of September, and one by one, other posts were abandoned to the enemy. Some further show of resistance was made by the remaining troops under command of De Lévis, still in hope of effectual succor from France; but as the invading armies invested Montreal, this illusion vanished, and that city capitulated September 8th, 1760; and thus Canada finally passed from French to British domination. De Vau-

---

* The Marquis de Montcalm was born near Nismes, France, in 1712, being thus 47 years of age at the time of his death. He was descended from a family of distinction, and had served successfully in the European wars; but possessed some defects of character. His personal courage and bravery were beyond question; but this could not avail against want of prudent foresight and strategic ability. He was impulsive even to rashness; full of vivacity and heedlessness; but not energetic or persevering. He liked to live luxuriously; but was unselfish, generous, and careless of expenditure.

E

dreuil sent orders to the chiefs of the French posts at the west, to surrender their commands to those authorized to receive them; and by the year 1761, all had been given up. Most of the privileges of the people were assured to them, but the principal French functionaries, and many of the prominent among the people, returned to France. The possession of Canada and its adjacent territories, was confirmed to Britain by the treaty of Paris, signed May 16th, 1763.

When the notorious Bigot appeared at Versailles, he was met with reproaches and indignities; then arrested, and after suffering a lengthy imprisonment, was tried and exiled for life and his estates confiscated. Several of his accomplices shared similar punishments; the ex-commissary Cadet, being fined 6,000,000 francs! Even the ex-governor did not escape imprisonment, which indignity he owed as much to the criminating insinuations of Montcalm's partisans, as to the perfidious calumnies of Bigot. He made a dignified defence; showed that he had sacrificed not only his salary, but property he had before accumulated, in order to supply deficiencies toward the close of the war; and best of all, the patriotic and high-minded De Lévis, stood his firm friend. De Vaudreuil was relieved from the accusations made against him, but died the next year, less from old age, than vexation of spirit.

State obligations to the amount of 40,000,000 francs were held by Canadians at this period, which became almost valueless to the holders in the end.

EASTERN TOWNSHIPS. 67

CHAPTER VIII.

CANADA AT THE CONQUEST.—MILITARY RULE.—QUEBEC GAZETTE.
—SIGNS OF THE AMERICAN REVOLUTION.—CANADIAN INTER-
ESTS.—LAW OF 1774.—PROVINCIAL CONGRESS. — GENERAL
CARLETON'S ADMINISTRATION IN CANADA.—THE CRISIS PRE-
CIPITATED. — INVASION OF CANADA BY AMERICANS.—LEGIS-
LATIVE COUNCIL OF CANADA. — INDEPENDENCE OF AMERICA
ESTABLISHED.—SUCCESSIVE GOVERNORS OF CANADA.—LORD
DORCHESTER.—PEACE. — A CONSTITUTION FOR CANADA.—
ELECTIONS APPOINTED.—SUCCESSIVE GOVERNORS.—THE WAR
OF 1812. — TREATY OF GHENT AND RETURN OF PEACE.—
DEATH OF SIR GEORGE PREVOST.

THE population of Canada at the time of the conquest is estimated to have been 69,275 souls. The British government proceeded to organize a regular colonial administration, and the colony was dismembered. Labrador, Anticosti and Magdalen Island were annexed to Newfoundland ; Cape Breton and Prince Edward to Nova Scotia ; the territories of the great lakes to the neighboring American colonies, and a part of Canada took the name of New Brunswick with a separate administration.

Sir Jeffery Amherst, the first British governor general, having returned to England, general Murray was appointed in his place, and in accordance with his instructions, formed a new Executive Council, in which, along with the governor, was vested all executive, legislative, and judicial functions. This body was composed of two lieutenant-governors, the chief-justice, the inspector-general of customs, and eight persons chosen from the leading inhabitants of the colony. What remained of Canada was divided into two judicial districts; a court of Queen's Bench was instituted, and also of Common Pleas. The judges of these courts were appointed by the Council, subject to royal confirmation. The Council itself was an appeal from decisions of the courts, and the awards of that body were liable to revision in the King's Privy Council.

For the first few years, the government was purely military, and probably more to the taste of the people than that which immediately succeeded it; self government, politics and legislation, being quite out of their sphere, and beyond their aspirations. It was during governor Murray's administration, that the first printing press used in Canada was imported; and No. 1 of the *Quebec Gazette*, with matter half French, half English, appeared June 21st, 1764. This journal started with a subscription list of only 150 names; merely noted passing events; and was neutral in politics.

An attempt was made to substitute the laws of England, for those hitherto in use in the colony; a change extremely unpalatable and offensive to the newly conquered subjects; which repugnance was openly manifested.

There were now unmistakeable signs of the American revolution looming up in the distance. Disputes were commencing between Great Britain and her old American colonies respecting the rights of imposition; and even in the Imperial Parliament great diversity of opinion existed and was expressed on the subject.

The American provinces were opposed to being taxed, and if they had before submitted to pretensions they held in aversion, it was because they did not think themselves strong enough to resist successfully. But their strength was rapidly increasing, and when a series of resolutions serving as the basis of a Stamp Act, were adopted in March, 1764, all the colonies entered protests against the principles thus laid down. The essence of their opposition was expressed in the assertions, " No taxation without representation. As British subjects, we assert that we are not imposable except through our representatives." They were also loud in their complaints on other points, which they considered as so many steps taken towards bringing them into subserviency. Notwithstanding this strong opposition, the Imperial Legislature passed a law in 1765, extending the provisions of the Stamp Act in Britain, to all its colonies. This brought the spirit of contradiction to a culminating point, and roused so strong an opposition that finally the obnoxious law was repealed; which had the effect of softening provincial hostility for a time; but with the advent of a new ministry, other troubles arose. In 1767, taxes were initiated on several articles for exportation to the colonies, and stringent measures were taken to enforce submission. This project was yet more odious to the Americans than the Stamp Act had been; overt resistance was manifested; and a general convention was proposed. The arrival of four regiments of soldiers with artillery, for a time put a stop to demonstrations of opposition; but the discontent only smouldered. In 1770, energetic measures were taken to carry out this new policy, but the ministerial agents were met by a system of such spirited and concerted resistance as effectually thwarted their purposes, and eventually led to the separation of the colonies from the mother country.

This state of things was rather favorable than otherwise to Canadian interests, as an important concession was made at this period, by the restoration of the civil jurisprudence of Lower Canada. This however, was done in the face of a strong and determined opposition on the part of the old subjects of the King, who had settled in the Province, expecting that in all cases wherein they were personally concerned, the laws of England were to apply.

While laws, enacted in 1774, thus tended to reconcile the Canadians to British domination, that which closed the port of Boston, infuriated the southern provincials to the utmost. This act had been passed in retaliation for the outrages and audacities committed by the radical colonists against the ministerial agents. It had become apparent that neither Old or New England would bate a jot of their respective pretensions, and that the sword alone must decide the quarrel. At the first provincial congress which met in Philadelphia, an address was drawn up inviting the Canadians to join the disaffected party; copies of which, found their way into the country; yet the effect intended to be produced by them, was to a great extent neutralized by expressions used in an address previously issued, which bore hardly upon the recognition of the Catholic religion in Canada, and the permanent establishment of French law. This, with the remembrance of old antagonisms, was the means of losing Canada to the new confederation.

General Carleton, now Major-General and Knight of the Bath, returned to Canada in 1774, and inaugurated a new constitution. He formed a legislative council of twenty members, eight of whom were Catholics. Several Canadians were placed in office; colonial feudality was respected, and the seminaries were recognized. But Carleton's situation was a difficult one at this crisis, as many, through widely different motives, became American partisans. " Liberty " and " Independence " are high sounding words, and in the present case, were not without effect. However, the clergy and seigniors were bound to British interests, and the majority following the lead of the superior classes, rejected the American invitations to revolt.

In the meantime hostilities between the British and their American colonists were precipitated by the casual conflicts at Lexington and Concord: blood had been spilt; the Americans were arming everywhere, also taking possession of forts, arsenals, and government stores. The battle of Bunker Hill was fought, in which the British, though twice repulsed, were finally successful in carrying the entrenchments of the provincials.— This battle, according to the numerical forces engaged, was the bloodiest and most obstinate of the whole war; and if eventually lost to the Americans, answered the parliamentary slightings of their opponents, and taught the British regulars to respect their courage and determination.

A project was now put on foot for the invasion of Canada, by a combined attack; one detachment was to enter the Province by Lake Champlain, while Col. Arnold was to make a descent on Quebec, by way of the Kennebec and Chaudière rivers. The details of this futile attempt to take Canada, also the more successful ending of American campaigns at the South, the " Declaration of Independence " in 1776; and the aid subsequently afforded by France in achieving that independence, are all matters of common history.

This independence having been established, negotiations for peace were opened in Paris, and the memorable Treaty by which Great Britain recognized that independence, was signed September 3rd, 1783,

General Carleton had been replaced by General Haldimand, who, after a short administration, had given place to Lieutenant-Governor Hamilton. The latter was superseded in 1785, by Colonel Hope, who soon after gave place to Sir Guy Carleton, raised to the Peerage as Lord Dorchester, and re-appointed as Governor-General of British North America.

A project for a constitution of Canada had been submitted to Lord Dorchester which divided the country into two prόvinces : the expressed design of hich separation was to put an end, if possible, to the competition between the old French inhabitants and the new settlers from Britain and the British colonies. A Council and House of Assembly were proposed for each division.

When the new law came into operation, Canada passed under the rule of the fourth government set over her during the thirty-one years succeeding the Conquest. First, there was martial law from 1760 to 1763 ; military sway from the latter date to 1774 ; a species of civil rule from 1774 to 1791 ; and finally, a partially elective system to commence in 1792.

After dividing Canada into two provinces, and apportioning the laws and regulations which were to prevail in each, the new constitution provided that all public functionaries, beginning with the Governor-General, should be nominated by the Crown, and be removable at royal pleasure ; and that the free exercise of the Catholic religion with the conservation of its rights should be guaranteed permanently. In each province there was to be instituted a legislative Council and a legislative Assembly. An executive Council, the members of which were to be of royal nomination, to advise the Governor, was instituted, with the powers of a court of appeal in civil matters.

In 1790, the division of the Province into three se- - parate districts, or departments, took place. In order to visit England, Lord Dorchester transferred his functions to Major-General Alured Clarke, who fixed the time for the election of members to the Assembly, in June.

Lord Dorchester resumed the duties of his office in 1793, and in the succeeding session of Parliament, gave great attention to efforts at equalizing the income and expenditure of the Province.

In 1796, Robert Prescott, Esquire, replaced Lord Dorchester as governor. Soon after his accession to office, difficulties arose with the council respecting the management of the public lands ; which troubles were the probable cause of his Excellency's return to England in 1799. He was succeeded by Robert Shore Milnes, Esquire, as Lieutenant-Governor. About this time, the government entered on possession of the Jesuit's estates. In 1800, an Act was passed to sanction the foundation of a royal institution intended to promote a general system of public instruction. The Protestant bishop of Quebec, himself the originator of the project, was called to preside over the new institution.

The first French newspaper *Le Canadien*, appeared at Quebec in November, 1806.

Events were now transpiring which seemed a forecast of coming war. Preparations were made for the crisis, which, however, was long delayed through the efforts of diplomatists.

At this critical juncture, Sir James Craig arrived as governor, and took the oaths of office in October, 1807. He was a military officer of some repute, but possessed some characteristics which made him unpopular as an administrator among the people to whom he was sent. Party spirit had been kept alive by the frequent introduction of vexed questions and angry debates upon them; and though a certain restraint was temporarily observed, adverse feelings grew stronger, each contestation having a tinge of national jealousy. An unfortunate antagonism between the Executive and the Legislative branches of the government, finally led to a dissolution of parliament, the suppression of *Le Canadien* newspaper, and the arrest and imprisonment of several persons, which gave great offence to the opposition.

Governor Craig was succeeded by Sir George Prevost, a veteran officer of Swiss origin. His first official acts restored to a great extent the good feelings between parties; and soon the most lively sympathy sprang up between the governor and people. War was now imminent between Britain and the United States.

The governor made a tour of observation along the frontier lines, examining the fortified posts, and noting the military positions; from which he returned satisfied with the spirit manifested by the people. Anxious to stand well with the clergy, Sir George had several conciliatory interviews with the Catholic bishop of Quebec; who profited by the occasion to obtain a full recognition of the legal existence of catholicism in Canada.

The Americans commenced the campaign of 1813, by a series of operations against Upper Canada, which, though at first attended with varying success, terminated in their being driven from the country. Invasions from other quarters were equally abortive; and after various attacks and defeats, ravages and retaliations, hostilities ceased; and in August, 1814, British and American envoys met at Ghent in the Low Countries, to confer on terms of pacification. On the 22nd and 24th of December, two treaties were signed; the first containing commercial, the second, political stipulations; both of which were ratified by the respective governments. Each party was to restore whatever territory had been taken during the war; and the subject of the rightful limits of Canada and New Brunswick was referred to a mixed commission, afterwards to be constituted, for its final settlement.

Sir George Prevost had been popular as a ruler among the people of Canada, and when summoned to England to defend himself against accusations preferred in consequence of the unfortunate ending of the Plattsburg expedition, he carried with him their deepest regrets and warmest sympathies. But before he was called to meet his enemies face to face, he died from the combined effects of fatigue, exposure, and a deeply wounded spirit. His health, never robust,. had been materially affected by an overland passage from Quebec to St. John, N.B., where he embarked for Britain; his death taking place shortly after his arrival in London: consequently the court martial appointed to try him, never met. The military reputation of the dead warrior was at last cleared of the stain attempted to be cast upon it, by members of his own profession.

CHAPTER IX.

RENEWAL OF POLITICAL DISCUSSIONS AND AGITATIONS IN CANADA.—SUCCESSIVE ADMINISTRATIONS.—DISORDERED FINANCES.—CONTINUED ANTAGONISM OF PARTIES.—THE EARL OF DALHOUSIE.—APPROACHING CRISIS.—DEPUTATIONS, ADDRESSES AND COUNTER ADDRESSES SENT TO LONDON.—CANADIAN AFFAIRS IN THE BRITISH PARLIAMENT.—SUCCESSIVE ADMINISTRATIONS.—COURSE OF CANADIAN HOUSE OF ASSEMBLY.—SESSIONS OF 1831-2.—RIOT AT MONTREAL.—CHOLERA IN CANADA.—INTENSE POLITICAL FEELING.—SESSION OF 1834.

THE war just terminated had, while it lasted, a calming effect upon the habitual discord between the executive and representative chambers. Peace having come again and Prevost being gone, the old dissensions began to re-appear.

General Drummond entered office as substitute *pro tem* for a regularly appointed governor; and while in the discharge of his official duties, his attention was drawn to existing abuses, and to providing means to regulate them. With these official probings, he was occupied till the opening of Parliament in 1816; soon after which, the house was dissolved by the governor in virtue of an order sent from London.

At this period Sir John Coape Sherbrooke, arrived as governor. His official career was begun by acts which seemed to indicate sympathy with the people, and augured favorably for his future popularity.

In a general way, his prudent polity greatly moderated the ardor of partisanship in the colony; and after the Parliament met, January 17th, 1817, the Assembly seemed well disposed toward the executive.

He soon after demanded his recall under the plea of failing health, and embarked for Europe shortly after the close of the session. It was confidently asserted that he was disgusted with the task he had attempted; and it is probable that he wished to avoid troublesome contentions.

Instructions had been sent him to stand firm against the opposition of the House, but in answer he had enlarged on the embarrassments of his situation, and the impossibility of carrying out such a course in the present unquiet state of the popular mind.

His immediate successor was the Duke of Richmond who arrived at Quebec in 1818, and at once assumed his official duties; but sickened and died suddenly, August 28th, 1819.

For a time the government was administered by the Hon. James Monk; and afterward by Sir Peregrine Maitland, until the arrival of the Earl of Dalhousie in 1820. Parliament had assembled in 1819, but was at once dissolved by Mr. Monk; a step which greatly increased the agitation already existing, and from the first it was foreseen that the government would have a more refractory Chamber to deal with in future. As soon as the New Parliament met, the representatives elected their speaker, but nothing further was effected, as on the demise of King George III, an immediate dissolution of both the Imperial Parliament and Canadian Assembly followed.

Lord Dalhousie arrived during the election of 1820 ; and on the meeting of the House in December, the new governor's opening address seemed to flow from the heart of a man who ardently desired that good-will and harmony should prevail.

Intelligence of the introduction to the House of Commons, of a bill for the reunion of the Provinces, at once awoke opposition, and was postponed for a time through the influence of some distinguished Commoners. When news of this reached Canada, public meetings were convoked among French Canadians in all parts of the country to enter a protest against the measure.

On the meeting of Parliament in January, 1827, it was found that the old animosities were still in force ; and when the supplies were asked for, the demand was met by a flat refusal, which act brought matters to a sudden issue. This was the most solemn censure that a country could pass against the administration. So Lord Dalhousie understood it, for the Chambers were prorogued the next day. In the elections which necessarily followed, the Assembly gained every possible advantage, and the liberal press were strong in condemning the Governor's polity. But that functionary grew only the more firm and unwavering in his course, and looked upon the opposition chiefs as so many incipient rebels. The Chambers met on the 20th of November, and M. Papineau was elected president of the assembly ; but the Governor refused to acknowledge him as such, and immediately prorogued parliament. The country was now in a state of intense agitation. The government party prepared an address, thanking Lord Dalhousie for the energetic measures he had taken, and for striving to put an end to the divisions that distracted the colony. On the other hand the partisans of the Assembly continued to agitate with ardor. Addresses were adopted for transmission to the King and Imperial Parliament, in which the abuses of power imputed to the governor were reproduced and denounced. Deputies were sent to London with petitions, to which a great number of signatures were appended.

Counter addresses were also despatched from Lord Dalhousie and his supporters. The governor, on his part, dealt vigorously with defective magistrates, militia officers, and the opposition press. The like agitations were also disturbing Upper Canada.

After prolonged debates, the House of Commons referred the Canadian petitions to a special committee of its members. The report of this committee was neither adopted nor yet repudiated.

Sir James Kempt replaced Lord Dalhousie at Quebec,

and matters were left to pursue their old train, as no permanent results followed the parliamentary debates.

The new governor had received ample instructions for his guidance from the Home office. The provincial legislature met near the close of the year 1828 ; M. Papineau was recognised as president of the Assembly; and Sir James assured the Chambers of a lively desire on the part of the Home Government to correct all abuses.

In 1830, the government passed into the hands of Lord Aylmer. The same course of conduct was pointed out to him, yet there was augmented opposition to encounter in the Assembly, and public feeling was far from being satisfied with an expression of good intentions. The reforming party was growing stronger, and the former assembly men in opposition had been re-elected by large majorities.

Several important concessions and reforms were proposed by Lord Goderich, now presiding in the British Colonial Department, yet they were met with apparent distrust, and finally with open rejection by the Assembly; a malign influence seeming to govern its actions.

The factiousness of the opposition was further manifested by acts as uncalled for, as pretentious and inconsistent.

The parliament which assembled in 1831, had among its members many younger men who had brought their exaggerated ideas into the Assembly, and pushed on the chief leaders of the debates, who rather needed restraining influences after polemic heats. They little thought that the British Government, more skilful and far-seeing than their own leaders, would make use of the course they were bent on pursuing, as a pretext of necessity for bringing about the very measure they most dreaded, viz., a union of the two Provinces : or, as best described, in the words of Lord Durham : " The settlement in this Province of a British population, having English laws and usages, and to confide its direction only to a legislature of thoroughly British character."

In this state of public feeling an election took place for a member for Montreal, which lasted through three weeks of obstinate partisan struggle, accompanied by fitful riotings. On one occasion the troops were called out and fired upon the crowd, killing several and wounding more : which event created painful impressions on the public mind.

The Asiatic cholera broke out at this period for the first time in Canada, and raged with great mortality, particularly in the cities of the Province : but terrible as the visitation proved to be, it had little effect in calming the political perturbations of the times.— Gatherings were common in various parts of the Province, and in some parishes particularly, matters were carried to an extent not before heard of in the country.

Too late, the leaders of this agitation sought to allay the fury of the storm they had conjured : for they found it as impossible to restrain as to guide the current of popular feeling, which they were now obliged to follow rather than lead.

The British party also had its meetings, in which counter resolutions and addresses of sympathy were moved for the governor and his supporters, as a set-off for the assemblages in the parishes.

The Provincial Parliament assembled January 7th, 1834, when it soon became apparent that neither party were in the least inclined to abate in their respective pretensions. Previous to the opening of the session, Mr. Stanley had replaced Lord Goderich as Secretary of State for the Colonies. The new minister had before become inimical to the French Canadians, and was by them considered a partisan of *Anglification;* and consequently, nothing that should emanate from him, could be expected to find favor with them.

After the preparation of an exposition of grievances and a bold avowal of political preferences by leaders in the Assembly, the Governor prorogued the House; which step roused the opposition party to a state of feeling indicative of incipient rebellion.

CHAPTER X.

THE CRISIS.—CANADIAN AFFAIRS IN BRITAIN.—ELECTION TROUBLES IN CANADA.—APPOINTMENT OF A ROYAL COMMISSION.— FAILURE OF EFFORTS AT RECONCILIATION.—RUPTURE WITH THE GOVERNOR PARLIAMENT PROROGUED.—PREPARATION FOR ARMED INSURRECTION—DEMONSTRATIONS FOR GOVERNMENT— MARTIAL LAW.—ARMED OPPOSITION PUT DOWN BY FORCE.— DEBATES IN THE BRITISH PARLIAMENT.—EARL OF DURHAM.— SIR JOHN COLBORNE.—RENEWED TROUBLES.—STRINGENT MEASURES.—PROPOSED UNION OF THE CANADAS.

The antagonistic courses pursued by the parties in opposition, sufficiently prove that the times were critical. Much uncertainty prevailed respecting the future policy of the British government, each party in Canada hoping and believing that a final decision would be favorable to their own views and wishes. Current rumors and journalistic hints, nourished the hopes of either in turn.

A new election of parliament members now took place, the returns of which were still more unfavorable to the government than before. The polling was attended with disorders in many places. Associations inimical to each other, were formed, and renewed petitions were preferred to the King.

Local demonstrations, fiery speeches, and efforts of political journalists, all manifested an increasing violence and passionateness. The provincial parliament opened February 21st, 1835, but its first proceeding was to enter a protest against the remarks made by the governor at the last prorogation, and to expunge the report of his speech from the journals of the House. This was a declaration of war at the outset.

Sir Robert Peel, then British minister, formally announced that he was about to send out a government commission of neutral colonial politics, charged to examine into the circumstances of the case, and report to the home authorities whatever it was needful they should know. The Earl of Gosford who was appointed Royal commissioner, had the reputation of being firm in character, yet liberal in his opinions. Two others, viz, Sir Charles Grey, and Sir James Gipps, were associated with him. They arrived at Quebec in August 1835. The Chambers opened on the 27th of the succeeding October. Lord Gosford made a long address to the Assembly, dwelling much on the reforms intended, and as his discourse breathed moderation and justice, it was hoped that the threatened storm might pass over. But during the debates of the session, the two branches of the legislature became more alienated in spirit and action than ever; their contentions ending only in the prorogation of Parliament. Commissioners

Grey and Gipp returned to England, and the report of the commission was laid before the Imperial Parliament early at its next session.

Notwithstanding current rumors, and threatening demonstrations, Lord Gosford was slow to believe that serious outbreaks would occur, and regarded as exaggerated the reports that reached him. He knew that the leading aspirations of the French Canadian people, were to preserve their usages and nationality, which would at once have been jeopardized by the annexation of their country to the United States. He also believed that things would mend if the two councils were liberalized, and in this faith, recommended the addition of seven French Canadians to the Legislative Council, and nine more to the Executive Council. The Chambers were summoned to meet on the 18th of August. In his opening address, the governor recommended the Assembly to make disposition themselves for the employment of the revenue; at the same time intimating that if they did not, the home government would order it to be done for them. Upon this, the majority of the members of the House, with a fatal obstinacy, voted an address protesting against the suggestions contained in the report of the commissioners, which being presented to the governor on the 26th of August, he immediately prorogued the Parliament by proclamation.

Concurrent circumstances had now convinced Lord Gosford that Papineau's partisans meant nothing less than to set up a republic. In several localities of the rural districts, the people were led away by agitators. Opposition discourses went on unceasingly in town and country. The young men of the movement party were especially violent, and great efforts were made to induce the humbler classes generally to join in a revolt: secret associations were formed and open resistance concerted. In several parishes, warlike preparations were in progress; clubs were formed and secretly armed; bullets prepared but kept hidden.

The Executive Council took immediate measures to quell the insurrection and cause the law to be respected. The authorities began to act with vigor against defective magistrates and militia officers. The catholic Bishops of Montreal and Quebec, issued pastoral letters to their flocks, enjoining them to be on their guard against evil counsels and inflammatory appeals; and reminding them of the duty of obedience to the powers that were established.

The whole district of Montreal was put under martial law, and the people in many places began to renounce publicly all participation in the revolt. The insurrectionary movements in the parishes had been summarily suppressed, and some of the leaders, now sensible that they had acted rashly, sought to persuade the governor to call the Assembly together; but Lord Gosford declined to do so. Similar troubles had also been experienced in Upper Canada, where bodies of Canadian malcontents and American sympathisers raised the standard of revolt, but were soon defeated and dispersed.

Lord Gosford had long solicited his recall. His resignation was now accepted, and Sir John Colborne who had from the first of the insurrection, been invested with command over the whole military force in the two Canadas, was appointed to fill the place of governor temporarily.

When the Imperial Parliament assembled, Lord John Russell explained what measures had been taken for the suppression of the revolt; soon after which, a bill was brought in for suspending the constitution of Lower Canada.

The provisions of this bill were brought forward successively, and led to discussions which lasted several days; yet the opposition was of a character not likely to result in any way favorable to the radicals. Nevertheless several prominent members of both houses of Parliament, blamed the conduct of ministers, and commended clemency for the insurgents. Another inquest was to be made on the spot, as to the state of the country: the Earl of Durham was chosen chief of the mission of inquiry, and made immediate preparations for his passage to Canada. Meanwhile, as soon as the Imperial Parliament had suspended the Canadian constitution, an order was sent to Sir John Colborne, then administering the government, to form a special council for despatch of the more pressing executive business. This body, 22 in number, part of whom were Canadians, met in April.

The mission of the Earl of Durham so auspiciously begun, was marked by acts which gave great dissatisfaction to the home government, and the occasion was eagerly seized to damage the credit of the cabinet under whose instructions he acted. Intelligence of the disapproval of his course, wounded him to the quick, and he at once renounced the further prosecution of his mission ; announcing his retirement in a proclamation to the people. The government was again left in charge of Sir John Colborne, Lord Durham returning to England in November.

At this period, refugees from Canada in the United States and the armed Americans who sympathised with them, organized an invasion which was to take place with a simultaneous rising of the disaffected people of both Canadas. Early in November, symptoms of this appeared in several of the parishes, and a corps of Americans and refugees entered the province with hostile intent. Such attempts were also made in different parts of Upper Canada. The acting governor who was prepared for these demonstrations, immediately assembled the council, proclaimed martial law, and with a sufficient armed force proceeded to the invaded region. There was little resistance, most of the disturbed districts being surrendered by the invaders on the approach of troops ; and whatever opposition was made, was soon suppressed. The American government sent an armed force to repress frontier disorders, and little was effected by the insurgents. Many arrests took place, however, for participation in the revolt; several were condemned to death, and many more were banished. Thirteen of the number thus condemned, suffered the extreme penalty of the law.

In May, 1830, a bill was introduced into the Imperial Parliament, providing for the union of the two provinces. The project was accepted by the Upper Canadian legislature ; but we need hardly say how distasteful the measure was to a majority of the Lower Canadians. Protests were drawn up against it in the districts of Quebec and Montreal.

CHAPTER XI.

ADMINISTRATION OF LORD SYDENHAM.—SIR CHARLES BAGOT.—SIR CHARLES (BARON) METCALFE.—EARL CATHCART.—THE EARL OF ELGIN AND KINCARDINE.—SIR EDMUND HEAD.—LORD MONCK.—CONFEDERATION.—SIR JOHN YOUNG.

THE union of the two provinces marks an era in Canadian annals. The law passed by the Imperial Parliament in 1840, took effect February 10th, 1841, when the Right Hon. C. P. Thompson, who had been in the country since 1839, was raised to the Peerage as Lord Sydenham, and became sole representative of the Queen in Canada.*

The first united Parliament was summoned to meet at Kingston in June, 1841. Several important measures were passed by it, relating to municipal institutions, popular education, customs, currency, &c. The

---

* Notwithstanding the political troubles, in 1840 the provincial revenue had reached the sum of £184,000, while the expenditure was but £143,000. In 1844, (the year nearest to the union wherein a census was taken) the population of Canada East was given as 697,000 souls, of whom 524,000 were of French origin, the remainder being of British or foreign blood.

session terminated in September under the most melancholy circumstances, occasioned by the violent and unexpected death of the Governor-General, who was thrown from his horse and mortally hurt. The accident took place on the 13th of that month. The deceased nobleman was deeply and universally regretted.

The new constitution of United Canada as embraced in the act of union, embodied several features not before introduced into colonial constitutions, the most important of which was *responsible government*, that is, a government controlled by colonial ministers of the crown having seats in the legislature, responsible to it for their official acts and for their advice to the Governor-General. Second in importance, was the concession to the House of Assembly, of a complete control over the revenue in all its branches, and the entire supervision of the expenditure of the country. This was just what the great liberal party had long been contending for; while to meet as far as possible the views of the other party, guards and checks were interposed, which have been gradually relaxed. Much had been accomplished in a short space of time by the late Lord Sydenham towards elevating and improving the country.

Sir Charles Bagot was his successor in office, becoming Governor-General of Canada in 1842. He had many difficulties to contend with, arising from the smouldering embers of party rivalries and passions which were some times fiercely roused. By a prudent and conciliatory course however, he succeeded in calming the heats of angry strife, and many useful measures were passed by the legislature during his administration. His health failing, he returned to England where he died in 1843, aged 63 years.

Sir Charles Metcalfe, who had distinguished himself as Governor of India and of Jamaica, succeeded Sir Charles Bagot. His efforts to mitigate what he felt to be the evils of mere party government, and his appointments to office, led to a difference between himself and the members of his cabinet, who resigned office. They maintained that appointments under the Crown should be made chiefly with a view to strengthen the administration, and upon the advice of ministers responsible to Parliament. Sir Charles, on the other hand, maintained that the patronage of the Crown should be dispensed according to merit, irrespective of party objects, and for the sole benefit of the country. Other points of difference arose, which widened the breach; on an appeal to the country, the policy of Sir Charles was sustained by a majority of the electors, and he was shortly afterward raised to the Peerage as Baron Metcalfe. He was compelled to resign his office and return to England, in consequence of disease, where he died of a cancer in the face in 1846, aged 61 years. It was during his administration that the government removed to Montreal. On his return to England in 1845, General Lord Cathcart, Commander of the Forces, assumed the reins of government, which he held till the arrival of the Earl of Elgin and Kincardine, early in 1847. This period was made sadly memorable by the prevalence of what was termed "ship fever," which had been induced by famine, and had spread desolation in Ireland and Scotland, driving multitudes to seek refuge in Canada. They brought fever and death with them; and for a time pestilence was abroad in the land. Measures which were promptly taken to provide for this calamity, in some degree mitigated the evil.

Lord Elgin entered heartily into his official duties, and soon public attention was drawn from the pestilence to the political state of the country. He exhibited a comprehensiveness of mind and a singleness of purpose, which at once gave dignity to his administration, and divested the settlement of questions then agitating the public mind, of much of that petty bitterness and strife which had before entered so much into the political discussions of the day. Under his auspices responsible government was fully carried out, and every reasonable cause of complaint was removed. Rarely had a governor so identified himself with the interests of Canada, or sought so ably and effectually to promote them; and the consequences were favorable in the highest degree to the general improvement and prosperity of the country. A general election took place in 1848, giving a large preponderance of the reform party in the House of Assembly. The governor at once surrounded himself with the chiefs of that party, and measures of great utility and importance were passed by the legislature.

One measure however, produced a sudden ebullition of party violence, which for a time disturbed the general harmony and brought disgrace upon the Province. In 1845, a former ministry under Lord Cathcart's administration, had issued a commission of inquiry into the losses sustained during the rebellion, by individuals, either from military necessity or from lawlessness. Their report was but partially acted upon at the time; but so great was the pressure brought to bear upon the government by parties who had suffered those losses, that in 1849, the matter came up before the governor in council, and subsequently before the legislature for final settlement. The measure proposed, being thought too indiscriminate and liberal by the party in opposition to the government, warm discussions arose in the house, and a violent agitation commenced throughout the country. The measure however, passed both houses, and was assented to by Lord Elgin in the Queen's name. No sooner had he done so, than he was assailed in the streets of Montreal, and as a crowning act of violence, the Houses of Parliament were set fire to, and with their valuable library almost totally destroyed. Beside the irreparable loss of the library, and of the public records, a fatal injury was inflicted upon the good name and public credit of the country, and popular violence for a time triumphed. The seat of government was at once removed to Toronto.

In consequence of this ebullition, Lord Elgin tendered his resignation; but the Queen declined to accept it, and raised him a step in the Peerage. After a time tranquillity returned; and with it the unfeigned respect of the great mass of the people for his Lordship, with an admiration for the courage and ability he had displayed during an eventful crisis in their history. Many measures of great benefit to the country became law during his administration, and at the period of his departure from Canada in 1854, the Province again enjoyed peace and prosperity. Before leaving, he procured the passage of the reciprocity treaty with the neighboring republic; which opened a ready market for surplus agricultural products, and for large quantities of lumber. *

Several important lines of railway, prominent among which were the Grand Trunk and Great Western,

---

* This treaty was concluded in June, 1854, between Lord Elgin, Governor of Canada, and Mr. Marcy on the part of the United States. Its design was to regulate commercial intercourse between the two countries; and it was to remain in force ten years from the time at which it came into operation; or further still, until the expiration of twelve months after either of the contracting parties gave notice to the other, of its wish to terminate the same.

It expired on the 11th of September, 1864, after which, either Great Britain or the United States were free to give notice of the termination of its provisions; to take effect twelve months after the date of such notice. Of this power the United States government availed itself, and the treaty came to a final termination in March, 1866. Steps have since [been taken towards negotiating a new treaty, but hitherto without any successful issue.

G

were also projected and commenced during this administration.

In the great International Exhibition which was held at London in 1851, Canada made a most favorable impression on the British public.

Sir Edmund Head succeeded Lord Elgin as governor of Canada in 1854. His administration was a memorable one in the annals of the country; being noted for the number and extent of public improvements effected; foremost among which, was the completion of the Grand Trunk Railway to Rivière Du Loup, and of the Victoria Bridge over the St. Lawrence river at Montreal. The Clergy Reserve, and Seigniorial Tenure questions, were also finally disposed of. In 1855, and in 1861, Canada again distinguished herself in the great International Exhibitions. In 1856, the Legislative Council was made a partially elective Chamber. In the same year, an ocean line of steamers running to Ireland and England was established. In 1858, the decimal system of currency with appropriate silver and copper coins, was introduced.

The closing period of Sir Edmund's administration was rendered still more memorable in 1860, by the visit of his Royal Highness the Prince of Wales, to Canada and other British North American Provinces as well as to the United States. The Prince met with an enthusiastic reception wherever he went; his presence as the especial representative of his august Mother the Queen, evoking feelings of the warmest enthusiasm and loyalty for Her Majesty. While in Canada, His Royal Highness inaugurated the Victoria Railway Bridge, and laid the corner stone of the Parliament buildings at Ottawa, that city having been previously selected by Her Majesty as the permanent seat of Government for Canada.

On the retirement of Sir Edmund Head, Lord Viscount Monck was appointed to succeed him. The civil war which commenced in 1861, between the Northern and Southern States of America, greatly deranged the trade of the country, and led to many difficult and embarrassing complications.

In 1864, the feeling of antagonism that had been kept alive in Parliament between the Upper and Lower Canada factions reached a crisis. In the successive elections that had been held during the preceding years, it was found that the hostile majority from either Province in the legislature, was increased rather than lessened. A project of confederation designed ultimately to embrace the whole of the British North American Provinces, was therefore set on foot, by which each was to have the management of its own local affairs; while to a general government it was designed to leave matters common to all. An Intercolonial Railway connecting Canada, New Brunswick and Nova Scotia, directly with each other, so as to afford a winter outlet for travel and commerce, has also been projected.

It was expected by friends of the enterprise, that should this principle of confederation be applied to the different Provinces, an impetus would be given to internal trade and foreign commerce, and a new era of social and political prosperity dawn upon the colonies ; and further, it was hoped that the bitter party personalities which had grown out of national rivalries and sectional jealousies, might give place to more enlarged and liberal views, and to a more enlightened statesmanship, and that our public men might feel that in representing parts of a great confederation, their policy and acts should be dictated by a higher and more dignified national standard than as yet they had attained.

By Act of Imperial Parliament the Provinces of Canada, Nova Scotia and New Brunswick, were constituted one Dominion under the name of Canada; which Act, according to Royal Proclamation, took effect July 1st, 1867. It was provided in the Act, that the new Dominion should be divided into four Provinces, named, respectively, Ontario, Quebec, Nova Scotia and New Brunswick.

The part of Canada known as Upper Canada, constitutes the Province of Ontario; the part known as Lower Canada, forms the Province of Quebec : while the Provinces of Nova Scotia and New Brunswick, retain the same names and limits as before the passing of the Act of Confederation.

In the autumn of 1868, Sir John Young arrived in Canada, to succeed Lord Monck as governor general.

EASTERN TOWNSHIPS. 101

CHAPTER XII.

UNITED CANADA. — ITS LIMITS AND BOUNDARIES. — SURFACE OF COUNTRY.—LAKE SUPERIOR.—HURON.—ERIE.—ONTARIO.— THE ST. LAWRENCE AND ITS TRIBUTARIES.—EXTENSIVE CHANNEL OF INTER-COMMUNICATION.—EXTRACT FROM EUROPEAN CORRESPONDENCE. — UPPER CANADA. — LOWER CANADA.— COMMERCIAL FACILITIES. — AGRICULTURAL PRODUCTS. — EXPORTS AND IMPORTS. — REVENUE AND EXPENDITURE. — DEBT AND ASSETS. — PUBLIC IMPROVEMENTS.—CONSTITUTION AND CIVIL GOVERNMENT.—EDUCATIONAL SYSTEM. — MUNICIPALITIES.—JUDICIARY.

THE country hitherto known as Canada, comprises but a small part of British America. Taking it lengthwise, its limits extend from the 60th to the 84th degree of west longitude; and from the 42nd to the 52nd parallel of north latitude. It lies in the form of a parallelogram extending north-east and south-west. The inhabited part of it is included in about 36,000 square miles ; the remainder being still in its primitive state.

The northern and eastern boundaries are Hudson's Bay Territory, Labrador, the Gulf of St. Lawrence, New Brunswick, and a part of the State of Maine ; the southern, are the States of Newhampshire, Vermont, and a part of New York, to St. Regis on the St. Lawrence, about 75 miles above Montreal ; that being the point where the 45th parallel of north latitude strikes the river, which then constitutes the division to Lake Ontario ; whence the countries are separated by the chain of lakes and connecting rivers, to Lake Superior at the north-west, where it must be confessed, the extreme limit seems rather undefined.

The surface of this vast extent of country includes every variety of scenery, from the bold and precipitous mountain with its snow-capped summit, in its rugged and unapproachable grandeur ; the magnificent river with its thundering cataract or foaming rapid ; the expansive lakes within which lie beautiful and fertile islands ; to the extensive forest plains or cultivated fields from amidst which have sprung up towns and villages ; while at many points on lakes or rivers, are cities of commercial or military importance.

At the further north-west is Lake Superior, said to be the largest body of fresh water in the world. It is 360 geographical miles in length ; resembles an irregular crescent in form ; while its surface is 627 feet above the level of the Atlantic, and its shores give indication of having been forty or fifty feet higher. Through this lake we are enabled to attain a distance of 2,000 miles by water, from the mouth of the St. Lawrence. Its surplus waters issue near its south-eastern extremity into St. Mary's channel, through which they are carried more than forty miles to Lake Huron. About midway are the St. Mary's falls (Sault Ste. Marie) around which a short canal has been constructed, so as to admit vessels into Lake Superior.

Lake Huron is the second in succession, as well as magnitude, of this great chain. It is about 240 miles in length, and not less than 220 in breadth; its circumference being nearly 1,000 miles. Its surface is only 32 feet below that of Lake Superior; being thus 595 feet above the sea level; and it is equally with that lake, distinguished for the clearness and brilliancy of its waters, and for an extraordinary depth of 900 or 1000 feet. This lake pours out its surplus waters at its southern extremity through the river St. Clair, which stream expands into a lake of the same name, about 26 miles in length, by about the same in breadth. Both this lake and the Detroit river which issues from it, are extremely shallow. The latter flows 26 miles, when it expands into Lake Erie.

This body of water is about 244 miles long, and at its centre, 58 miles in breadth; its circumference being estimated as somewhat less than 658 miles. Its surface is said to be 565 feet above the level of the ocean; making it thirty feet lower than Lake Huron. The depth seldom exceeds 270 feet; which shallowness is accounted for by the supposition that the basin of the lake is becoming filled with deposits carried down by the rivers. It is the most dangerous of the lakes to cross, being very subject to storms and sudden gusts of wind, rendering the navigation at all times insecure.

Here the great channel of communication changes to the north-east. The Niagara river issues from Lake Erie, between Fort Erie and the city of Buffalo. It is about 33 miles long, steam navigation ending at Chippewa nearly opposite Navy Island, where the Welland river enters it. Below this point, the current rapidly increases; the roaring of the yet distant and unseen Fall is heard; a misty cloud rises and hovers over the waters; the sound grows louder; the banks rise higher; and with swiftly concentrating force, the mass of waters rush, foaming and furious, to their tremendous leap, the world-renowned Falls of Niagara. Some seven miles below this, the river again becomes navigable, till it enters lake Ontario. These obstructions to the passage of vessels are overcome on the Canadian side, by the Welland Canal, which joins Lake Erie at Port Colborne, and enters Lake Ontario at Port Dalhousie.

Ontario is the last and most eastern in the chain of these "Inland Seas." Its length is given as 172 miles through the centre from south-west to north-east. It is 750 miles from the sea, and 234 feet above it. The name "Ontario," which signifies "The Beautiful," is considered peculiarly appropriate; as the surrounding scenery partakes of the calm and peaceful order, rather than the striking and sublime in nature. It lies in the midst of a highly cultivated country; and numerous cities and towns on its bays, inlets and tributaries, are fast growing into importance. At its eastern extremity, through the mighty stream which now for the first takes the name of St. Lawrence, the surplus waters of this vast connection of lakes and their numberless tributaries, pour their resistless flood, hastening "Onward to the Ocean." After a short distance the channel of the river expands and takes the name of the " Lake of the Thousand Isles ;" given in consequence of the innumerable islands of every variety of size and form which are here grouped together. Passing these, with somewhat contracted channel the river continues on its course till an island causes the rapids of *Long-Sault*, to avoid which the Cornwall canal was constructed. Past this point, the river again expands to the width of five miles, and is here called lake St. Francis. Below this, the channel is obstructed by rapids in a degree that makes navigation difficult and dangerous for some distance ; to avoid which, and enable vessels to ascend as well as descend the current, the Beauharnois canal has been constructed. Below this the river spreads out into Lake St. Louis. Here at the point opposite where the waters of the Ottawa mingle with those of the St. Lawrence, is situated the Indian village of *Caughnawaga*, or "the village of the rapids." Passing this the river again contracts. when the Lachine rapids, or *Sault St. Louis* of Jacques Cartier memory, are formed by the body of water which rushes foaming among rocky obstructions for a distance of nine miles; to avoid which, the Lachine canal was built. We now pass the city of Montreal, the commercial metropolis of Canada; below which, the river is navigable for sea-going vessels. But about 40 miles down, where it receives the waters of several large rivers from the south side, it expands into Lake St. Peter and becomes so shallow that it has been found necessary to dredge and deepen a channel which is extremely intricate at best. This lake is 25 miles in length, with a breadth varying from one to ten miles. Immediately below this, on the northern side, is situated the town of Three Rivers; up to which the waters of the great river rise and fall at the regular ebb and flow of the ocean tides. Now expanding, then contracting, and occasionally receiving the waters of some considerable tributary, the mighty flood nears Quebec, and flows majestically past the " Stronghold," in a somewhat narrowed channel, yet with a deep strong current. Twenty miles below this, the waters begin to have a saline taste which naturally grows stronger till they acquire the briny saltness of the ocean. At Kamouraska the river is twenty miles in width, which continues increasing till it reaches the island of Anticosti, where at what is usually termed its mouth, it has acquired a breadth of 60 miles.

This island is 135 miles in length, by about thirty miles in width at its broadest part. It has but few inhabitants, little of the land being fit for cultivation;

but contains two light-houses for the benefit of mariners; two depôts of provisions in case of shipwreck; and a permanent hunting and fishing establishment. The Gulf of St. Lawrence from the coast of Nova Scotia to that of Labrador, is 300 miles in width.

The northern shore of this river for more than 200 miles up from its mouth, is said to present nearly the same primeval range of forest as when first penetrated by the early French navigators : the only exceptions to this, being Tadousac at the mouth of the Saguenay river, and a few other unimportant settlements. Tadousac owed its former importance to having been for a long time a chief fur trading post. The southern coast, however, from Gaspé up, gives more sign of civilization and advancement, and the further we ascend, the improvement becomes more apparent. Some points along the coast of the lower St. Lawrence, have more recently become fashionable sea bathing resorts.

This noble and majestic river, which carries in its moving flood all the surplus waters of an immense extent of country, likewise bears on its surface those " White-winged messengers," which take away our own staples of commerce, and bring back to us the products of more genial climes. Up to Quebec the largest class of sea-going vessels ascend without difficulty ; and those of 3000 tons go up as far as Montreal, from which city an inferior class of vessels can reach the Upper lakes, by the course above described.

In magnitude and importance, the Ottawa river

ranks next to the St. Lawrence. It has its sources among the lakes of the north, and may safely be said to exceed 500 miles in length. It was formerly the great thoroughfare by which an extensive traffic in furs was carried on with the natives of those regions; the *voyageurs* avoiding the numerous rapids, and passing from lake to river by *portage;* till according to previous arrangement, they met another class of messengers called *couriers des bois,* whose business it was to collect and bring the furs to an appointed rendezvous.

More recently, however, the valuable timber on the banks of this river and its tributaries, has drawn the attention of those engaged in lumbering, and immense quantities of saw-logs are every year floated down to the cities of the St. Lawrence, whence much manufactured lumber finds its way to European markets.

The channel of the Upper Ottawa is much broken and obstructed by islands and rapids, among which may be found many points of interest to the lovers of beautiful natural scenery: yet it is hardly probable that either the *voyageurs* of old, or the hardy raftsmen of the present day, had either time to admire, or taste to appreciate them: more probably thinking of them as greatly multiplying their labors and fatigues.

Near the location of the city of Ottawa, are the famous Chaudière or Kettle Falls, said to be eighty feet in height by about 212 feet in width. The peculiar shape of the impeding rock turns the current toward the centre of the river, and thus concentrates its force as it plunges into a chasm, or kettle as it is termed, which has been found to be of extraordinary depth. The supposition that there exists a subterraneous passage beneath the bed of the river, which receives part of the mass of waters, is increased by the fact that half a mile lower down, they come boiling up as if from the kettle.

Below this, the navigation is obstructed at points, rendering it perilous except to boatmen of strength, skill and experience. Sections of canal have been constructed to avoid these dangers. Still further down, the river expands into the "Lake of Two Mountains," so called from two hills in the vicinity; after which the channel of the Ottawa is separated; which division forms the island of Montreal. The part of the river passing back of that island, joins the St. Lawrence below at Repentigny; while far the greater volume of water enters it above at Lake St. Louis.

The St. Maurice which enters the great river from the north, is composed of two principal branches, the most westerly of which has its source in a remarkable chain of small lakes situated far to the north. Cataracts occur upon this river, one of which is said to be 150 feet in perpendicular height. The waters of the St. Maurice are divided at its mouth by two small islands into three distinct channels, giving it the appearance of Three Rivers, which is the origin of the name given to the town near its junction with the St. Lawrence. Much valuable timber is found on the banks of the St. Maurice and its tributaries, and floated down to Three Rivers.

Further down toward Quebec, but on the same side of the flood, comes the Jacques Cartier River, which, issuing from the distant mountains in the north, rushes rapidly in with its tributary waters, as if hastening to swell the mighty current.

The Saguenay river issues from Lake St. Johns, which lies directly north of Quebec, and is said to be just 100 miles around. This lake receives the waters of many large rivers and streams, but discharges only through the Saguenay; which accounts for the extraordinary depth of that river. Though some distance north of Quebec, the climate in the vicinity of this lake is said to be far preferable to that on the sea coast, and the land is of excellent quality for cultivation. The scenery is thought unsurpassed in any section of Canada, and settlements are rapidly springing into life. Ships of the largest size can ascend the Saguenay river 70 miles, and schooners go up to the head of tide water 15 miles further, to the foot of a series of rapids ten miles in length. The Saguenay flows in a southwestern course, till it enters the St. Lawrence at Tadousac.

The chief tributaries of the St. Lawrence coming from the southern side, are described elsewhere. This great river with the connecting lakes thus affords immediate and direct water communication for about 2,000 miles of inland coast, without reference to those affluents which come from all parts of the interior.

A European, writing on the resources of Canada and

their availability through these natural and improved facilities for inland navigation, says : " Their waters transport the produce of the settler's labor to distant markets, and lay open to his enterprize the wide-spread forests and plains, that but for them would still have remained the heritage of the Indian hunter and his brutal prey. Among the greatest proofs of enterprize in the world are those canals by which navigation is made practicable from the ocean to Lake Superior.

" The display of the natural products of the far-reaching lands, watered by the giant St. Lawrence and its tributaries, at the great Exhibition of 1862, came to the eyes of most of us with a sort of shock. It was surprising, indeed, to behold such evidences of wealth given by a dependency which was associated in the popular mind with frost and snow,—with Niagara, Labrador, and French insurrection—Moose, moccasins, and Indians.

" There we saw an exuberance and excellence of growth in timber and in the cereals—in all kinds of agricultural produce, combined with prodigious mineral riches, showing what a future Canada may expect when population and capital combined, shall disinter its treasures and develope its resources."

UPPER CANADA (ONTARIO).

This Province is about 750 miles in length, and from 200 to 300 miles in width. Its surface is generally undulating rather than mountainous, the most elevated portions being the Laurentian hills, which appear at intervals running west, and north-west, but are generally mere water sheds rather-than bold prominences. The magnificent chain of lakes which form the southern and western boundaries of Upper Canada have a total length of 1085 miles, and cover an area of more than 70,000 square miles. The principal rivers are the Ottawa, separating it from Lower Canada; the Niagara, dividing it in part from the United States; the Grand River which flows into Lake Erie; the Trent which discharges into the Bay of Quinté; the Thames, which falls into Lake St. Claire; and the Aux Sables, Maitland, and others which enter Lake Huron.

Upper Canada was originally settled mostly by the United Empire Loyalists of America and their descendants, and by emigrants from the British Isles. It was constituted a distinct government under the name of Upper Canada in 1791; the first Parliament being opened at Newark (Niagara) in 1792, by Col. J. G. Simcoe, the first Lieutenant Governor. The House of Assembly consisted of only sixteen members, and the Legislative Council of only seven.

The chief cities and towns of Upper Canada are Toronto, Hamilton, Kingston, London, Brantford, Belleville, and Cobourg; while many others are fast growing in population and importance. Ottawa city, on the river of that name, is the seat of government of the Dominion of Canada.

The climate of Upper Canada, though somewhat

inclined to extremes both in winter and summer, is yet sensibly tempered by the influence of the great lakes; and is milder than that of Lower Canada. Wheat is the staple product; and barley, oats, rye, peas, buckwheat, Indian corn, and the common domestic vegetables are raised in abundance. Some sections also, particularly the south-western parts, produce fine fruits.

LOWER CANADA (QUEBEC).

This Province is about 600 miles in length, by about 300 miles in breadth. Though not strictly speaking a mountainous country, its scenery is more imposing than that of Upper Canada, on account of the magnitude of its rivers, and the greater height of its mountains. A range enters the Province from the south, known here as the *Notre Dame* Range, and continues at intervals to the lower St. Lawrence; while on the north is the Laurentian range, extending west and north-west, from the Gulf of St. Lawrence into the interior. Some of those mountains are from 3000 to 4000 feet high.

The chief rivers are described elsewhere. The chief cities and towns are Quebec, the ancient capital; Montreal, the commercial metropolis; beside which, are Three Rivers, St Hyacinthe, and the towns of St. Johns, Sorel, and Sherbrooke; while others are growing apace.

The climate of Lower Canada is more steadily severe in winter, and warmer in summer than that of Upper

H

Canada. Spring usually opens late, but vegetation grows rapidly. The agricultural products of the Provinces are similar, with the exceptions that less wheat is grown and less choice fruit is raised here than in Upper Canada.

COMMERCIAL FACILITIES.

In addition to the natural advantages possessed by Canada, commercial facilities have been increased by the construction of numerous canals, railways and telegraph lines. Steamboats and other lake and river vessels are now numerous. The first steamboat built in Lower Canada, was launched at Montreal, by the Hon. John Molson, in 1809, and was named the Accommodation. On the first trip, she left Montreal on the first of November, and reached Quebec, on the morning of the fourth; the return trip occupying a week.

The first steamboat built in Upper Canada, was launched at Ernesttown, in 1816, and named the Frontenac. The first trip was made May 30th, 1317. The postal system of Canada is now quite efficient. Reciprocity arrangements exist for the free exchange of natural productions with Great Britain and her other North American colonies.

AGRICULTURAL PRODUCTS.

In addition to the different kinds of grain and vegetables, hemp, flax, hops, tobacco, &c., are successfully cultivated in many parts; and maple sugar, Canada

Balsam, Gensing, &c., are extracted from our forests. The total quantity of wheat produced yearly in united Canada, is about 30,000,000 bushels; of oats about 35,000,000; rye about 15,000,000; barley 4,000,000; peas 15,000,000; buckwheat 4,000,000; Indian corn 5,000,000; potatoes 20,000,000; turnips 25,000,000; flax and hemp about 4,000,000 lbs; tobacco 15,000,000 lbs; and maple sugar nearly 10,000,000 lbs. Vast quantites of dairy produce are also sent to market from Upper, and from parts of Lower Canada. The value of occupied farms in both Provinces is about $425,000,000; and of farm stock about $80,000,000.

EXPORTS AND IMPORTS.

Lumber and grain form the chief staple of Canadian exports. In 1863, the timber shipped from Quebec was valued at $10,000,000. In addition to the convenience of having open lakes and rivers for reaching sea-ports, slides are constructed when there are falls and rapids on rivers where timber berths exist. It is estimated that at least 25,000 men are engaged in the lumber trade of Canada. The value of exported grain is double that of the timber. In 1862, nearly 9,000,000 bushels of wheat alone were exported from Canada at an estimated value of about $10,000,000. Aside from these resources may be mentioned the products of the forest, the sea, the mine, ship building, and domestic manufactures. The annual value of our exports is from $30,000,000 to $40,000,000. The chief imports into Canada, are Woollens, Cottons, Silks, Iron, Tobacco, Tea, Wine, Sugar &c. Their annual value is estimated at from $40,000,000 to $50,000,000. The Revenue and Expenditure are about $11,250,000 each. The total debt of the Province about $76,000,-000; total assets $77,000,000.

PUBLIC IMPROVEMENTS.

The public improvements of Canada consist of canals, railroads, public buildings, harbors, light-houses, roads and bridges; the most important of which are canals and railroads. The total length of the canals altogether is 235 miles; their cost $21,000,000. The aggregate length of railway is near 2000 miles; constructed at a cost of over $100,000,000. The two principal lines are the Grand Trunk and Great Western. The former includes the celebrated Victoria bridge over the St. Lawrence: the suspension bridge over the Niagara river, connects the Great Western and New-York Central railways. A Canadian line of mail steamships, running to England and Ireland, from Quebec in summer, and from Portland (Maine) in winter, has been established. The Telegraph was introduced in 1847, and extends to all the principal places in the country. Post-offices are also generally established, and are increasing in number. A uniform postage rate of five cents was introduced in 1851; which has been reduced to three cents since the passing of the Confederation Act.

Civil Government.

In Canada, the system of government is monarchical in its most popular form. The Queen is represented by a Governor-General, who is aided and advised by a Council styled the "Queen's Privy Council for Canada."

The Constitution is founded upon and is identical with that of England, with the single exception that the sanctioning of any law may be reserved for the supreme authority of the "Mother Country," whenever the Governor-General thinks proper.* This prerogative is only exercised to maintain the principal of colonial dependence ; for in point of fact, the Imperial Parliament grants the fullest liberty to the colonial Assembly, and the management and enjoyment of all their revenue.

The Parliament of Canada consists of the Queen, an Upper House styled the Senate, and the House of Commons. The Queen is represented by the Governor-General, aided and advised by the Queen's Privy Council for Canada, the members of which are chosen and sworn in as Privy Councillors by the Governor-General, and may be removed by him.

---

* The assemblage of laws, termed the constitution (says an eminent Jurist) is distinguished from the term government in this respect, viz: the constitution is the rule by which the sovereign *ought* to govern at all times; and the government is the machinery by which he *does* govern at any and at all times.

SENATE.

This body consists of seventy-two members styled Senators ; twenty-four of whom are appointed by the Governor-General to represent each of the three divisions named in the constitution of the senate of Canada ; viz : Ontario, Quebec, and the Maritime Provinces.

The qualifications of a Senator are as follows : He must be full thirty years of age ; a natural born or legally naturalized subject of the Queen : must possess lands or tenements to the value of four thousand dollars free from all incumbrances ; and must also be a resident in the Province for which he is appointed. A Senator holds his place during life, subject to the provisions of the act, but may resign it by addressing a writing to that effect, to the Governor-General. Cases are also specified in which the place of a Senator becomes vacant; when the Governor-General is empowered to fill the vacancy.

Questions arising respecting qualifications, &c., are heard and determined by the senate. Fifteen senators including the speaker are necessary to constitute a meeting of the senate for the exercise of its powers.

HOUSE OF COMMONS.

The House of Commons consists of one hundred and eighty-one members. The several Provinces are divided into Electoral Districts, each of which returns one member to the House. Eighty-two are elected for Ontario; sixty-five for Quebec; nineteen for Nova Scotia; and fifteen for New Brunswick. The presence of at least twenty members are necessary to constitute a meeting of the House for the exercise of its powers; the speaker elected by the House, presiding on all such occasions. Questions arising are decided by a majority of voices; the speaker being entitled to a vote only when the voices are equal.

PROVINCIAL CONSTITUTIONS.

For each Province there is an officer styled the Lieutenant-Governor, appointed by the Governor-General, and holding office during his pleasure. The Executive Councils of Ontario and of Quebec, are at first composed of the Attorney-General, the Secretary, Registrar, and Treasurer of the Province, the Commissioner of Crown lands, and the Commissioner of Agriculture and Public Works; and in Quebec, the Speaker of the Legislative Council, and the Solicitor General. The Constitution of the Executive authority in each of the Provinces of Nova Scotia and New Brunswick, are to continue as they existed at the union, till altered by authority. The seat of government for Ontario, is the City of Toronto; for Quebec, the city of Quebec; for Nova Scotia, the city of Halifax; and for New Brunswick, the city of Fredericton. The Legislature of Ontario consists of the Executive and of one House styled the Legislative Assembly of Ontario, which is composed of eighty-two members, representing the several Electoral Districts.

The Legislature of Quebec consists of the Exccutive and of two Houses, styled the Legislative Council of Quebec, and the Legislative Assembly of Quebec. The Legislative Council is composed of twenty-four members, appointed by the Lieutenant-Governor in the Queen's name, one of whom represents each of the Electoral Divisions. These Councillors hold office during life, unless the Legislature otherwise provides. Their qualifications are the same as those of Senators. The Speaker is appointed from among the members of the Council, ten of whom, including that officer, are necessary to constitute a meeting for the exercise of its powers.

The Legislative Assembly of Quebec is composed of sixty-five members, elected to represent the sixty-five Electoral Districts.

The Legislative Authority of "The Parliament of Canada," extends to that class of subjects which are considered of general importance ; instance, the public debt and credit ; the regulation of trade and commerce ; the postal service ; such public improvements as extend beyond the limits of one Province ; the issue of paper money ; the regulation of intercourse with other countries ; bankruptcy and insolvency and numerous other matters affecting the interests and prosperity of the Dominion as a whole ; while to the respective Provincial Legislatures are assigned matters of a more local nature, or such as involve the regulation of the internal affairs of the Province. This class of subjects includes the raising of a revenue for provincial purposes; the regulation of municipal institutions; the supervision of educational matters; the appointment of provincial officers; the management and sale of the public lands belonging to the Province; the establishment and maintenance of hospitals, asylums, &c., with many others of like nature.

EDUCATIONAL SYSTEM.

The earliest educational efforts in this Province were confined to the Roman Catholic institutions of Quebec and Montreal. A Legislative Act in 1801, establishing a "Royal Institution" for the promotion of English education, received the royal sanction in 1802, but failed of accomplishing much. The next step in legislation was in 1805; when an act was passed facilitating the establishment and endowment of elementary schools, and making it lawful for the *Fabrique* (that is, the Roman Catholic priests and church-wardens of each and any parish,) to establish one school in each parish, and to increase the number in proportion to the increase of the inhabitants. This, however, failed of accomplishing the desired object. In 1829, another step was taken in legislation by an appropriation of lands for the establishing of schools; and provision was made for the election of trustees for their management. This is the earliest date of the introduction of the popular element into our educational system. In 1832, a further appropriation was made by government, and the sum of £20 each, was granted to a limited number of schools in each county. Reading, writing, and arithmetic were the only branches required of the teachers.

In 1841, a permanent fund was erected for the establishment and support of the schools, and an annual grant of £50,000 voted for their continued maintenance. In 1843, other changes were made, resulting in the enactment of separate schools for Upper and Lower Canada, adapted to the prevailing religious elements in each section. In Quebec (Lower Canada) the general local municipalities have the direct control of the schools, and elect commissioners for their management. They are supported partly by government and partly by local taxation, a monthly scholar fee being laid to cover deficiencies. It is provided that in communities composed of mixed religious elements, minorities may dissent from majorities, and on going through certain prescribed forms, are entitled to a proportion of the school money for the establishment and support of the dissentient schools.

In 1856, the whole school system of Lower Canada underwent a comprehensive revision under the direction of the Hon. Dr. Chauveau, Superintendent of Education for the Province. There are now three Universities in Lower Canada, viz: McGill college at Montreal, Laval college at Quebec city, and Bishop's college at Lennoxville: also four special schools, viz: two institutions for Deaf Mutes; one Agricultural school, and one

School of Arts and Manufactures. Besides these are eleven Classical colleges; fifteen Industrial colleges; sixty-two Academies for boys and mixed; sixty-eight for girls; one hundred and eighty-four Model schools, and three thousand five hundred and eighty-nine Primary schools; under the supervision of twenty-eight school Inspectors. All of the above receive Legislative aid. Three Normal schools for the training of teachers have been established; two of which (one French and English each) are at Montreal and one (French) at Quebec city: the three being under the direction of the Superintendent of Education, who divides among the colleges, academies and schools, the annual legislative grants, and administers the school laws generally.

Two "Journals of Education,"—the one French and the other English—are published by the Department.

By the late Union Act equal powers and privileges are extended to the dissentient schools in each Province, and should questions arise respecting the rights of minorities of the Queen's subjects on this point, final appeal is open to the Governor-General in Council; and in case of the neglect of the steps necessary to be taken by the Provincial authorities, the Parliament of Canada reserves the right to make and enforce remedial laws.

MUNICIPAL SYSTEM.

Up to the Union of the Provinces of Upper and Lower Canada in 1840, there had existed no municipal system in the country. Special acts were passed for incorporating cities and towns, but there were no local representative bodies in the rural districts. From the year 1796 till 1841, all matters relative to the opening of roads, building of bridges, &c., were under the direction and superintendence of the Grand Voyer or his deputy ; and as these officials usually lived in the cities, it can be readily conceived that the opening up of a road in those days was a work involving time and expense.

Soon after the above named union, municipal districts were established in which district councils were formed ; and in addition to other powers transferred to those bodies, was that hitherto vested in the Grand Voyer. During the few subsequent years, other changes were made, and in 1855, the present system of parish or township and county councils was established.

Each parish, township, or village corporation elects seven councillors, who may hold monthly or quarterly sessions, choosing a mayor and secretary-treasurer.

The business of this council relates to the valuation and assessment of property ; the preservation of public order ; the imposition of fines, and the general regulation of the internal affairs of the municipality.

The Mayors of the different local councils within the county, form a county council, which holds quarterly sessions, from among their number electing a chairman or Warden. A secretary-treasurer is also chosen.—

This body has supervision of those matters within the county in which more than one local council is interested, and also acts upon such appeals as are made by the township, parish, or village councils.

The object sought by the repeated changes that have been made in the order of municipal affairs, has been their better regulation; and as new views and improved plans were presented, to adopt and incorporate them into the system; till at length it has become so thoroughly improved as to operate to the very general satisfaction of the people.

A city must contain at least 10,000 inhabitants to entitle it to an act of incorporation as such; and have a mayor, aldermen, and common council men.

A town must contain 3,000 inhabitants, and have a mayor and town councillors.

A village is a smaller municipal division. The members of the corporation are elected once in two years by the assessed rate payers.

With the extension of settlements in the country, counties were formed for representation in Parliament, and as inhabitants increased, have been divided as occasion required. The counties of Lower Canada were assigned their present limits by Act of Parliament in 1853; the new counties being formed for electoral purposes, while the old divisions remained for convenience in registration, till the new counties were furnished with Registry offices.

Where the population is sparse, two counties are

sometimes united for the return of one member. Townships are divisions of less extent, and are formed into municipalities as soon as found to contain the required number of inhabitants.

JUDICIARY.

From a very early period, Lower Canada has been divided into districts for judicial convenience. On account of the great extent of these divisions, the steady increase of inhabitants within them, and the necessity there existed for a more ready and efficient administration of justice, other divisions have been made, and new limits assigned the respective districts from time to time. Each of these divisions comprise two or more counties, and contain a court house, jail and public offices. The place where these are located is called the *chef lieu* of the district.

The superior courts of the Province are the Queen's Bench, which has one Chief Justice, and four Puisné Judges. It hears appeals, and also gives judgment in serious criminal matters.

The Superior Court has one Chief Justice, and eighteen or more Puisné Judges. It gives judgment in important cases, and in appeals referred from the Courts below.

The third in order is the Circuit Court, the jurisdiction of which is limited to sums not exceeding $200. The circuit at the *chef lieu* of a district, has concurrent jurisdiction with the circuit courts in and for the various counties in the same districts.

The Admiralty Court which tries maritime cases, has one Judge residing at Quebec.

Commissioners' courts having jurisdiction in sums not exceeding $25, are held in the several townships and parishes, the first Monday of each month, by commissioners appointed by the Government.

Justices of the Peace are also appointed from among the prominent inhabitants, and invested with the power of deciding on all rural and other matters of police.

There is a final appeal in important cases, from the superior courts of Canada, to the Judicial Committee of Her Majesty's Privy Council, in England.

Part Second.

CHAPTER I.

THE ABORIGINES OF OUR OWN SECTION. — HOSTILITY TO THE ENGLISH BEFORE THE CONQUEST.—USUAL ROUTES OF TRAVEL. —SETTLEMENT OF VERMONT RETARDED.—DANGERS ATTENDING IT.—A MORE EASTERN ROUTE.—FINDING OF INDIAN RELICS.

IT appears that the territory now known as the Eastern Townships, before the conquest was the hunting ground of tribes belonging to the Algonquin nation, as the Abenquis, or St. Francis Indians, and the Coossucks were known to have occupied the section lying on the St. Francis and Beconcourt rivers and their tributaries, with the northern parts of Vermont and Newhampshire.

The absence of any town or village of Indians within this section, may be accounted for from the fact that a race of men subsisting entirely by the chase, required a large field from which to draw even a scanty sustenance, and, notwithstanding the great extent of forest land in North America, its aborigines were often in straits from the difficulty of finding a sufficiency of game for their support.

Their frequent depredations upon the frontier settlements of the English colonists while the European nations were at war, is matter of history; and it is also well understood that in their predatory excursions, their usual routes lay through Lake Champlain; and if the settlements to be attacked were located on the Connecticut river, they passed up one of the larger streams entering the lake from the east as far as that was navigable for their canoes, and thence by *portage* to the Connecticut or some of its largest tributaries. All the streams falling into the lake being known to them, there were several frequented routes; but between the navigable head waters of Otter Creek which enters Lake Champlain, and those of Black River which discharges into the Connecticut, was a way so much frequented by these hostile parties as to be called the " Indian road."

The obvious reason why no Indian villages were located within the tract now known as Vermont, was the near proximity of several powerful tribes, who were almost invariably at war with each other. During the Colonial and Indian wars, that territory was the great thoroughfare through which most of these warlike expeditions proceeded, and where hostile parties often came into collision; and being situated at nearly an equal distance from the English or French frontier, it might

I

have been exposed to the depredations of either party, as it was the frequent battle ground of their Indian allies; nor was it till after the conquest of Canada by the English, that any considerable settlements were made. True, several points were at times occupied by either, but rather as military posts than actual settlements.

In 1752, townships were surveyed and stockades erected by the British at Coos, on the Connecticut river, the object of which was to form a barrier against the incursions of the St. Francis Indians in case of war; but the effort was of little avail and was finally relinquished. Before the year 1754, several settlements had begun at different points along the Connecticut, but they were effectually checked, and some of them entirely abandoned at the breaking out of the war, which lasted till the conquest.

The instincts of these settlers were sharpened to keenness by the dangers and vicissitudes of their manner of life. "There were seasons when the deer furnished the best venison; the bear, the richest tongue and steak; and when no lurking enemy was near to be attracted by the click and report of the rifle, those sounds were the sure premonitions of a repast, which, but for the meagreness of its appointments, might have been a feast for an epicure. In places where the settlers risked remaining, their houses were fortified to withstand the attacks of musketry. In the spring when poughing was to be done and seed put into the ground, a guard was stationed near so as to give warning in case of danger ; and in going to their work, the settlers would as soon have left their implements of husbandry at home, as their fire arms, for it often proved to be the case, that the same wood which surrounded their little plot of ground and sheltered their dwelling, was also the lurking place of their deadliest foes."* These continued depredations had the effect of arousing the united strength by which the conquest of Canada was finally effected, and an end put to scenes of massacre and devastation.

* History of Vermont.

CHAPTER II.

DESTRUCTION OF THE INDIAN VILLAGE OF ST. FRANCIS.—RETREAT OF ROGERS' PARTY UP THE ST. FRANCIS.—THE PURSUIT.—REPULSE OF THE INDIANS WHO CONTINUE THE PURSUIT.—THEIR FINAL DEFEAT AT THE LOWER FORKS.—DISPERSION AND SUFFERINGS OF ROGERS' MEN.—FINAL END OF THE EXPEDITION.

DURING the interval between the taking of Quebec by Wolfe, and the final cessation of hostilities, a large body of French troops had taken possession of Isle-aux-noix at the north end of Lake Champlain; a post that commands the entrance into Canada in that quarter. The forces there collected being well supplied with munitions of war, made an effectual stand against the entrance of the English at that point. The French had still several vessels on the lake, and General Amherst who at this time commanded the British colonial forces at Ticonderaga and Crown Point (which places the French had successively abandoned), thought it best to delay his advance till he had prepared a superior naval force.

In the meantime he took the opportunity of carrying into effect a project long before determined on, viz., that of punishing the St. Francis Indians (Abenquis) for the frequent and fearful depredations and atrocities they had been guilty of. These Indians had always been firm allies of the French, and as persistent and bloody foes of the English colonists. Major Rogers, a brave and experienced officer of the colonial force, was therefore selected to command and conduct the expedition which was to put an effectual end to their depredations and cruelties.*

" He embarked at Crown Point with 200 men, and proceeded down the lake in batteaux. On the fifth day, while encamped on the east shore of the lake, a keg of gunpowder was accidentally exploded, by which a captain and several men were severely wounded. They were sent back to Crown Point with a party to attend them, and with a force thus reduced to 142 men, Rogers moved forward to Missisquoi Bay, where he concealed his boats among the bushes that overhung one of the inlets, and left in them provisions sufficient to carry the party back to Crown Point.

" Leaving two of his rangers to watch the boats, the party advanced into the wilderness, but on the evening of the second day, were overtaken by the trusty rangers,

---

*In one account of this affair, it is related that Rogers had been driven to the verge of madness by having returned to his home after an absence, to find his wife and children murdered and scalped by a party of these savages; and that in his burning indignation, he sought and obtained the command of an expedition that was to wreak a summary vengeance on the perpetrators of that and other kindred atrocities. The attacking party was composed entirely of provincials accustomed to Indian warfare.

and Rogers was informed that a party of 400 French
and Indians, had discovered the boats and sent them
away with fifty men, and that the remainder were in
pursuit of the English. He kept this intelligence
a secret, but despatched a lieutenant and eight men
with the two rangers to Crown Point to inform General
Amherst of what had taken place, and request him to
send provisions to Coos on the Connecticut river, by
which route he intended to return. He then determined to out-march the pursuing enemy, and pushed on
toward St. Francis with the utmost expedition.

" Rogers came in sight of the village on the evening
of the fourth of October, and leaving his men to
refresh themselves, disguised himself in an Indian
garb brought for the occasion, and went forward to reconnoitre the town. He found the savages engaged in
a grand dance without apprehension of danger, and
returning about one o'clock, led forward his men within
500 yards of the village. At four o'clock the dance
was ended and the Indians retired to rest.

" Having posted his men at the most favourable points,
at day-break they commenced the assault. The place
was completely surprised; the Indian method of warfare was adopted, and wherever the savages were
found, without regard to age or sex, they were slain
without distinction and without mercy. As day-light
increased, the ferocity of the provincials was roused to
intensity, by discovering the scalps of several hundred
of their countrymen suspended on poles and waving in

the air. They were determined to avenge the blood of their friends, and resolved on completely destroying the village and its inhabitants. Of the three hundred souls it contained at the time, two hundred were slain on the spot, several were taken prisoners, and some English captives were recovered. It appears that most of the warriors of the tribe were absent on a hunting and fishing expedition, so that comparatively little resistance could be made.

" The English had only one killed and six slightly wounded: when having reduced the village to ashes, and refreshed his men, Rogers set out on his return at eight o'clock in the morning, with the retaken captives, and such articles of plunder as were of value and could be easily taken away.*

" In order to avoid the party of Indians he knew to be on his track by the way of his entrance into the country, he commenced his retreat up the St. Francis river, directing his course towards Coos on the Connecticut. He was several times attacked in the rear by a party of warriors who had followed in pursuit, and lost several men by them ; but finally formed an ambuscade on his own track, and fell upon the enemy with such success as to put a stop to further annoyance.

* Tradition says that this plunder was taken from the church in St. Francis, and the probability is, that if so, it consisted of valuable articles which according to a very common practice in those early times, had been sent from France by pious devotees, to the native church. Other articles may also have been collected.

"In the meantime, by order of General Amherst, four persons proceeded from Charlestown on the Connecticut, up that river, in two canoes loaded with provisions. They landed on a small island at the mouth of the Passumpsic river, where they encamped for the night; but in the morning, hearing the report of guns and supposing Indians to be in the vicinity, they were so terrified that they reloaded their boats and hastened back to Charlestown.

"Rogers at this time was encamped but a few miles up the Passumpsic, and about noon reached the mouth of that river. Observing fire on the island, he made a raft and crossed over to it; but to his great surprise and disappointment, no one was there, nor was any provision left. The men with him, already reduced to a state bordering on starvation, were so disheartened by the prospect before them that they gave up in despair, and before the next day several of them died. Rogers now gave up command, telling the men to take care of themselves. Some were lost in the woods and perished miserably: but the leader and several of his party, after the most incredible hardships, succeeded in reaching Charlestown, and after having collected and refreshed the survivors of his band, proceeded with them to Crown Point, where they joined General Amherst's command about the first of December. Upon examination, Rogers found that his loss after leaving the ruins of St. Francis, was three officers, and forty-six privates."

The foregoing narrative of the destruction of St.

Francis village by Rogers and his party, which was taken nearly verbatim from Thompson's " History of Vermont," gives but a meagre description and conveys but a faint idea of the difficulties and dangers which he really encountered on his retreat through the wilderness.

The subjoined account was received from the late Jesse Pennoyer, Esq., who, while on a professional tour of exploration and survey in the townships, was accompanied by Captain St. Francis, late Chief of that tribe of Indians, and one of the *few* survivors of the pursuing party. This Captain St. Francis gave Mr. Pennoyer the following relation of the affair, which was corroborated by a person named Bowen, son of one of Rogers' men ; and still further in its main features, by the descendants of a person named Barnes, one of the recovered captives mentioned. A little discrepancy exists between this and the published account respecting the number of survivors, but at this distance of time, we can do no better than to receive both, and weigh probabilities. Mr. Pennoyer's account is as follows.

" On the morning of the fifth of October, 1759, the assault took place ; 200 Indians of all ages and sexes were slain ; some few taken prisoners, and a number of English captives retaken ; when Rogers with his party, prisoners and rescued captives, made a hasty retreat up the St. Francis river. The Chief of the tribe (father of the Capt. St. Francis above named)

with a number of his warriors had come in during the
day and immediately held a council of war, at which
it was decided that all present should start in pursuit the
next morning; and that as many more of their warriors
as they could call in, should start with canoes on the
second day. Accordingly on the morning of the sixth,
about fifty warriors, each armed with a gun, tomahawk,
and scalping knife, started up on the north shore of the
river; and on the 7th, about forty-five more, armed like
the others, set off in seven large canoes. These overtook the party that had started the day before, at the
rapids in the township of Wendover, where the first
detachment had waited the arrival of the canoes; and
at day break on the morning of the eighth, they all set
off together. They came up with Rogers' men in
Kingsey, and in the skirmish that ensued, the Indians
lost several men, while only three or four of the other
party were slightly wounded. As soon as the Indians
discovered any of their enemies, they fired and often
missed aim; in fact, their shots seldom took effect, and
before they had time to reload they were shot down,
or if the savage was separated from his fellows, his
enemy quickly rushed up and dispatched him with the
bayonet. The Indians sustained considerable loss in
this manner throughout the day, though they succeeded
in doing but little injury to their enemies. On the
morning of the ninth, they held a council, at which it
was proposed and urged by quite a number of their
party, to abandon the pursuit and return. Well

would it have been r them had they done so; but the majority of them were for pushing forward to the 'Little Forks,' (now Lennoxville) where they intended to give their enemies another battle. On the tenth, Rogers crossed with his men to the opposite shore of the river, near Brompton Falls, and while the Indians were making the *portage*, pushed on toward the 'Big Forks,' (now Sherbrooke) and gained an elevated point (near the present residence of Mr. Sheriff Bowen). His experienced eye at once saw the strategic importance of the position thus gained, and he at once determined to avail himself of the advantage, to attempt the defeat of his enemies, and put an effectual end to further annoyance from them.

" The river, which here makes a short turn, on one side has a high bank which was then thickly wooded ; while the opposite point was low, and then covered with a thin growth of stunted bushes. From this height Rogers had a fair view of the river for a distance of two miles down. For the purpose of deceiving and misleading the enemy's scouts, he sent a small party of his men on to the ' Little Forks,' with instructions to build fires, in a manner similar to what had been done in their former camping grounds, and then return to join the main body at the heights beyond the mouth of the Magog.

" In the mean time the Indian scouts passed up the north shore till they saw the fires at the ' Little Forks,' and thinking that Rogers' party were encamping there, returned to the falls with the intelligence. Those who had completed the *portage* immediately set out in the canoes, leaving the others to follow up the north shore, expecting to find their enemies in camp at the ' Little Forks,' and hoping to surprise and cut of their retreat. But their vigilant foe had not been idle.— During this time he had posted his men in such a manner that while they were out of sight themselves, they had full view of the approaching canoes a long way down the river, and as they came near, could tell about the number of savages on board of each, by the number of paddles. He then arranged for the attack by appointing a certain number of men for each canoe, equal to the number of paddles in each; and detailing a man to fire at each Indian separately from the first to the last, gave strict orders to aim well and not to fire till the signal was given by himself. Everything was quiet until about one half of the canoes had turned the point, when the signal was given and the men fired with such sure precision and deadly effect, that almost every savage in the canoes was either killed or mortally wounded. The Indians on the north shore had got a little in advance of the canoes by crossing the point with the intent of fording the river, but on hearing the firing they hastened back to the point. By this time Rogers' men had reloaded, and being still in ambush, again fired and killed several, while the others retreated up to the crossing, and forded the river. The English still kept on the heights, and a general and irregular skirmish followed ; but as the savages were in the open woods on the intervale below the mouth of the Magog river, while the others were covered by the thick forest on the hill, the result was, that most of the whole Indian force was either killed or badly wounded, while but few of their enemies were either killed or hurt.

"It being now near sunset, the English party crossed the Magog, and proceeded up to the ' Little Forks,' where they encamped for the night, and the next day Rogers addressed his men thanking them for their bravery and obedience to his orders, and for their faithfulness and perseverance from the first of the difficult enterprize which had been undertaken and carried out, in order to pay their savage foes in their own coin, for their repeated cruelties to the colonists in former years.

" This, they had now achieved by the almost entire annihilation of that tribe of their enemies.

" Then ordering the remaining prisoners to be shot, he resigned his command, advising the men to divide themselves into small companies, each of which should take a somewhat different route to reach the appointed rendezvous on the Connecticut river. This method he deemed best, as affording to small parties a greater chance for game, on which all had now to depend for food. The advice was followed, some of the men going up the St. Francis to the mouth of the Eaton river, others taking the Massawippi or Coaticook.* After several days,

---

* One account says that a party started on their return by way of the Magog and lake Memphremagog; and all are agreed in

Rogers and those of his command still with him, reached the appointed place, but were disappointed and greatly disheartened at finding the still smoking brands and warm embers of a camp fire, and other unmistakeable evidences of the recent departure of those who had been sent to their relief; but no food was there, and the fainting men, wearied, sick and starving, gave way to despair.

" But three of them with their brave leader,—himself the most courageous and persevering of the whole,— leaving their sick and starving comrades to gather such subsistence as the forest afforded at that inclement season, went forward with what remaining strength they had, in search of help. The four formed a raft on which they descended the river to the first rapids, where they lost their raft and barely escaped being drowned. They then formed another, on which they came to the second fall, which by effort almost beyond their strength they succeeded in passing, and then floated down the current to where they obtained relief. Food was at once sent to the famishing men left behind ; and persons were hired to go up the river with canoes and provisions, and with orders to bring in any of the straggling survivors who might have reached the river, or to leave provisions at points where there was the least probability that they might find their way. Having

---

saying that it was only after great privation and suffering that the survivors reached the confines of civilization, while many perished miserably.

attended to this duty, and rested and recruited the remnant of his command, Rogers started on his return to Crown Point, to rejoin the army under General Amherst."*

Thus ended an expedition which has been seldom equalled in the wildness of its conception, the boldness and daring with which it was undertaken, the skill with which it was managed, or the deadly determination by which it was carried out to the end.

We turn from the meditation of such barbarities, connected though they be with the past in our country's annals, with unmitigated horror and disgust; thankful that no further recitals of the kind will be required: rejoiciug that in our day no *necessity* can be urged in extenuation of such acts. The only approach toward a justification of the course then pursued, lies in that special plea. Such was the only mode of warfare recognized by the Indians; they knew no mercy; with them, clemency was cowardice, and pity was contemptible weakness.

It will be observed, that in Mr. Pennoyer's account no mention is made of the *plunder* spoken of by the historian. Reference was made to it however, by Barnes, one of the recovered captives.† He stated that when

---

* We subsequently hear of Rogers as a "Famous Partizan," to whom the commandants of the French posts in the lake country were to surrender by order of M. De Vaudreuil, the last French Governor of Canada.

† So says tradition.

Rogers decided to make a stand and give the Indians battle, a small party, of whom himself was one, was detailed to carry this treasure to a given point on the Connecticut river; and that on hearing guns and being in doubt as to the success of their comrades in repulsing their enemies and fearful of being overtaken by the savage victors, they buried the treasure in what they considered a safe manner, and hastened on without such wearisome incumbrance. Tradition has also assigned various localities as the place of this deposit; and though search has been made by parties professing to possess instructions left by the survivors of those engaged in burying it, nothing approaching any description of this property has ever been found. The more reasonable supposition is, that if ever such articles were buried here, they were subsequently carried off by parties who had obtained a knowledge of the locality, and had the hardihood and shrewdness to effect the removal and turn it to their own advantage.

Some years previous to the destruction of St. Francis, in a descent of those Indians upon one of the frontier towns of New England, among other captives they brought away two young children, a boy and girl, belonging to different families. The boy, who was the eldest of the two, remembered that his family name was Gill.— After the cessation of hostilities for the time being, the surviving friends of the children, sought to reclaim them; but their captors had become their protectors, and being attached to the little ones, refused to give them up.—

An appeal was made to the legal authorities in hope of recovering them by force, but the children were suddenly missing, and were kept in hiding till the parties seeking them were obliged to abandon the search as hopeless and return without them. They were therefore left to grow up among their captors, who had them carefully educated in the French language, and Roman Catholic religion.

When of proper age, these two young people, thus strangely associated, were united in marriage, and from this union have sprung a numerous and highly respectable progeny, who in time, have become so wealthy and influential, as in a great measure to supersede the owners of their captive ancestors in the proprietorship of the soil, and to become, in fact, the largest landholders in the vicinity. Fortunately the captive boy's name had been retained; his posterity have honored it, and risen to enjoy a high social standing in the country; one of them having represented his county in the Provincial Parliament. Our informant had the pleasure of a personal interview with a late member of this family, whom he found intelligent and cultivated, affable and prepossessing. From him (Mr. Gill,) he received the facts above given, and was likewise told that he (Mr. Gill) had visited the place of his ancestor's nativity, and had instituted inquiries respecting any surviving members of the family; but up to that period without other success than learning that all of the kindred had long before left the place, and if any were still living, it was at a distance. The whereabouts of these young people when the village of their captors and protectors was destroyed, is not known; but the supposition is, that they were absent at school: and as they were universal favorites and *protegés* of these Indians, an event so disastrous to the tribe generally, might have contributed to their material benefit and worldly advancement.

CHAPTER III.

THE SEIGNIORIES, THEIR LAND TENURE, &C.—COMMENCEMENT OF
AMERICAN REVOLUTION.—GREAT INFLUX OF POPULATION.—
DIFFERENT CLASSES.—EFFECTS OF CIVIL COMMOTION.—U.
E. LOYALISTS.—STEPS NECESSARY TO OBTAIN GRANTS OF
LAND.—RELATIONS OF AGENT AND ASSOCIATE.—ERRORS OF
THE SYSTEM.—EMIGRATION.—PIONEER LIFE.

WHEN the French began their settlements in Canada, land was granted in extensive lots called seigniories, stretching along either coast of the St. Lawrence far below Quebec, and above Montreal, comprehending an extent of several hundred miles ; and as time progressed, spreading along the principal rivers of Lower Canada. These seigniories each contained from 100 to 500 square miles, and were parcelled out into lots in a freehold lease to the inhabitants, as the persons to whom they were granted had not the means of cultivating them. The proprietors were generally officers of the army, gentlemen of limited means, or religious communities, who were not in a state to employ workmen and laborers. The portion assigned to each inhabitant was three acres in breadth, and from 70 to 80 acres in depth, commencing on the bank of the river, and running back into the woods, thus forming an entire and regular lot of land.

To the proprietors of seigniories, some powers as well as considerable profits were attached. Their grants authorized them to hold courts and sit as judges in what was termed *haute* and *basse justice*, which included all crimes committed within their jurisdiction, treasons and murders excepted. The seignior's income was derived from the yearly rent of his lands, from *lods et ventes* or a fine on the disposal of property held under him, and from grist mills, to the profit of which he had an exclusive right. The rent paid by each tenant was considerable, and those who had many inhabitants on their estates, enjoyed quite a handsome revenue. In the event of the sale of any of the lots of his seigniory, a proprietor might claim a preference of right to re-purchase it; but this power was seldom exercised unless with a view to prevent frauds in the disposal of the property. The seignior had also certain rights respecting timber for building mills, &c.; and tithes of all the fisheries on his domain belonged to him. With these advantages, seigniors might in time have attained to a state of comparative affluence, were their estates allowed to remain entire. But by the practice of divisions among the different children of a family, they became in a few generations reduced in circumstances. The most ample share which retains the name of seigniory, was the portion of the eldest son, the other partitions being denominated fiefs. In the next generation, these were again divided, and thus in the course of a few descents, seigniors became possessed of little more than their titles. This is the condition of most of those estates that have passed to the third or fourth generation.

The inhabitants in like manner make divisions of their small tracts of land or houses, and it is from these causes that many of them are retained in a state of poverty, a barrier to industry and emulation interposed, and a spirit of litigation excited. Some of the domiciliated savages also held land in the right of seigniors.

The townships have all been granted since the conquest of the country by the British, and are settled by a mixture of English, Scotch, Irish, French Canadians, and Americans, with a slight infusion of other national elements in their population. The people of the townships hold their lands by a tenure denominated "free and common soccage."

A period of fifteen years had elapsed from the conquest of Canada by the English, to the breaking out of the American revolution, which time had passed in measurably successful efforts toward a reconciliation of existing differences between conquerors and conquered: and when the troubles between Great Britain and her older American colonies culminated in open war, and attempts were made to induce the Canadians to join the standard of revolt, they were ineffectual. These efforts failed principally through the entire alienation of feeling caused by the old feud between them, and from the distrust born of religious differences.

Many sought refuge in Canada, from the troubles of that distracting period. Prominent and influential men among those who favored the royal cause, then left the country which had ceased to be to them a home. Some of them were native Britons who had crossed the ocean and established themselves in the colonies, expecting still to enjoy the protection of their country's laws, and end their days under the sheltering influences of the flag they honored and loved. But this hope proved an illusion to be quickly and rudely dispelled, and the alternative which remained to them was either submission to what was distasteful and highly offensive ;—was to some an unbearable indignity;—to return to the land of their fathers, or seek an asylum in the wilds of Canada.

Many foresaw the gathering tempest and wisely withdrew in time to escape its fury. Others who had ever been accustomed to regard the yeomanry of their country in the light of dutiful and obedient subjects, and to consider those who should rebel against constituted authority as worthy of the direst punishment, only brought trouble upon themselves in attempting to reason with their opponents, or to coerce them into submission. Warmly and sincerely attached to the Royal cause, it was with mingled excitement, indignation, and disgust, that they beheld people demanding redress for wrongs which seemed to them more imaginary than real, and enforcing those demands with threatening manifestations. These men had vainly striven to stem the tide of popular feeling, and had brought suffering upon themselves and anxiety and distress upon their friends, by interference in the disputes of that troublous time. Not only persecutions and indignities, but arrest and close imprisonment, was often the measure meted out to them in consequence of their loyal principles; yet, as is usually the case, these only increased their attachment to the government of their choice and in like degree prompted dislike and hatred of its enemies. A short experience of life in the midst of such commotions was sufficient, however, to convince them that all efforts to stem the current were unavailing, and desirous of avoiding like repetitions, they withdrew, while yet there was time.

Many who had remained to share the vicissitudes of war, in hope of the retrieval and ultimate triumph of what they believed to be the right, were finally glad to secure a safe retreat. In some cases, through the influence and address of friends who were favorable to the popular cause, their property was saved from confiscation and finally transferred to them in this country.

But still more common were the cases when after prolonged attempts to subdue a power already too strong for them, they were forced to yield to inevitable necessity, and resign house and lands, home and friends, wealth and station, all that men desire in this life, aside from that precious boon itself.

Still another class, more cautious and less impulsive, while hopeless of a successful resistance of the prevailing powers, wisely avoided the heat of party strife, and waited till the fury of the storm was spent, when they quietly disposed of their effects, and transferred their interests and allegiance together. Additions of worthy and desirable inhabitants were made in this undemonstrative manner.

But it cannot be denied that many were brought in by the exigencies of the times, who could only be regarded in the light of unavoidable evils, being of that irresponsible, ill-regulated class that accumulates and thrives amid scenes of tumult and commotion, and constitutes a disturbing element in any community.

It is well understood that for many years before the revolution reached a culminating point, a numerous floating population representing many different nationalities, had been accumulating in those Colonies which offered not only an asylum for the oppressed of all grades and distinctions, but a hiding place for the refugee from justice. This class of people, without fixed principles, or permanent interests in the country, on the breaking out of the war, at once sided with the party which could offer the most tempting inducements. Some were drawn into it by a morbid taste for exciting adventure; others may have had some private pique to be gratified, or some personal quarrel to be avenged, and but waited the opportunity for giving vent to a long nursed wrath; while others still, who were but designing and unscrupulous adventurers, rushed into the conflict with the mere hope of gaining some advantage.

The associations into which such characters were thrown during the long and bloody struggle which preceded their advent into Canada, had anything but a softening and humanizing effect, as all the angry and vindictive feelings were kept fully roused: and when in the course of events the scale turned in favor of the popular party, the bitterness of disappointment and the humiliation of defeat were added to intensify the already over-wrought and over-mastering passions.

Such of the colonists as preferred exile to a surrender of their allegiance, were encouraged to come to Canada. Numbers of them entered the British service, and when the end came, settled in the country. Some of character and ability had offices of trust and profit conferred on them, while others received special grants of land in reward for service rendered, or in remuneration for losses sustained. Large accessions were thus made to the population of the country. It would appear however, that up to the year 1791, unless along the immediate frontier of the Province, the part known as the Eastern Townships was an almost unbroken wilderness. In order to facilitate its settlement, lands were granted on conditions specified, to such as would locate there.

The preliminary steps to be taken in order to obtain the grant of a township of land, were for a number of individuals intending to become settlers, to organize themselves into a company called associates, and select one from their number to act as their agent in the transaction of the business with the government. In this arrangement the agent was to bear all expenses incurred in the survey of the township; to open a road to, and through it; to erect mills within it; and to obtain the signatures of a certain number of persons, pledging themselves to become actual settlers on the premises. The number of associates required, corresponded with the size of the tract petitioned for; forty being the usual number designated for a township ten miles square.

As a first qualification, the person acting as agent for the associates, was to procure a certificate from some source considered reliable, to the effect that he was a responsible character; and furthermore he must show his authority for acting as agent of the associates, by presenting a petition for a certain tract of land designated; in which petition, the peculiar claims of those who preferred it, were set forth; which claims almost invariably related to embarrassments and losses suffered in consequence of the then late American rebellion; and redress was asked for these grievances, in the manner above related. Then followed a description of the size and location of the tract asked for : " Which petition was referred to the land committee for consideration."

The power to issue " Warrants of Survey" rested with the Governor in Council, who for the convenience of parties interested, appointed a board of commissioners at a convenient location, whose duty it was to make the requisite examinations into the characters of parties presenting the petitions, to administer the necessary oath of allegiance, and attend to the business in its various details. The examinations were to be made and the oaths taken, before the parties could be accepted and have their names entered in the Letters Patent.

The arrangements between agents and associates were personal and private agreements by contract between the parties who shared equally, to the effect that of the number of lots drawn by the associate, he should re-convey to the agent, in consideration of the expense incurred and the latter's services in the business, all received over a certain number of acres agreed upon between them, on which " Actual settlement " was to be made. This number was usually 200, and the settler was entitled to his choice of the lots falling to his share; yet exceptions to this were very common, especially if the associate had sons growing up who were considered desirable acquisitions to the community in process of formation, and extra inducements were thought necessary, when a larger proportion of land was offered ; the matter admitting of great latitude.

The prosecution of the business relating to the grant of a township, was often attended with serious delays and great expense, as intricate and vexatious questions were frequently raised, to the great annoyance of parties interested in bringing the matter to a speedy close.

The items of expense involved in the necessary surveys, opening of roads, building of bridges, &c., were almost constant calls upon the time and means of the agent, for which he was not too well repaid by the land that reverted to him, as it often proved to be of a quality unfit for sale or cultivation. In this manner small fortunes were often laid out, without anything like adequate returns ; a statement of the items of expense in a single township, being sufficient to do away with the impression that these arrangements might have been a source of profit to the agent. Indeed the very reverse was almost invariably the case.

Upon the reception of the petition, if all was satisfactory, a warrant of survey was issued by the governor to the surveyor-general, requiring that functionary, " At the proper cost and charges " of the agent and his associates, to make a faithful and exact survey of the tract of land described in the petition. After specifying the various restrictions, limitations, reservations, &c., which were to be made, the surveyor-general was required to report to the person administering the government, within six months from the date of the warrant issued; and to return that document, with a plot or description of the tract, annexed, specifying the outlines, divisions and subdivisions, severally numbered, and the reserves distinctly indicated. *

In the report which accompanied the returned warrant, the surveyor-general certified that he had " Set off and caused to be actually surveyed, marked, measured, and bounded in the field," all the tract designated ; and after indicating the survey into superficial acres, division into ranges, and sub-division into lots, these latter with their numbers were given, with particular descriptions of such as were of irregular conformation ; which were the crown and which the clergy reserves ; then the lots in their respective ranges falling to the agents and associates severally ; the number and size of lots in the tract with the number of acres altogether, exclusive of an allowance for highways. Particular care was had that the reserves were of the same quality and value as the granted lands ; and moreover, it appears to have been so arranged that the titles of such lands as has been located upon by associates, were confirmed to them. Accompanying this report, was a certificate from the surveyor-general of woods, to the effect that no part of the lands thus described, was included in any district marked out as a reservation for masting or other timber fit for naval use.

---

* In all these grants, two-sevenths of each township were reserved from the alienation; viz one-seventh for any future use or disposition of the crown, and one-seventh for the support of a Protestant clergy : which reserves were systematically distributed through the grant.

At the expiration of a given period after the oath was taken, the parties again went before the board of commissioners to represent the state of matters in relation to the fulfilment of the conditions. In very few if any cases were they fully complied with, but the government was lenient and compromises were effected.

Such steps were preparatory to granting the charter which was a formal and wordy document, filled with the details of survey; with a reference to the petition, the certificate of the surveyor-general of woods, and the steps successively taken; when it was declared that the tract thus petitioned for, surveyed and described, " Was created, erected, and constituted a township, to be called, known, and distinguished by the name of——."

It was expressly stated in the charter that if the grantees, their heirs or assigns, should not within one year from the date of the Letters Patent, settle on the premises granted to them, so many families as should amount to one family for every twelve hundred acres; or if they should not within three years, effectually cultivate at least two acres for every hundred acres of such of the lands as were capable of cultivation; and should not within seven years plant and effectually cultivate at least seven acres of such of the premises as were capable of cultivation; that then and in any of these cases, the grant and everything therein contained, should cease and be absolutely void, and the land and premises therein granted, revert to the Crown. Or if any part of the grant was found to be within any previous reservation made by the authorities, it was declared " Null and void and without effect." Still further, it was required, that within six months from the date of the Letters Patent, a copy should be registered in the office of the Provincial Registrar, at the seat of Government, in default of which, the whole should revert to the Crown.

The following are the closing sentences entire :—
" And we do, moreover, of Our special grace, certain knowledge, and mere motion, consent and agree that these Our present Letters being duly registered and a docket thereof made as before directed and appointed, shall be good and effectual in law, to all intents, constructions and purposes whatsoever, against Us, Our Heirs and Successors, notwithstanding any mis-reciting, mis-bounding, mis-naming, or other imperfection or omission, or in anywise concerning the above granted, or hereby mentioned and intended to be granted, lots of land and premises, or any part thereof. In testimony whereof, We have caused these Our Letters to be made Patent, and the great Seal of Our said Province of Lower Canada to be hereunto affixed."

To this document were added dates and the signatures of both the governor and his secretary. It may be proper here to say that though there were exceptional cases, when townships or parts of townships were granted to individuals and parties, without many of the formalities above described, the course pursued was very nearly uniform throughout these townships.

Subsequent events have caused doubt as to the expediency of the methods then practiced of granting lands. There is evidence that at an early stage of the proceedings, the evils that would inevitably follow in the wake of this system, were in a measure foreseen and pointed out; and that in fact, this was at times a cause of very serious disagreement between parties high in official life. However well conceived it might have been in some respects, it was essentially lacking in such guarantee or safeguard as might have effectually prevented the intriguing and corrupt conduct of some engaged in the business; and have secured the upright and honest-minded who were acting in good faith, from being defrauded and victimized by the designing and unscrupulous adventurer. Much fruitless and vexatious litigation might have been prevented, and the government saved the trouble and expense of appointing special commissions to examine into claims and correct abuses which have been a standing disgrace to our section of country. Many appeared to regard these transactions merely in the light of a speculation; assuming all the obligations of asociates without thought of ever becoming settlers on lands to which they thus acquired a claim. The duplicity and intrigue often practiced and sometimes brought home to guilty parties, had frequently the effect of throwing suspicion and distrust upon the innocent, and causing them to suffer unjustly.

It was during the later years of the previous century and the earliest years of the present, that most of the settlements were made in accordance with these arrangements. That party resentments were cooling, is evident from the fact that a majority of those who came to this section at that time, were from the New England States. As a general thing, they were men of large families and limited means, and were no doubt induced to take this step by the feasibility with which land could be acquired. These New England men were mostly of that energetic, self-reliant, and independent temperament, that gave assurance of success in any enterprise they might undertake. Some of them had been inured to backwoods life, and thus had received a training which fitted them to depend on their own exertions; yet it is more than probable that new features of this life were met with in their Canadian experiences.

In many cases the elder sons were of an age to join the company of associates, and thus draw land for themselves, and in all cases there was room enough, good land being both plenty and cheap. The advantages thus offered answered the double purpose of drawing attention to the country, and of encouraging the timid approaches of those disposed to prefer a residence where they would enjoy the protection of British laws.

Of the different motives that prompted our forefathers to give up home and comfort, and enter upon the severe labors and meet the perilous adventures incident to forest life in a country like this,—whether prompted to the change by a spirit of ardent enterprise, restless ambition, or hope of gain—it is not our province now to judge. We only know that they did so; and that in many instances, delicate and tenderly reared women were called to give up the enjoyments of social life, and with young and rising children around them, follow their hardier husbands to the comfortless homes provided for them in the wilderness; that they were forced to bear their part of the self-denials and privations which were invariably the lot of the early settler; and that both their strength of mind and their physical energies were often tasked to the utmost in caring for their families, and in those departments of domestic industry where their services could be made available.

The soil in these townships was fertile, as could be plainly seen from the majestic trees and luxuriant shrubbery with which it was covered. The woods were filled with game, and excellent fish abounded in the streams and lakes; yet with all these helps to a living, those who ventured on the trial knew that for years they should be subjected to the most laborious toil, and though some shrank from the prospect before them, few gave their decided voice against the change.

There appears to some minds a sort of fascination in the incidents and perils of forest life. Cases are common when love of exciting adventure strengthens with indulgence until it becomes a mastering passion. While most of these men were strong in manhood and health, their hearts were buoyant and hopeful of long life, successful effort, and years of enjoyment.

Of pioneer life,—that enigma to many,—one writer says that " Danger seems only to sharpen the spirit of adventure, and attract rather than repel emigration." Another with something of a cynical sneer, remarks that " The great mystery of pioneer life is but a greed for newer, wilder, and more dangerous adventures than as yet had been met with ;" while another with still greater causticity, says that " A great deal of what is called the pioneer spirit, is but the working of a shiftless discontent; as when inefficient men become very uncomfortable, they are quite likely to try emigration as a remedy."

Either of these sententious paragraphs may be true to some extent and in some cases, yet neither of them are suited to universal application. There may be reasons for change foreign to those that are given above; causes known only to the parties most interested and most affected by it, which not only justify but render it highly desirable and expedient.

CHAPTER IV.

TOURS OF EXPLORATION; CHOICE OF LOCATION, AND PREPARATIONS FOR SETTLEMENT.—JOURNEY OF EMIGRANT FAMILY. — DIFFERING ROUTES AND METHODS OF TRAVEL, DELAYS, EXPEDIENTS, &C. — HOUSEHOLD FURNITURE. — FORAGE FOR DOMESTIC ANIMALS. — KNOWLEDGE OF MECHANICS.—MAPLE SUGAR.—SEASONS OF SCARCITY.—HIGH PRICES.—SUFFERING IN CONSEQUENCE.—DESTITUTION.

WHEN the idea of coming to Canada was seriously entertained, the first step to be taken was to open negociations with some person acting as agent for a company of associates in obtaining the grant of a township of land. Next, the father of the family of intending emigrants, usually made a tour of observation and inspection ; when if pleased with the situation and decided to become a settler, he made choice of a location, and some sort of preparation for moving in his family; unless some friend was already on the ground whose shelter they could share while preparing a cabin of their own.

These tours of exploration were usually made on foot, sometimes alone, but more frequently in company with one or more who like themselves, were looking out the land ; and as there were then no " Houses of entertainment" on their route, it was needful that travelers went prepared with whatever they might want in the way of provisions, which in addition to the necessary axe, gun and ammunition, with the indispensable camp-kettle, formed no slight burden: this however, was divided, each bearing his share with great good humor. If fire-arms and fishing tackle were taken, they were depended on to furnish from the woods and streams, whatever was wanting of "fish, flesh or fowl," when only bread and seasoning articles were required to be taken. The travellers were guided to the tract they sought, by *marked trees*, or as they were otherwise called *spotted lines*: which method of pointing out the way to any particular locality had been adopted generally by surveyors and those using the compass, whose business called them through the woods.

Fire was indispensable, both to cook the food when taken, and as a safeguard against the approaches of wild beasts. In those days before the introduction of the useful " Lucifer," fire material consisted of flint, steel and spunk, which were carried in the pocket ready for use. Unless providentially led to the covert of some friendly cabin, these wayfarers were obliged to pass their nights in the woods with their mother earth for a bed, the wide spread canopy of heaven for a shelter, and perhaps the sighing of the wind, the rustling of the trees, the screeching of the owl, or the howling of the distant wolf for a lullaby : the camp-fire being depended on for keeping away the last named dreaded denizens of the forest.

In addition to the fatigues of such a journey, these travellers often suffered excessive annoyance from the swarms of venomous insects with which these woods were then infested at certain seasons of the year. The largest and most troublesome of these was the moose-fly, so called from its being particularly obnoxious to that creature. It is said, when fully grown, to exceed a honey-bee in size, and has a sting so acute that horses rear, plunge, and become quite unmanageable, when bitten by them. Happily they were but a short lived nuisance; but during a reign of about one month, comprising the two last weeks in June, and the two first in July, they were the torment alike of man and beast. So much were the early settlers annoyed by them, that they were often obliged to confine their horses and cattle in darkened stables, and if it was necessary for themselves to go out, to anoint such parts of their persons as were exposed to be bitten by the fly, with some substance distasteful to them. Beside these, were smaller insects, equally numerous and troublesome. Smudges which had the effect of keeping them away, were made of dry touch-wood, which is an excresence taken from the trunks of trees growing in damp soils, or of several pieces of cedar bark firmly bound together; either of which retains fire and emits smoke without kindling into a blaze. At night, the smoke of the camp-fire did good service toward keeping away these merciless intruders, but without the necessary precaution, travellers by day were often nearly blinded by them.

If streams of water were to be crossed on these excursions, the axe was brought into use to cut down a tree on which to pass over, which quickly constructed bridge was left for the use of successive travellers, till some flood carried it away.

The camping ground was usually chosen near some stream of clear water, and while one of the party lighted the fire, another perhaps was busied in gathering hemlock boughs for their bed, while the third was engaged in compounding a savory supper. Partridges which were then exceedingly numerous, often made the principal share in these repasts.

The camp-kettle was suspended over the fire on a shcrt pole supported at either end by small crutches driven into the ground, when with the aid of axe and pocket knife, such articles of table furniture as were indispensable were readily and rudely shaped from the clean hard wood which grew so plentifully at hand. Notwithstanding the simple appointments of the feast or its lack of tasteful surroundings, hunger which is said to be the *best sauce*, quickened the appetite, and novelty gave zest to the entertainment; while the bottle, which was an indispensable accompaniment of such excursions, no doubt added to the general conviviality of the party, as each in turn boasted of the share of adventure he should have to recount on his arrival home; and the song and jest passed round, till the invisible influences of the drowsy god were softly stealing over the senses; when stretching before the fire, they resigned themselves to the arms of "Tired nature's sweet restorer."

The dwelling which was prepared for the emigrant family was but a shanty or cabin, often not more than twelve or fifteen feet square, with log walls and bark roof, and without floor other than the smoothed earth; it being designed as a shelter only till a dwelling of more comfortable dimensions and convenient arrangements could be erected. Yet it answered the purpose intended, and though very primitive in appearance, had the double virtue of being readily and cheaply constructed. It was invariably built of logs uniform in size and length, laid one above another, with the ends so notched as to fit into each other and thus bind the whole structure firmly together. The interstices between the logs were filled with bits of wood and moss and then plastered with clay; a space being cut out for a door and window -each. The roof was covered with hemlock bark which was best obtained for the purpose in the spring of the year when it peels off readily. An opening was left in the roof for smoke to pass out; flat stones so placed as to keep the fire from the logs; blankets or skins hung at the door and window, and the cabin was ready for occupation. If, as was often case, the it too small to allow of a fire, or a bed within, the ground was thickly covered with hemlock boughs as a substitute for the latter, and near the cabin was a frame of poles covered with barks, under which was a fire-place built of stones.

When the time came for the family to move in, a road which had been surveyed and marked, was bushed out along the line of entrance, so as to prepare the way for the sleds which at that early period were the only vehicles that could penetrate into the country. The mother and younger children occupied the front part, leaving the back for bedding, provisions, kitchen ustensils, or such small articles as were brought with the family, while the men and elder boys came in on foot. Winter was often chosen for these journeys, as the roughness of the way was then lessened by the snow which covered the ground, and streams could be crossed upon the ice. Horses were sometimes used at this season, especially if the location to be reached was near the margin of some lake or river, on which the ice afforded an easy way of transportation; but the roads into the interior were so rough in consequence of stumps, stones and like obstructions, that the patient plodding ox was oftener employed for the labor.

If the journey was made in summer, streams which were too deep to be forded, were crossed by means of a raft formed of light timbers firmly bound together by withes. On this, the sled and loading were embarked, while the oxen which had been detached from them, swam over.*

As there were few dwellings on these routes of travel, and perhaps several nights were to be passed in the woods before reaching their destination, the family were made as comfortable as possible in camp, and the animals were turned loose to browse. If the journey was made in winter, the men of the party cleared away the snow from a space of ground, kindled a fire, and gathered a quantity of hemlock boughs, which are said to prevent taking cold from exposure. The largest of these were set in a circle a little back of the fire so as to keep out the wind, while a bed was made of the small branches. This custom is said to have been derived from the Indians and like many of their other practices, was adopted by hunters, surveyors, and others obliged to pass their nights in the woods.

As there was then no hay in the country, cattle were left till spring, except such as drew in the sleds ; and for these, a supply of forage had also to be brought in. People settling in the various localities, came in from different sections, by different routes and modes of

---

* After the lines of road leading into the various sections had been bushed out, much of the travelling done by parties in search of a location, was on horseback ; when if the rider was obliged to camp out for a night, he turned his horse loose to browse, perhaps tied a small bell around his neck to help in finding him, and then with the saddle for a pillow, laid himself down to sleep. If the streams were too high to be forded or too broad to be crossed upon a fallen tree, the horse had to swim and carry his master.

conveyance. Those coming to the townships near the north borders of Vermont, usually came by land directly to their new homes: those locating along the course of the St. Francis, came up that river : while many came in by way of Lake Memphremagog and the rivers through which it is drained. This method of travel, from the necessity there was of making frequent *portages*, was fatiguing and dangerous at all seasons of the year, and distressing casualities were by no means uncommon.

. Those journeying in this manner were usually provided with a sort of tent made of blankets, which they spread on a frame of poles cut and driven into the ground, at any point where they chose to land and pass the night. Under this, a bed of hemlock was prepared, while a fire kindled near, at which their supper and breakfast were cooked, completed the arrangements for their comfort. On frequented routes, a rudely constructed frame was sometimes covered with boughs or bark, and left for the use of successive travellers.

Much persevering and patient labor was necessary in overcoming the serious and unforeseen obstacles which were at times encountered on these journeys. Such hindrances as severe storms, drifted snows, fallen trees, swollen streams, &c., were by no means unusual, and in some instances, as many as fifteen or twenty days elapsed before the travellers reached their destination ; during which delays, it was well for them if they found occasional shelter beneath the roof of some friendly cabin. Unlooked for and unthought of emergencies would frequently arise to make necessary a resort to ingenious and amusing expedients.*

The household furniture in use at that period, necessarily partook of the style and character of the dwelling. If no table had been brought in, one was readily formed by driving four small crutches into the ground at proper distances, on which were laid poles of the length required to support the pieces of board forming the leaf. Every bit of board, box, or whatever had been brought from the former home, was made of great account. An iron pot or kettle, and a frying-pan were indispensables ; but a tea-kettle was a luxury; and many of the kitchen utensils in daily use in the family, were roughly shaped by unskilled hands from the hard timber which grew so plentifully near. A bedstead, dignified by the name of *Catamount*, was also improvised in a manner similar to the table. It stood in a corner

---

* After the more general opening of roads, women often came in on horseback, a distance of one hundred miles or more, bringing infants in their arms, with perhaps a feather bed or other bulky article, bound on behind; while the husband on another horse, with perhaps one or two other children, carried the necessary provisions and other indispensables which were to serve them till the arrival of the lumbering ox-sled. Those coming from a distance often had long tent-like wagons which, as far as the roads were passable for them, served the double purpose of vehicle by day and lodging place at night; but on approaching the newer sections, these were exchanged for sleds. The milk of cows driven in at the time, was also used by the way.

of the cabin, where at a distance from the wall proper for length on the one hand and width on the other, crutches were driven into the ground to support poles that formed the frame. Elm bark stripped into proper widths was then woven around the poles something after the manner of basket work, when this piece of furniture was also ready for use. The space underneath was used for the storage of trunks, boxes, &c., or whatever might be laid aside. Similar make-shifts also supplied many another real want.

The only hay in the country at the coming of these first settlers was the wild grass which grew upon the "Beaver meadows," some of which were found in all parts of the country. They were low, level spots of land lying upon some stream of running water, on which these industrious little proprietors, with an instinct almost amounting to human intelligence, had built dams which set back the water and thus flooded a space often several acres in extent, from which, for their own use and convenience, they had cleared away the timber. On the abandonment and destruction of this dam, the land thus drained was left open, and in time was covered by nature with a verdant clothing. If these meadows were at any considerable distance from the farm buildings of the settler, the grass was cut in season and stacked on the ground, for want of a road by which it could be taken home. Until land was cleared and seeded down, which was not usually till the third year, little could be done in the way of raising stock. Between this wild grass, straw, cornstalks, prepared leaves and browse, forage was supplied for the few cattle that were driven in, till the new farms could be made to produce such as was needed. Grains, seeds, and the smaller domestic animals and fowls, were brought in with the settler's family.

Some knowledge of the use of tools was indispensable to the settler, who brought in with him such as were in common use at the time, these being not only necessary in building and furnishing their dwellings, but in making all the implements of farm labor. There was therefore almost constant use for the axe, saw, auger, adze, plane and shave.

In many sections of the townships, the rock or sugar maple was found in great abundance ; indeed, in some portions it was the most common timber. This was an inducement to some of the early settlers who knew beforehand the product of these trees in spring time, and accordingly chose locations on land covered with them. For many years small wooden troughs, roughly hewn out of almost any kind of timber, were used to receive the sap as it fell from the tree, when it was gathered in buckets and boiled in kettles to the consistency of syrup, then strained and cleansed before being boiled down to sugar. Aside from the taste of the article produced, the making of sugar is by no means a *sweet* or agreeable employment, as it involves an amount of hard work of such a nature as to take away all romantic interest in it. A very short experience of sap gathering, or boiling with eyes blinded by smoke, would convince a novice in the art that the only sweet is the sugar made. Seasons have always varied in the quantity and quality of the article produced, which from the first has been made to contribute materially toward family supplies. Improvements in its manufacture have been made from time to time.

The necessary provisions for one year were brought in with the family, and when once settled in their cabins, it was felt to be most important that as much land as could possibly be cleared, should be prepared to receive seed, as on the proper improvement of seed time, depended the harvest and much of their future comfort : yet as a general thing, it was not till the second or third year that grain enough was raised to furnish bread for the family, and it was no unusual event for this harvest to prove a failure, either through the depredations of bears or destruction by frosts. Those who had been thus unfortunate, or from any cause had been unable to provide against such emergency, were often obliged to go on foot thirty, forty, fifty miles, or even more as the case might be, before finding what they sought, and then return laden with all they could bring for their destitute families. During seasons of scarcity and high prices, much suffering was experienced by these poor people.

Until the introduction of sheep and the raising of flax, such clothing as had been brought in with the settler's family had in most cases to suffice, as there were then no ready means by which the supply could be renewed. We are told that in some of the more remote sections, before wool and flax could be produced and made into cloth, mothers of families were sometimes driven to the necessity of cutting up the blankets they had prepared with great care for bedding, in order to clothe their needy little ones; and furthermore, that the clothing of the men had often to be patched with the skins of animals, for want of cloth.

CHAPTER V.

IMPROVEMENTS IN DWELLINGS, FURNITURE, AND OTHER CONVE-
NIENCES.—MECHANICAL LABOR.—METHOD OF CONVERTING
CORN INTO FOOD.—ERECTION OF MILLS.—OPENING OF ROADS.
—CLOTHING IN USE.—FEMALE EMPLOYMENTS.—SOCIAL
GATHERINGS.—DRINKING HABITS.—FERTILITY OF SOIL.—SUR-
PLUS PRODUCE.—WANT OF A MARKET.—EARLY PRODUCTS.—
TRADING ESTABLISHMENTS.—PUBLIC HOUSES.—WHEELED VE-
HICLES.—WILD ANIMALS.

AFTER the first year's scanty crops had been put into the ground, attention was usually given to the erection of more convenient dwellings, which to a great extent superseded the cabin, though years elapsed before many of the poorer class of settlers had more comfortable habitations. The new buildings were necessarily of the same material, and had the same covering as the cabin, but were a decided improvement on the score of size, being designed to correspond in this with the numbers and circumstances of the families which were to inhabit them.

A cavity for the cellar was made in the centre of the spot chosen, and at one end was a large open chimney which was built up a short way with stones and

M

clay, to resist the action of the fire, and thence carried up through the bark roof, with small split sticks crossed at the corners and filled in with clay, when the whole inside of the chimney was plastered with a thick coating of the same substance, and the largest flat stones that could be procured were laid around the fireplace for a hearth. If the dwelling was put up before the advent of a saw mill in the vicinity, the floors, doors and partitions, were made of hewn planks, fastened together by wooden pins. Hand-saws were often passed lengthwise through the joints of these floors while the timbers were in a frozen state, in order to prevent any unevenness of the sides, and of course, when thawed, the natural expansion of the wood made them tighter still. If in these houses there were either nails, iron door latches, hinges, glass windows, or other fixtures of the kind, they had been brought at great trouble and expense from the older settlements. A log barn and shed completed the farm buildings, as these were required for storing the grain and fodder that might be raised, and for sheltering the domestic animals and fowls.

The furniture of the new house was also an improvement on that of the cabin, at least it had the added convenience of being *moveable;* both the table and bedstead described in the foregoing chapter being firm fixtures ; but as there were floors in the new building, " the mother of invention" prompted such change as was effected in the bedstead, by having four posts of proper height, bored near the top so that poles of the right length for the sides and ends, could be inserted to form the frame, when the whole was bound together with bark woven as before described. The tables, benches, and other articles in daily use were improved accordingly, as necessity had taught these people to rely on their own efforts.

Beside their bedding and a few utensils of iron and earthenware, some small articles of furniture found their way in with the family, most of which had been kept as mementos of departed friends, or relics of bygone and better days. These were generally more prized for their connection with past associations than for any intrinsic value, and were cherished with a care amounting almost to veneration.

The necessity of a supply of tools has already been adverted to, but these articles when in constant use will wear out or get broken, and this made the blacksmith a most necessary adjunct to the new settlement. At first, men wore mocassins of the imperfectly tanned hides of animals; but in time the shoemaker made his appearance, and in addition to his legitimate calling, was both saddle and harnessmaker. The saw mill called in carpenters and joiners, and many of the persons named as associates had more or less knowledge of some one of the essential branches of mechanics.

After the people began to raise corn and before the general erection of mills, an article of domestic use known as the "*Plumping mill,*" was brought into requisition to convert the grain into meal. It was made of a section of log standing upright, with a cavity in the top into which the corn was put. The pestle was a long piece of wood rounded at the bottom, of convenient size for the hand in the middle, and fastened at the top to a spring-pole, so that after one stroke upon the corn in the mortar, it would rebound for another. When the corn was sufficiently pounded, a scive separated the coarse and fine meal, the former of which was made into *hominy*, * and the latter into wholesome coarse bread, or used in various ways known to housekeepers in this country. The plumping mill was probably an improvement upon the Indian method of pounding corn in order to convert it into food, there being otherwise no way except the process known as hulling, and was in use only till the erection of grist mills. Settlers who lived near the lakes and streams which were navigable for canoes, often took their grain a long distance to be ground, as in some localities there were no streams sufficiently large to carry mills. †

But the first practiced methods of converting grain into food by pounding, boiling or sending it a long distance to be ground, were found to be much too incon-

---

* An Indian dish made by boiling the coarse meal when separated from the bran.

† At a very early period in the settlement of Bolton, Nicholas Austin procured a large coffee mill, which when propelled by the water of a small brook near his residence, would grind corn at the rate of six bushels in twenty-four hours.

venient and laborious, and a more general erection of grinding mills was called for by the increasing wants of the people. In the building of these, heavy iron castings and mill-stones were required, and must be brought from a distance. If there was no route by which they could be transported at least part of the way by water, all such weighty articles were usually brought in on sleds in winter. In some places however, stones were found in the vicinity, which by being brought into something of the required shape, were made to answer a purpose, and though as soon as circumstances favored the change, they were replaced by others of improved quality, it must be claimed for them that they did good service for the early settler. Saw mills in time were greatly multiplied, and then came a very decided improvement in the building line, as a well covered barn in which the hay, grain, and farm stock, might be well secured, was of little less importance than a comfortable dwelling.

When the first locations were made in these townships, the roads leading to the several settlements were merely bushed out, and the next step in advance was the opening of cross roads from one section to another, but from the nature of the soil and the imperfect manner of their construction, they were in a bad state for years. As regarded local convenience these early people had to depend upon themselves, and any efforts to improve their roads were of course voluntary; the usual course pursued being to meet and tax themselves so much labor yearly.

Most of the clothing worn by the early settler and his family, was necessarily of home manufacture, spun, woven, and made into garments by the industrious hands of our grand-mothers, mothers and aunts; for this branch of work belonged exclusively to the female department. To them a practical knowledge of the use of hand-card, distaff, wheel and loom, was indispensable. To a great extent it was their education, and presented a field for emulation in efforts to excel in making the various kinds of cloth, yarns, bedding, &c. The winter and summer clothing were products of the home farm, both of them being often finely spun, woven and colored with skill and taste. The house keeping and cooking departments were also under their charge; for to the domestic sphere and the care of the sick, their faculties and energies were devoted. Few resources or opportunities for religious instruction or intellectual culture were theirs to enjoy. These were reserved for their children and grand-children.

It was customary from the earliest formation of settlements, for the scattered inhabitants to assemble at times for the cultivation of a neighborly intercourse, and the gratification of a natural desire for companionship. Where people had so few sources of enjoyment, it is probable that these gatherings were looked forward to with pleasurable anticipations. Old people who in youth shared in these merry-makings, assure us that in those days a more hearty good feeling and a more unconstrained freedom prevailed, than in later years ; and that less of the unamiable and unloveable spirit of envy, rivalry, or detraction, existed at that time, then has since been the case. Though dancing was much practiced, it is hardly probable that the music whether of the *fiddle* or the human voice, was subjected to any very close criticism. For years there were no public houses; every man's dwelling was open to the traveller, and a cordial welcome was extended alike to friend or stranger.

A mutual regard and consideration for each other's comfort and convenience is said to have been characteristic of society at that early day ; the people seeming bound to each other by a community of interests and sympathies as well as trials. Each felt the necessity of cherishing a spirit of mutual accommodation, as this seems to have become almost universally diffused among them. Many came into the country who were not fully supplied with teams, farming implements, mechanic's tools, &c ; and as there was no place in this section where such could be readily procured, resort was had to the practice of borrowing. This system which has its evils and abuses, had its origin in necessity, and in time came into very general use. A man would hardly feel justified in refusing to lend his property if not using it himself, when his neighbor was in want; and even money was often regarded as valuable only in contributing to the general convenience and comfort. He would often loan it without bond or interest; and such was the mutual confidence, that there was no thought of fastening doors at night, or of otherwise confining or secreting property. And yet instances of dishonesty or theft were extremely rare. When they did occur however, they were regarded with unaffected horror and disgust. Notwithstanding the many disagreeable peculiarities which characterized life in the woods at that day, this mutual confidence, common sympathy, and generous feeling, made amends for much.

In the days of which we write, spirituous liquors were considered essential as a beverage, and no doubt the stimulant went far toward promoting the general enjoyment and hilarity on their festive occasions: but however the practice of drinking to excess might have been indulged in at other times and places, we are assured that such was seldom the case at these social gatherings.

An examination into this subject, would reveal the fact that a most astonishing quantity of whiskey was manufactured and consumed by these early people. As their land was new and generally very productive, after the first few years the farmers raised a large surplus of grain, which, till a market was available, was mostly converted into whiskey and taken as a beverage. Distilleries became exceedingly numerous; the making and selling of this article being pursued and recognized as a respectable and legitimate employment.

After the introduction of taverns, selling whiskey became the most lucrative and of course the most important branch of the business. Although this whiskey was not then adulterated and drugged as at the present day, its effects on those who became slaves to their appetites, were in most respects the same. The way was thus gradually but too surely prepared for drunkenness, poverty, and the various forms of vice which often culminated in crime and its fearful penalties.

But notwithstanding the many drawbacks and disadvantages with which these settlements had to contend in the days of their infancy and for a period of years, persevering effort was finally rewarded by a measurable success. The new land produced well, and after the first few years of labor, grain was usually plenty. In the more rapidly increasing settlements there was also abundant use for the surplus produce that was raised. But in the more isolated parts, many trying and discouraging influences were at work, and the poor settler had to struggle for a bare subsistence. Though the soil might produce ever so luxuriantly, there was little use in raising more grain than was needed for home consumption, as for a long time there was no market available for the surplus.

The game in our woods, the fish in our streams, and the maples in our forests, being the most readily available natural resources of the country at that day, had contributed largely to the living of the settler, till farms could be cleared and made to produce. As soon however, as this was the case and a necessity was felt for a market, efforts were made in many sections to open winter roads that would give the people that advantage once in the year at least. Those living west of Lake Memphremagog sought a market in Montreal by different lines of road through the interior, while inhabitants along the line of the St. Francis and its principal tributaries found their way in canoes down that river to its mouth, and thence across the St. Lawrence to Three Rivers. Along the rivers and streams which afforded transportation by canoes, this had been carried on to some extent from the first, and as the population increased, it was pursued with enlarged and improved facilities.

For several years the only available routes to Montreal, had been either around by Missisquoi Bay and St. Johns, or down some navigable river to the St. Lawrence and thence up to the city. But in the course of time it was ascertained that by going through the wilderness to the French seigniories, a considerable saving in the distance would be made, and winter roads were opened connecting with different lines leading direct to Montreal.

Settlements had first been commenced in localities chosen for good land and valuable timber, rather than in reference to any facilities for communicating with other parts ; but the necessity for such connection in time became apparent, and the more enterprising among the settlers met and agreed upon concerted action for the good of the whole. On some of these routes there were few indications of settlement for many miles, and a still more unpromising feature of the case, was that some of the proposed routes lay through sections of swamp, hitherto penetrated only by the foot traveller who picked his way through on fallen trees and mossy formations. Such enterprises were not effected without the most laborious toil and many discouraging adventures. After the commencement of cold weather, the streams were sufficiently frozen to cross upon the ice; but owing to the shade of heavy trees, or the peculiar nature of the soil, the ice in swamps was not so firm, and many places had to be filled with logs, brushwood, &c., before a passage could be effected. While engaged in this work the poor beasts would often sink so deeply into the mud that their drivers had to cut poles and pry them out; but perseverence at length accomplished the task and winter roads were opened. This partial success had the effect of stimulating the people to further efforts toward improving their condition; an ambition which seemed to have reference to the future opening before them, rather than the pressure of any existing necessity.

The next steps in the work, were to bridge the streams and construct causeways over the swamps, when ox-sleds could pass in summer to the navigable rivers, or to travelled roads in older settled sections. Those who had money gave it to these enterprizes, and those who had none—which was much oftener the case—gave their labor.

In the two principal lines leading from the east to Montreal, were two large rivers in the way ; and as there were then no bridges either at St. Johns or Chambly, that river (the Richelieu) was crossed by means of scows; a large flat boat formed of planks, the sides being some fifteen or eighteen inches high, while the ends of about the same height rise gradually, to facilitate the embarkation and debarkation, and to pass more readily over the surface of the water. Teams could thus be ferried across without detaching the animals in case they were quiet and manageable ; but if otherwise, great care and pains were necessary to effect a safe passage. In case of storms, travellers were obliged to wait till the wind subsided before the boatman dared venture upon the water, and often whole days or even several days were spent waiting for a change of weather, as the elements could not be braved, and there was no remedy.

Batteaux were necessary on the St. Lawrence, as the greater depth of that river and the consequent strength of the current, required differently constructed boats ; though this as well as the scow, was managed by oars and setting poles. These boats were more in the form of a canoe, being curved toward the end so as to present nearly a point to the surface of the water over which they were to glide; usually about twenty-five or thirty feet in length by seven or eight in width at the centre; built of ship timbers covered with boards and planks. They were brought up to the shore against a projection or wharf, and strongly fastened; when planks were laid so as to form a sort of bridge descending toward the centre of the boat, over which walk animals were led in and securely tied; or whatever was to comprise the loading was taken on board and stowed away as compactly as possible. If very bulky substances were to be taken over, two of these boats were often bound together firmly so as to prevent rocking, when a large body of freight could be carried to the opposite wharf, whence it was taken by carters up to the city; or a boat could be towed up against the current by men who took the end of a cable attached to it and drew up along the shore, while others on board with setting poles, kept it at floating distance from the bank. On returning, the current favored descent to the place of crossing, when the journey homeward was simply in reversed order.

In illustration of the difficulties and labors encountered in getting to market at that early period, we give the simple experience of two settlers living about seventy miles from Montreal. This was their first effort in this line. In the days of the famous " *Embargo*," when potash commanded a high price, they started from their homes with each a sled drawn by cattle, on either of which were two barrels of potash. These they took to the Yamaska river where a ferry had been established, whence it was carried by scows six miles to the Montreal road; thence by hired carters across the Chambly river in scows, and from there to Longueuil; thence across the St. Lawrence in a batteau, and from the landing, taken by truck-men to the inspection office, when after the necessary examination it was ready for sale. Notwithstanding the labor and expense of the journey, the times were so favorable that they realized a very considerable profit, each receiving one hundred dollars for his load. Household necessaries were taken back by the same route reversed, when after an absence of eighteen days and an expense of twenty dollars each, the travellers reached their homes.

Beside surplus grain and the products of wood ashes, the furs of wild animals taken by hunting or trapping, were carried to market. Black salts however were the poor settler's principal dependence, as they bore a high price, and were always in demand. It has been estimated that the product of the ashes thus sold, paid for the labor of clearing the farm; and this was certainly a great help to the poor people when money was scarce and resources were few. So profitable was it at particular times, that at the less busy seasons of the year, men would go into the woods, fell trees and burn them for the simple purpose of making salts: or in cases of emergency when money was greatly needed, this was the readiest and surest way to obtain it.

For many years pot and pearl ashes were the staple articles with which to make remittances in trade, and for a long time were the principal products which could be spared from sections of the country where a non-producing population was rapidly multiplying.

Trading establishments on a small scale, were opened at a very early day in localities which served as a sort of centre where the surronnding inhabitants could exchange their potash, pork, furs, sugar, or surplus grain, for salt, tea, tobacco, whiskey, or such other necessaries as were required. The goods kept in these stores were not generally of a very superior quality, but the prices asked for them were exceedingly high; often exorbitant. To some extent this was a necessity, as an offset to the trouble and expense involved in bringing them from market; and in further palliation of this apparent extortion, was the undeniable fact that in order to convert this ready pay into money, time and labor were both requisite. But in some cases the prices asked were out of all proportion to the original cost even with this just allowance; and this injustice fell upon those whose necessities obliged them to supply their wants in this manner. The following instance is given, not with the view of reflecting upon a useful and honorable class of men, but in illustration of the system then pursued by some who disgraced their calling, in making " their neighbor's necessities their opportunity;" and further as an individual case of a certain order of intelligence, by no means exceptional at that period; and which is nearly always allied to, and associated with an unscrupulous disregard of the rights and convenience of others. On occasion of the visit of a certain country trader to Montreal for the purchase of goods, the merchant with whom he was transacting business, very naturally inquired what profit the other made on his goods. " Only three or four per cent," was carelessly replied; when the merchant looking up with an expression of surprise, doubt, and inquiry, repeated in a tone indicative of all these: " Three or four per cent! what do you understand by three or four per cent?" "*Only three or four times as much as they cost*," was the characteristic rejoinder.

An ungenerous advantage was often taken of the temporary scarcity of some article of necessary use, to demand an exorbitant price for it, when the pressure of necessity favored sale at an unreasonable rate. Instances occurred when seven or eight dollars per bushel were asked for salt; and a case is related where a settler was obliged to give twenty four bushels of such corn as weighed sixty pounds to the bushel, *for just one hundred weight of nails*.

Some of the men engaged in this business accumulated wealth, while others accomplished little or failed entirely; and at best it was attended with a great deal of uncertainty and anxiety. An ashery where black salts were refined and prepared for market, was usually an appendage of the store.

After a period of years, taverns or public houses were generally introduced into the more thickly settled localities, and on the more frequented routes of travel. But in numbers of places purporting to be houses of entertainment, liquor selling and its concomitants in time usurped an unmerited prominence, often to such an extent that the wearied traveller failed to find the quiet and repose he needed ; and what was in itself a reputable and legitimate calling, was thus let down to the level of the common grog-shop.

The first wheeled vehicles that penetrated the country were ox-carts, of course constructed with a view to strength and durability, and as far as finish was concerned, in perfect keeping with the high-ways over which they were to pass. The first that penetrated to a certain locality some distance north of the Province line and west of Lake Memphremagog, was loaded with iron castings for a mill then in course of erection. The load was so heavy and the road so rough, that the axle-tree of the cart gave way three times and was on the point of the fourth break-down, when arrived at its destination ; being replaced each time by the driver who carried with him both axe and auger, from the hard timber which grew so plentifully by the way. As the cart rolled on over all obstructions, the iron load, which was fastened on with chains, created an unusual and unaccountable noise which with its echoes could be heard reverberating and resounding through the forest, long before the lumbering vehicle appeared in sight to explain to the astonished and expectant people living along the way, the simple cause of such an uproarious din.

Among the wild animals found here, the panther or catamount though the largest and most ferocious, was by no means the most numerous or destructive among the flocks and herds of the early settlers : indeed we incline to the opinion that they were occasional visitants, rather than frequenters of these wilds. Their appearance in any locality was always a signal of terror, and though they may not have destroyed human lives in these parts, men have been closely pursued by them and were only saved by reaching a timely covert.

Domestic animals used to disappear in a mysterious and unaccountable manner; but if killed by these creatures, retreat was made by them to some far distant and inaccessible spot. In some of the mountainous sections, panthers of an enormous size, were seen and killed.

But of all the denizens of these woods, the black bear became the most destructive, as he not only killed the domestic animals, but ravaged the grain fields of the settler ; and became so bold and encroaching as at times to break into enclosures thought secure, when the destruction was often terrible ; as if the creature's bloody instincts sought revenge for not being allowed his prey at will. It often appeared as if this animal required the promptings of hunger or rage to attack and destroy ; at others, as if he could really discern signs of alarm and distress, and even play upon the fears of those who were terrified at his appearance. Unless in self-defence or when they consider their young in danger, they are not thought particularly formidable to man ; but let their cubs be attacked, and they will appear to forget themselves and fight with ferocity and desperation. When completely subdued and in the power of their captors, they have been known to "*play possum*" or feign themselves dead ; but whatever instinctive object prompted such cunning, could only be conjectured. They finally became so bold and encroaching that many expedients were devised to extirpate them. At times they were caught in steel-traps which were chained to logs that they might not be carried away d lost; but both trap and log have been dragged to a distance, while the torn up earth, trees bitten and scratched, and sapplings broken off or torn out by the roots, gave evidence of inconceivable strength and fury. It has occurred that when thus taken by the leg, and the bone of the limb was broken so that the foot was only held by skin and muscle, the beast would savagely gnaw these off and escape on three feet, in which case his path was marked with blood.

Bears often grow to an enormous size, and seem to learn cunning with age, as was evident from the w ays in which they would evade the efforts made to des troy them. Often large domestic animals and sometimes colts in the pasture were killed by them; and breaking into enclosures, they would carry off their living, struggling victims, clasped tightly in their arms as they walked away erect. Some years since, a monster of this species came out of his hiding place in the wilderness near the township of Eaton, and for a length of time evaded all efforts to kill or take him, while he carried on his work of destruction. Traps were set for him and guns fired at him in vain, as he was cunning enough to avoid the one, and his skin seemed impervious to the other. His death which was finally effected, was a matter of public rejoicing, as his depredatious had not been confined to one locality. Several balls were lodged in him before he finally yielded, and on examination of the skin, the tanner found others imbedded in it, over which the wounds had healed, showing that they must have been made some time previously.

As the country became more generally settled and a bounty was offered by government for killing these creatures, such as escaped destruction were driven to take refuge in remote and unfrequented regions; yet even at the present day, one occasionally strays from his mountain home and finds a hiding place in the vicinity of some tempting flock, among which he usually succeeds in doing a deal of mischief before he can be discovered and destroyed.

Wolves were also numerous in the country at particular seasons, and often roamed about in *packs* or companies, as if " seeking what they might devour," when if any unlucky creature came in their way, it was sure to be attacked, and if not too formidable or fleet of foot, was destroyed; but when single, they seldom attacked animals larger than sheep. Among flocks in the field, they killed all they could catch, and often made great havoc; but if by any means they found their way into yards, it would seem as if an instinctive cowardice prompted them to hurry away as soon as their hunger was appeased. For persons camping in the woods, fire was considered a protection from night attacks, as it is thought that they have a dread of that element; though as the early settlers had good reason to know, the bears care nothing for it.

The early people had frequent occasion for learning that, when together, wolves will attack men; and likewise, to observe the peculiar sounds by which they communicate with each other; which perhaps might aptly be termed howls of inquiry and response.

At some particular seasons, deer were very numerous in this section, and old people tell us that when such was the case, their natural enemy, the wolf, followed in overwhelming numbers. They are very prolific, and multiplied to such an extent, that government was obliged to come to the rescue and offer a bounty for their destruction.

On one occasion as a settler was out in the woods, he came upon a large hollow log lying horizontally, into the open end of which a beaten path led in such a way as to indicate it a frequent resort or den for some wild animal. Having a gun with him, he looked well to its priming, and on taking a peep into the open end of the log, two glaring eye-balls met his gaze. Nothing daunted, however, he took aim at them, pulled the trigger, and then hastened to block up the entrance with stones and rubbish. Returning with help the next day, he found all as he had left, and on cutting into the log it was found that the two burning eyes which had served as a mark the day before, had belonged to a she-wolf which now, with one of her young, lay cold and stiff in the midst of seven others still warm and living. They were but partly grown and were easily secured; and the old male was soon after taken in a trap. The bounty on this family of ten wolves was just one hundred dollars.

The lynx was also seen often when the country was new, and was sometimes destructive to sheep, calves, and other small animals, but was neither so numerous or mischievous as some of the other species.

The fox seemed to regard domestic fowls and young lambs as his especial prey; and being one of the plagues following civilization, multiplied as settlements, and consequently his means of living, increased. Numbers, and even whole broods of turkeys or chickens would often disappear in one night, which was a pretty sure indication that reynard had by some means found access to the roost; and instances of cunning were often exhibited which would have been amusing had they not been so very annoying. These nightly thefts were sometimes committed on a large scale as if the design was to supply numerous young with food ; and at other times it would seem as if instinct prompted them to kill all within their reach, and bury what they could not eat, as a provision against future want; but others still go to show the existence of a thievish instinct in these creature, which can bear no relation to a natural care for themselves or their young.

Besides those mentioned above, are the racoon, wolverine, otter, martin, weasel, ermine, mink, skunk, shrew, mole and bat, all of which belong to the order *Carnivora* or carniverous animals, distinguished from others in having three kinds of teeth and living principally on flesh.

Of the order *Rodentia* or gnawing animals, having large incisory teeth and grinders, are the beaver, muskrat, rabbit, woodchuck, rat, hedgehog, squirrel, and mouse. Their food is principally vegetables, roots, grain, nuts, and the bark of trees.

The order *Ruminantia* or ruminating animals having cloven hoofed feet and chewing the cud, are the moose, caribou, and common deer, beside domestic cattle and sheep.

There is also the order *Pachydermata*, which includes several of our domestic quadrupeds, as the horse, the ass, and the hog.

Only three of these orders are found in our country in a wild state.

Watchdogs were considered indispensable among the early settlers, and if they failed to keep this faithful sentinel at his post, they were pretty sure to pay the penalty of their negligence ; and even with all the care and forethought possible, depredations were frequent and vexatious.

CHAPTER VI.

WANT OF MORAL AND INTELLECTUAL CULTURE AMONG THE PEOPLE. — CHARACTER OF A MAJORITY OF THE EARLY SETTLERS. — SABBATH BREAKING, INDIFFERENCE, IRREVERENCE.—FIRST TEACHERS OF RELIGION.— PARTIAL SUCCESS.—EDUCATIONAL INTERESTS.— FIRST SCHOOLS AND THEIR TEACHERS. — DOCTORS AND THEIR PATIENTS. — SUFFERINGS AND CASUALTIES.

OF the many disadvantages which fell to the lot of the early settlers in these townships, the most unhappy and deplorable in its after results, was the lack of moral and intellectual culture which they suffered so long. Generally speaking, the class of men who comprised our earliest population were anything but religiously inclined : indeed, it has been said, and we fear with too much truth, that a really God-fearing man was a very rare exception among them ; and it is painfully evident that the whole train of influences to which many of them had been subjected, even before coming to this country, were in the highest degree unfavorable to the formation of correct principles and habits.

It will be remembered that a part of our earliest population was made up of that class who had then but recently been engaged in scenes of strife and blood, and though the tranquilizing influences of time had operated to cool resentments, and had brought a degree of order forth from the chaos of conflicting passions, many characters had been permanently affected by the demoralizing influences long prevalent. Intemperence with its attendant train of vice and misery very soon found its victim here. Sabbath breaking became very general, as many who in earlier life had been subjected to a restraining home influence, had by degrees fallen in with the prevailing practice of spending Sunday in idleness, or of regarding it as a season of mere relaxation and amusement. Frequently it was spent in reviewing the labors of the past, in forming plans or laying out work for the future, or perhaps some friend in another locality was to be visited, or some business might be attended to in order to save time; all which practices were common. They were in part the result of circumstance, as in that day there was little to interest the mind. Few books were to be had, even if there had been a taste for reading them; religious worship was a thing long unknown in many localities, or at best was held only by some passing stranger at long intervals of time; and even then perhaps was of a nature to excite the imagination and emotions, rather than to enlighten the understanding and regulate the life. To such as understand the natural perversity of the human heart, it is hardly matter of wonder that those who had been better taught, should have yielded to surrounding influences. Habits of indifference and irreverence toward the teachers and institutions of religion, were also in part the growth of false and perverse views received into the mind, in efforts at self-justification for a known wrong.

At a very early day, ministers of the different religious denominations occasionally made their way into these wilds, and among the inhabitants found some of their own people. These they formed into societies which first met for worship in some private dwelling, but in course of time adjourned to the school house. During intervals between the visits of these ministers, meetings were often conducted on the Sabbath by the few religiously disposed among the people ; and thus, God's holy day was kept from entire desecration. Notwithstanding the active opposition of some, and the stolid indifference of many others, a remnant " who feared God and worked rightousness" stood firm in their allegiance to truth ; the habit of attending public worship was to some extent formed, and a foundation was laid for established religious services.

Little attention could be paid to the interests of education in those early times, most of the instructions our fathers and mothers were blessed with, having been received from their mothers, unless they had friends in some more favored locality, to whom they could be sent for a period. A few months of schooling was all that many of them ever received. Few if any school houses were built before the year 1805 ; and the first teachers who were chosen from among the best instructed of the people, were expected to teach little more than spelling, reading, writing and arithmetic. Many of us can well remember the roughly constructed, dimly lighted and miserably inconvenient buildings where we first learned our ABC, and how pleased we were when they gave place to a better class of school houses.

The Doctor was a most important acquisition to a new community; and it was sometimes the case that both professions, viz, minister and doctor, were united in the one person. Moreover, instances were known when the duties of school-master were super-added.

Many of the more remote settlements were without a resident physician for years, and if sudden sickness or severe casualties occurred, much suffering often ensued for want of proper medical or surgical aid. When sent for to attend patients at a distance, the doctor was often obliged to find his way through the woods guided by marked trees; perhaps to walk on snow-shoes over the drifts; or to go up or down the river or lake in bark canoes. After the opening of lines of road, these distant visits were usually made on horseback. When infectious diseases prevailed, many were carried off, or were beyond help, before a doctor could be got to them.

Instances were known when parties were lost in

the woods and never found or heard of; while the remains of others thus lost were found and identified by their surviving and sorrowing friends. Persons became bewildered and lost for days and even weeks, during which time they were suffering keenly from the hunger which could be only partially relieved by such scanty subsistence as the forest afforded. Alive to the horrors of their situation, and wandering almost without hope or aim, they would perhaps fall in with some remembered object, or a well connected train of ideas might form in the mind and lead them out of the labyrinth.

CHAPTER VII.

WANT OF AN EFFICIENT ADMINISTRATION OF JUSTICE.—CHANGES AND IMPROVEMENTS IN THOSE AFFAIRS. RELIGIOUS MATTERS.—RESULTS OF IRRELIGION AND INDIFFERENCE—FANATICAL THEORIES.—UNION MEETING HOUSES.—LINES OF SEPARATION. — RELIGIOUS CONTROVERSIES. — BETTER STATE OF FEELING.—CHOICE OF CHURCHES.—CONDITION OF SOCIETY.— REMEDY FOR THREATENED EVILS.

A VERY serious hindrance to the moral and social improvement of the early settlers in these townships was the want of such an administration of law, as would have proved a more efficient " terror to evil doers." Among the mass gathered here, comprising representatives of various nations, and altogether forming a heterogeneous collection which was constantly receiving recruits (from south of the Province line) of the class who had "left their country for their country's good," such restraints were imperatively called for. A mere change of locality could not effect a change of nature or habit, and these refugees from justice *there* might fall into the same or similar errors *here*. The exigencies of those times demanded a more discriminating and energetic enforcement of law against offenders, than circumstances then favored.

Montreal and Three Rivers were not only the commercial marts where most of these early people did their trading, but were also the seats of those tribunals of justice which held jurisdiction over these parts of the Province ; and of course, all matters requiring judicial interference must be referred to one or the other of those places for adjustment. Owing to the sparsity of the population, many years elapsed before a properly constituted authority even in the form of a sufficient number of civil magistrates was furnished the country; a deficiency which was but in part remedied by the appointment of militia officers to act in cases where a magistrate's warrant could not be readily obtained. Though a sergeant of militia could execute a warrant if issued by a magistrate, or the justice could appoint special constables for that purpose, these deputed powers fell short of what was required ; and serious delays so frequently attended such proceedings, that the guilty often escaped merited punishment. If a crime had been committed, the culprit was to be arrested and sent to jail, (in Montreal or Three Rivers, as the case might be) till he was tried and punished, or released. In matters of a purely local nature, causes of complaint were numerous and called loudly for redress, as an application to those distant tribunals involved such delay and expense as instead of advancing the ends of justice, seemed to retard if not defeat them. To such an extent was this the case, that multitudes of people chose rather to suffer grievous wrong, than subject themselves to the inconveniences, annoyances, and perhaps humiliations, which would be risked in an attempt to seek redress by course of law. These things are still fresh in the minds of our people; yet we have now reason for congratulation, that such improvements and modifications have more recently been made in our judiciary, as have remedied faults and supplied deficiencies, till little is left us to wish in relation to them.

It is well known, that in earlier days, the townships along our southern frontiers were more or less the resort of a certain class of lawless and unscrupulous adventurers, who usually chose some isolated spot near the boundary line for their scene of operations, and probably had a hiding place on either side, in order the more readily to evade such officers of justice as were sent to arrest them for counterfeiting or other violations of law. Many traditional accounts are given of the shifts and expedients to which resort was had to hide the work which " sought darkness rather than light." Places which were the habitual resorts of this class of persons, suffered in reputation accordingly. With the lapse of time, however, public sentiment relative to the propriety of encouraging or allowing these practices, has undergone a radical change for the better; and pursuits which, to say the least, were once winked at by a certain class of the community, are now frowned down; indicating the existence of a more healthy moral feeling and the prevalence of more enlightened views. Such as still continue to follow these practices, have been driven to seek other hiding places ; and characters of questionable antecedents, find it necessary to assume at least the appearance and profession of honesty.

Among the first, if not the very first ministers of religion who followed these early settlers into this " *Moral waste* " and established their worship permanently, were the American Methodist preachers. Of the same origin as many of the people, and intimately acquainted with their peculiar characteristics, they could all the more readily command their sympathies, and accommodate themselves to their circumstances. Some few of the people had been connected with these societies before their coming hither ; others who had in youth received religious instruction, without questioning whether the doctrines now taught, were in consonance with what they had heard in earlier life, at once united with these people. Much interest was aroused by their preaching, and the fact, that in purity of life, self-denial, and in devotional zeal, they were singularly consistent with their profession, gave great weight to their teachings. The peculiarly simple ceremonies which characterized their worship ; their earnest and searching appeals to the hearts and consciences of their hearers, and the spirit-stirring strains of their sacred melodies, had often a most thrilling effect.— Many profligate characters were reformed through their instrumentality, who gave after evidence of corrected lives.

These preachers who came into the country as early as 1802, commenced forming societies in some of the frontier townships, and previously to the war of 1812, a circuit comprising the settlements east of Lake Memphremagog and north to Melbourne and Shipton, called the St. Francis circuit, was regularly visited by those connected with the New England conference; while another including the townships west of that lake, with the seigniory of St. Armand, and Caldwell's and Christie's manors, named Dunham circuit, was supplied from the New York conference. During the war, the visits of these preachers were necessarily discontinued; but when the political horizon was again clear, they were resumed and continued, till superseded by the arrival of Wesleyan missionaries from England. The first of these, who came to the country about the year 1821, were men of superior piety and ability, some of whom have long since finished their earthly career, and have left lasting monuments in the hearts and affections of those to whom they ministered. The names of Catterick, Squire, Lang, and others, will long be remembered among the people.

In time this body of Christians has become numerous and influential. In later years the Canada conference has been formed, which now controls their general interests.

Representatives of other religious bodies also found

their way here at a very early period, gathering congregations and organizing societies in connection with the various denominations to which they belonged.

But it was often the case that the efforts of Christian ministers and teachers were met either by violent opposition and direct insult, or a stolid indifference. Encased in an armory of self-satisfaction and assumption which called sophism and perversion to its aid, the latter was perhaps quite as effectual as the former in silencing the arguments of reason, or appeals to the heart and conscience. If such were possible, it would indeed appear as certain that this class of persons had really succeded in satisfying themselves that *they* could have no conceivable interest in matters thus urged upon them; any plea on the ground of duty or responsibility however forcibly represented, being set aside as fitting other cases rather than theirs; while any punishment involved in an evasion or neglect of these, was regarded as either visionary or parabolical. In their own words " We had no voice in our own creation, and our business in this world is to please and gratify ourselves."

It could not be otherwise than sure, that such a course of reasoning and conduct, communicated by precept and example from parent to child, should lead to certain results and bear its legitimate fruits. This it has done, and is still doing, as we may often see in the coldness, distrust, and marked irreverence sometimes manifested toward the teachers and the institutions of religion.

Wild and fanatical theories have at times been introduced, and disseminated by such as give their time and talent to hearing and telling things new and strange; and as there is in every community an element of weakness equally unstable and excitable, such persons were more or less successful in sowing the seeds of disaffection and disunion. What begun in doubt and distrust, grew into open estrangement and disruption, with all its unhappy consequences to societies and communities. Probably those engaged in this disorganizing business, considered portions of our country as offering an inviting field for such operations; and perhaps some of them are entitled to the credit of having believed in the truth and consistency of theories they advanced and urged upon others; but the event has proved, that not all thus employed have been deserving of even this consideration.

With the Book of Truth and the Spirit of Inspiration to enlighten, restrain, and regulate us; with the proper use of our own powers of reason and conscience; and a thoroughly humbling sense of our own imbecility and inefficiency, there is no danger that we become either unsound in faith or unsettled in mind. In the cultivation of a spirit of true humility, and an understanding of *self* in all its forms and guises, our views on subjects of practical moment will become clearer, our faith " established, strengthened, settled :" and we shall also better appreciate the injunction, to " hold fast a form of sound words."

Yet, notwithstanding all the untoward influences that opposed the spread of truth among these early people, or the evils that grew out of any form of fanaticism, a foundation of religious society was laid, and a work commenced, which in time has resulted in the permanent establishment of churches and their auxiliaries.

The first houses of worship built in the country were small wooden edifices, erected by the united efforts of parties professing different faiths. They were called " Union meeting houses," and were occupied as occasion required by each alternately, or by such preacher or lecturer as visited the locality. In process of time, however, the lines of separation between the several sects became more clearly defined ; preferences became prejudices ; controversies were introduced begetting rivalries, jealousies, and the deplorable spirit of detraction which is so prolific of evil. One of the results of this we may see in the number and variety of sects among us ; some of which, however, are but *distinctions* with very little *difference*.

To some extent, the circumstances of former residences and associations may have contributed to their increase ; but on the whole, it is to be regretted that such prominence should have been given to mere matters of opinion. Between such differences and alienation of feeling there is but a step, and then the door is open for a conflict of interests. Forbearance, moderation, and those mutual concessions which are perfectly consistent with decision of character, should prevail in the intercourse of Christians.

As evidence of improvement in these matters, we now see ministers of different creeds, meeting on terms of amity and good feeling, and side by side pleading in behalf of some work of benevolence or mercy, as brethren of the same family and children of one common Father. Distinctions and orders may never be done away from among Christians, yet we await with hope the time when religion shall appear freed from the mists of blinding passion or the trammels of prejudice, and when sectarian bigotry shall give place to an enlightened and comprehensive catholicity.

The inhabitants of our towns and larger villages can generally have their choice of churches in which to worship, and in the smaller country villages, some Protestant church edifice is usually found. As a rule, if a man is in health, and has a disposition to attend the public worship of his Maker, by a little exertion he may find such as are of his own way of thinking; but if the case be such that he cannot well have his choice, let him meet with others and acommodate himself to the necessity, rather than contract that miserably unhappy and unsettling habit so common, of regarding religious worship of no account.

The seeds of irreligion, long since sown among our people, having taken deep root, have borne a plentiful and fully matured harvest. *Then*, however, there was apparent excuse for much of this; now there is *none*:

yet we hear the same self-complacent assumptions, and the same cynical fault finding among them ; which is in fact, but the poorly concealed effort to justify to themselves and others, what they cannot but feel to be doubtful and unsatisfactory.

There is much to awaken appehension, in the insensibility and irreverence ; in the disposition to throw off restraint and regard obligation lightly, which is so deplorably prevalent at the present day; for in these the germs of insubordination and anarchy are painfully evident. The pulpit, press, school-room, and social circle, are the remedial agents by which these great moral evils are to be eradicated, and should be of one accord in forming correct views, and establishing a proper standard of thought and action upon this subject.

CHAPTER VIII.

INFLUENCES ADVERSE TO THE MATERIAL PROSPERITY OF THE COUNTRY.—DIFFERENT CLASSES OF EMIGRANTS.—DESTITUTION AND SUFFERING AMONG THEM.—LOCATION OF THE RICE FAMILY.—POOR EMIGRANT FAMILY.—IMPROVED FACILITIES.

PROMINENT among the adverse influences with which these early people had to contend at different periods, were seasons unfavorable to the growth of grain, vegetables and grass; when cold and frost either late in spring or early in autumn, entirely cut off the crops or materially injured them; beside which, they were often destroyed by wild animals. Though of course all felt the consequences of these evils and were obliged to submit to much that was inconvenient and uncomfortable, it was among the poor class of settlers and those living in the remote and newly opened sections, that the greatest suffering was experienced. At one time flour was eighteen dollars per barrel, wheat four dollars per bushel, and corn proportionally high in the markets; which with other necessaries at corresponding prices, came hard upon them. There was no help for it however, and the only resource for the poor was the making of black salts, which were carried by some one of the circuitous and laborious routes before described to market, where it was exchanged for breadstuffs and other necessaries. This made the most self-denying economy necessary, and resort was often had to new and unheard of expedients to increase the amount of eatables. During the season of wild berries they were made to contribute their utmost to the means of living ; and in some localities the poor people were driven to the necessity of gathering the tops of growing vegetables, cowslips, nettles, pig-weed, brakes, and even to resort to the forest for such leaves as could be boiled, beside the various kinds of wood-nuts, ground-nuts, wild onions, or whatever would relieve the pangs of hunger and prevent starvation.

Not only women and children, but strong-handed and stout-hearted men were often reduced to a pitiable state of suffering from hunger. Yet though thus reduced at times and often obliged to live without bread, there are few if any records of death from immediate starvation.

As has already been stated, many of these early people were from New England, where some of them had been inured to poverty, toil, self-reliance, and the usual incidents of pioneer life ; and in consequence of this training to the work, they were better fitted to meet its vicissitudes and endure its hardships, than the more refined and delicately nurtured, who, for reasons which we may not seek to know, sometimes found their way here when the country was new. This latter class,—proud, refined, and sensitive, as they often were, and all unused to depend on their own exertions, —were altogether out of place in the life they had undertaken, and were often sufferers to an extent utterly inconceivable to the less susceptible and more practical natures of those by whom they were surrounded. A case bearing strongly upon this point, is related of a family of English emigrants who by some misfortune had been reduced from a state of affluence to actual poverty, and thought to hide this from the world by a voluntary exile. They had come to this country entirely destitute of means to live without labor, yet all unused to self-denial or exertion, and as unfitted as possible to enter upon the life they had in view. Having moved in " good society" at home, they brought with them much of the natural reserve and dignity of manner which is characteristic of the class to which they belonged, and retained it in the little intercourse with others which was unavoidable. The people among whom they settled, though not wanting in common understanding, had been too intently occupied with the cares of daily life, and were too much absorbed n *getting a living*, to pay much attention to a culivation of the social proprieties and amenities ; or perhaps they were careless and rudely inattentive to these matters, as many such people think them of little importance. They were not slow however, in understanding the wish of their new neighbors to hold themselves aloof from intercourse with them; and with a characteristic readiness to suspect what they could not understand, and condemn what they thought savored of *pride*, they had allowed a partition wall of coldness, prejudice and distrust, to rise between themselves and the new comers. This state of things had continued for some time as neither showed the least sign of yielding, when one morning Mrs. S., the wife of a farmer in the vicinity, was greatly surprised by a call from the English lady who asked to see her in private. The interview was readily granted, when a case of destitution and real suffering was disclosed. The lady had brought a small but beautiful and costly article from her own wardrobe, which she wished to exchange for potatoes, as *her children were crying with hunger, and she had nothing to give them to eat.* Their suffering had induced her to break through the restraints which had held her, and seek the readiest relief. The occasion appealed directly to the sympathies of the other, and the wall that had risen between them as neighbors, was effectually broken down. In an after confidence, the lady told Mrs. S., that when she reached home with the potatoes, the famishing children would not be prevailed on to wait till they were cooked, but fell *to eating them raw.*

Emigrants of the poorer and uneducated class, though inured to labor and often to want, met with so much that differed from anything in their former experiences or what their minds had been made made up to expect, that some gave up to the disappointment and became utterly disheartened. Much suffering and complaint existed not only on account of the rigors of the climate, but of the scarcity of food; yet no doubt these evils were in many cases aggravated by a thriftless improvidence and a general unfitness for the life they had undertaken; and not unfrequently the whiskey bottle was the secret of extreme destitution.

In 1830, Israel Rice and family located in South Ham, on a line of road then in course of construction through from the townships to Quebec. It was called the Craig road, from having been surveyed and commenced during Governor Craig's administration. For the accommodation of laborers on the road through an extensive tract of unsettled country, temporary dwellings or *shanties* were built along the line, and moved from place to place as the work progressed.

Here at a distance of nine miles from any permanent neighbors on the one hand, and eighteen miles on the other, the Rice family lived for thirteen years, during which time their house was necessarily the stopping place for every description of travellers. One class of these were drovers who had collected cattle in the townships south, and were taking them through to Quebec; but a far more numerous class were emigrants who had landed at that city, and were on their way either to the townships or through to the United States. Much suffering existed among these latter, many of whom were wretchedly poor. The workmen in their shanties along the way had orders to supply the passing wants of the needy strangers by giving them food or shelter when required; and when the different sections of the road were finished, the cabins were left standing and were often used as temporary refuges, for such of these poor wayfarers as needed the shelter they afforded.

The family inhabiting this "lodge in the wilderness," (as Rice's house was in reality) were often called to minister to the needs of such poor people as fell ill through want and exposure, and had found shelter in the cabins. Instances occurred when children were born to these strangers in circumstances of great destitution. Common humanity required that they should be cared for, and in warm weather, this was comparatively easy; but during the cold and sudden variations to which our climate is subject, it was a more difficult task. In a situation like that occupied by the Rice family, all the evils of ignorance and inexperience on the part of emigrants, were seen in their full force, and the scenes often presented were heart-sickening indeed, as poor creatures with frozen feet and festering sores, hardly able to drag their weary way along, came to the door seeking food and rest. Often days and sometimes weeks elapsed before they could proceed on their journey; during which time the house was a hospital. Some were hastened to an untimely end through these sufferings; others disabled for life;

while the most unreasonable and unjust prejudices were raised against the climate and country.

One of the many cases of peculiar suffering which came to their knowledge, is related by them as having excited their deepest sympathies.

About the first of March, or at that period of the year when in consequence of sudden thaws, a break-up of the winter road was expected and the through travel for the winter had ceased, an emigrant family consisting of father, mother, and six children, who had arrived at Quebec the autumn before, were induced to undertake the journey through to the townships on foot; apparently in entire ignorance of the difficulties and perils to be encountered at such a season. There was still a great depth of snow upon the ground, and for the most unfrequented part of the way, the only visible track was that made by hunters and others on snow-shoes. The man carried a large bundle, the woman an infant about nine months old, and each of the elder children had such things as they were able to carry, or helped the little ones along. When the snow was stiffened by frost, they made some progress, but after the rising of the sun and thawing of the crust, they gained ground but slowly. Up to a distance of twenty three miles beyond the dwelling of the Rice family, there were houses at intervals along the way, where the travellers had found shelter at night, but the above named distance was at that period a solitary wilderness. On entering this, their progress was so slow that they were obliged to camp out two nights. On the third day, the elder boy arrived at Rice's house bringing his little brother on his back, when he told the family of the cold and hunger of the party he had left behind, and proposed to leave the little boy that he might return and assist the others. In the meantime he had taken off his shoes to warm his feet more readily, but in trying to get them on again, found that his feet were rapidly swelling, and on making the effort, was unable to walk. Unfortunately there was no man on the premises; Rice was away, and his eldest son absent from the house, so that no one could be sent to the help of the party coming in. Very soon however, the emigrant father came in alone, and appeared to feel so little anxiety about the others, that the family were entirely deceived in the supposition that as he said, " they would soon be in." When young Rice came in from his work, the day was far advanced, the weather was becoming colder, but the expected travellers had not arrived; and on hearing from his mother what she knew of the case, and furthermore, what she feared, (for she was already distrusting the man) he proposed to go out in search of them. Taking bread to feed the hungry children, and his hand-sled to draw them in, accompanied by his younger brother, he went out to meet the wanderers. After going some distance without seeing or hearing anything of them, and calling without getting any answer, he cut a stick, set it in the snow directly in the path, fixed the bread upon it, and returned with his little brother to the house. It was now about 8 o'clock in the evening, and after thoroughly warming and wrapping himself up, he returned to renew his search, this time accompanied by his sister, a young woman of seventeen, who fortified herself against the cold to help her brother in his work of mercy.

Following the road about two and a half miles, they came upon the objects of their search, where, wearied, chilled, and unable to proceed farther, they were closely huddled together under the snow-laden branches of a fir-tree, where they had resolved to pass the night. The rescuers were guided to the spot by the cries and moans of the baby which missed its accustomed nourishment as its poor mother had been so long without food. The little girl was vainly endeavoring to hush its cries, while the mother who had taken off a stocking and shoe, was rubbing her foot with snow to take out the frost. But a little boy seven or eight years old was missing from the number expected, and on inquiry they learned that he was dead.

When in the early part of the day, the elder son had started on for help with his little brother, Jimmy (the missing boy) had started with him, leaving the father, mother, and other three children together; but finding the little one on his back beginning to suffer from cold, and Jimmy unable to keep up with the pace it was necessary he should take, the elder brother had pursuaded him to wait and go with the others, promising to hurry on and return with help as soon as possible ; and accordingly Jimmy had waited. By this time the father had found his wife and little ones too slow in their movements, and leaving them to get on as they might, started at a more rapid pace. He must have come up with and passed Jimmy, (as the child was found directly in the path) but arrived at the house alone ; and without showing any real interest, or properly representing the state of the others, seemed only intent on securing his own comfort. When young Rice and his sister started out on their errand of mercy, he refused to accompany them, stupidly insisting that he *couldn't*, though more warmly clad than the others of his family.

After this desertion by her husband, the poor woman and her remaining little ones got on as they were able, till toward evening they espied a dark object in the path directly before them, which at first they thought to be a bear; but on looking more closely and seeing that it did not move, the mother approached it till in the gathering twilight she discerned the form of a child ; and coming nearer, with a great throb of heart agony, she found it to be her darling Jimmy whom till then, she had supposed safe with his elder brother. How this had occurred she had no means of knowing ; for though the boy was not dead, he was in a dying state ; and when in her distress she called him by name, he turned his wistful but fast dimning eyes upon

P

her and attempted to speak, but could articulate no word. Giving the baby to the little girl, she seated herself upon the snow, drew the dying boy into her lap, rubbed his limbs, breathed into his face, and sought by every means in her power to impart warmth and produce circulation; but he only moaned and looked into her face as the life-blood oozed from his mouth and nose. In half an hour he was dead; and the poor woman was recalled from her stupor of grief to action, by the cries and moans of the survivors. She drew the corpse aside from the path, straightened its limbs, and conscious that she could do no more, yet with the great fear at her heart that some ravenous beast of prey might devour the precious remains, reluctantly left the body to attend to the living, and started on with them. When arranging the corpse of her dead boy, she heard the calls of young Rice, but thinking them the cries of such wild animals as had already scented their prey, she neither made nor suffered the children to make any answering sound. And when they came to the bread, thinking it had been poisoned and placed there to destroy wild beasts, she would neither touch it herself nor allow them to do so. Coming at length to a cluster of fir-trees, the bent branches of which seemed to promise a sort of shelter from the wind, in utter weariness and exhaustion, she resolved to pass the night there. This would in all probability have been her last on earth, for the event proved that help had come none too soon to save her. The foot from which she had taken the covering, had been so badly frozen that she was unable to get on the shoe in consequence of the swelling. But the young people wrapped it carefully in their mufflers, took the little boy on the hand-sled, and causing the little girl to go before them, while the sister took the crying baby in her arms as she supported the exhausted mother, they started on their way to the house. But the poor woman's remaining strength gave out; the little girl sought to lie down continually, declaring she *had as lief die as not;* so taking the little boy on his back, and driving the other child before him, young Rice left the exhausted woman and baby with his sister, hastened to the house, and giving the children into his mother's care, returned to the others with refreshment and cordial. About midnight, all the living had been brought in.

During all this time, the brutal husband and father could not be prevailed on to leave his warm berth by the fire, to go to the help of the others, though quite able to do so, as he was neither frozen nor otherwise disabled. Indeed his conduct throughout, had given evidence of an unfeeling selfishness if nothing worse. The fact that his poor boy was found dying in such a manner, when it was clear that his father must have been the last with him, created a strong feeling against the man. Whether in order to hasten the child's movements, still his entreaties or complaints, or force him to wait and go with his mother, a blow had been struck, which under the circumstances of weakness took deadly effect, was known only to Omniscience and to the wretched man himself; but surmises all pointed to this, and the suspicions thus aroused, received strong confirmation from rumors respecting his antecedents, which subsequently reached the country.

The next morning young Rice went out with his hand-sled in search of the body of little Jimmy, which he found frozen stiff, though it had escaped injury from wild animals. Coming in with it, he was met by his father and others who had arrived in his absence, and together they drew it to the house.

Exhausted and suffering as was the poor woman, the grief of her boy's death under such circumstances had nearly driven her wild ; and till the corpse was brought in, imagination was constantly picturing her darling boy as torn and disfigured by beasts of the forest; a fear which was only quieted by sight of the body. That was decently laid out, a sort of coffin prepared, a grave dug, and all that remained of the unfortunate emigrant child was committed to the frozen earth. The mother and children were sent on to a point where they received the necessary assistance, but the unworthy father had little favor shown him and was obliged to go to work.

Yet notwithstanding the many mistakes that were made and the suffering that ensued, many emigrants did succeed by a course of persevering industry, and have now their reward in homes they can call their own, with all the essentials and many of the comforts and conveniences of life:

At the present day, there are places where all necessary information may be obtained respecting any particular section; direct routes of transportation either by water or railway to points in the vicinity of the newly opened portions; available resources near them; with which facilities and the most ordinary prudence and forethought, the difficulties above recounted may be entirely avoided, and should therefore be considered as belonging exclusively to the past.

CHAPTER IX.

EXTENT OF TERRITORY INCLUDED WITH THE EASTERN TOWN-
SHIPS.—PHYSICAL CHARACTERISTICS.—GOLD REGIONS.—AGRI-
CULTURAL CAPABILITIES. — DIVISION INTO TOWNSHIPS.—CO-
LONIZATION ROADS.—CHIEF RIVERS.

THE Eastern Townships are considered as including the belt of hilly country south of the St. Lawrence, extending from the southern and eastern frontiers of the Province, to the Bay of Chaleurs. As hitherto known, they have not embraced this north-eastern extension, but as it appears to belong to them both geographically and geologically, it has been found convenient to include it with them.*

Unlike the level country bordering the great river, this region abounds in hills and valleys, lakes and ponds, rivers and streams. The ridge which enters the Province from the south as a continuation of the Green mountains of Vermont, appearing at intervals running

---

* For many items of information contained in this chapter, we are indebted to a pamphlet published " By authority of the Bureau of Agriculture," which contains a Geographical, Agricultural, and Mineralogical Sketch of Canada,

in a direction a little east of north, is called in this country, the *Notre Dame* range. In places, they attain a mountainous height of near four thousand feet above the sea ; and three of the principal lakes on the south side of the range, viz, Memphremagog, Aylmer, and St. Francis, are from 750 to 900 feet above that level. South-east of Montreal these hills appear at a distance of fifty miles or more from the St. Lawrence, but seem gradually to approach it, as at a point opposite Quebec, they come within thirty miles of the river.

Parts of this section have been brought into more extended notice by recent developments of mineral wealth, and in consequence of the great attention drawn to that subject, important regulations for the sale of mineral land, have been made; two gold mining districts erected, named the Chaudière and St. Francis divisions, and an inspector appointed to each ; one item of his duties being to afford any requisite information pertaining to the business.

Most of this region is well wooded, possesses an abundant soil, and when the labor of clearing a farm has been accomplished, the sandy loam of which it is mostly composed has been found well suited to the production of grain and vegetables. Root crops, flax, hops, &c., are grown to a considerable extent.

Though some of the townships into which the section has been laid out, are tolerably well settled, and particular localities even thickly inhabited, a large part of the tract is still in a wild state, Numerous roads extending in different directions and connecting various points where settlements are commenced, have been constructed or are projected by government, with the view of opening up the country and still further facilitating its settlement.

This region is watered by numerous small streams and rivulets which unite to form rivers of considerable magnitude; and these, with the single exception of the St. John, after flowing in a general north-west direction through valleys which at intervals separate the hills, enter the great river at different points, and in draining this large extent of country, contribute to swell the mighty flood.

The Richelieu river, though not flowing directly through the townships, may yet be properly mentioned as the channel through which the surplus waters of Lake Champlain are discharged into the St. Lawrence. It is about 70 miles in length, and unlike many of the rivers of Canada, flows for the most part through a cultivated and populous country. Near the point where it issues from the lake, is situated the American Fort Montgomery; and a little below, are the British naval station and garrison of Isle-aux-noix. Navigation is unobstructed to St. Johns, where commence a series of rapids which extend twelve miles; which obstacle to navigation has been overcome by the construction of a canal, through which the smaller class of steamboats pass directly to Chambly Basin at the foot of the rapids. This expansion of the river is said to be about one and a half mile in diameter; from which, the river flows north into the St. Lawrence at Sorel.

The Yamaska and St. Francis rivers, which come from the southern sections of the Eastern Townships, will receive suitable attention in connection with the districts which they drain.

The next coming into notice in this order is the Nicolet, consisting of two main branches, distinguished respectively by the initials N. E. and S. W., both of which are receiving frequent accessions to their waters. The sources of the N. E. branch consist of small streams and rivulets uniting in one, which after winding through several townships, enters Nicolet. The S. W. branch has its extreme source in the far off highlands of Dudswell, whence it winds through the townships into Nicolet, where at a point near La Baie, it unites with the N. E. branch, when after flowing together a short distance they again separate and enter the St. Lawrence by two distinct channels, near the lower extremity of Lake St. Peter.

The next in course is the Becancour, a large river having its sources in the many small lakes and streams abounding in Leeds, Ireland, Somerset, and the surrounding townships; when passing through Becancour, with a continually augmenting volume of water, it enters the St. Lawrence opposite Three Rivers. Between the Becancour and Chaudière, the rivers entering the St. Lawrence are few and unimportant.

In September 1775, Col. Benedict Arnold of the American revolutionary army, received instructions to take command of a body of men and effect a passage through the wilderness, by proceeding up the Kennebec river in Maine, thence across the highlands to the head waters of the Chaudière river, and down that stream to its entrance into the St. Lawrence near Quebec. The object of the expedition was to co-operate with the forces of General Montgomery in the reduction of that city. Arnold and his men entered the Province at the southern extremity of Woburn, and followed up the stream which still bears his name to where it enters Lake Megantic, thence down that lake to the point where its surplus waters are discharged through the Chaudière. The unfortunate ending of an expedition as boldly conceived as bravely carried out is matter of history, and Quebec then remained as it still continues a British stronghold.

Lake Megantic the chief source of the Chaudière, is a fine body of water about ten miles in length, lying between the tracts known as Marston and Ditchfield. It has of late become a favorite resort for hunting and fishing excursionists, as an excellent quality of fish are taken from its waters, and the deep solitude in which it is environed, affords abundance of wild game. It receives the waters of Arnold stream on the south, those of Spider lake from Ditchfield on the east, the Megantic river from Marston on the west, while its outlet, the Chaudière river, issues from the north-east, and for a considerable distance flows in the same direction. Gradually it diverges towards the north, as it does so receiving the waters of many streams from the east and north-east; the largest of which are the Samson, Du Loup, Gilbert and Famine. Innumerable small tributaries fall into it along its entire course. It inclines a little towards the west on approaching the St. Lawrence, into which it falls a short distance above Quebec.

The next river in the course designated, and the last to be mentioned as tributary to the St. Lawrence is the Etchemin, the head waters of which come from Roux and Standon, and after flowing some distance and diverging a little toward the south and west, constantly receiving accessions to its waters, it finds its way through other townships into the St. Lawrence opposite Quebec.

The next and last we shall mention in this connection, is the river St. John, known as forming the boundary for a certain distance between Canada and the State of Maine. Parts of the gold region are washed by this river and its Canadian tributaries. Its head waters are the outlets of ponds and small streams coming from the highlands on and near the boundary line, and as it flows a little to the east of north, it separates portions of Canadian and United States territory; but turning more directly to the east, it crosses the northern part of Maine, diverges to the south-east, and passing through New Brunswick, empties into the Bay of Fundy. In its course along the boundary and through the north of Maine, it receives the waters of several considerable tributaries from the Canadian side.

CHAPTER X.

ADVANTAGES OFFERED TO EMIGRANTS.—WILD LANDS.—CLASS BEST ADAPTED TO THE COUNTRY.—ELEMENTS OF SUCCESS. MISTAKES AND FAILURES.—BUSH LIFE.—EARLY SETTLERS.— PARTIALLY IMPROVED FARMS.—EXTRACTS FROM DR. RUSSELL'S WORK ON CANADA.

PROMINENT among the advantages now offered by this country as a field for emigration, may be enumerated a facility and cheapness of access; a loyal and peaceable population; healthy climate; liberal institutions; moderate taxation; a free press; free schools; fee simple of the soil which only awaits occupation; an abundance of fuel; the necessaries of life at a moderate cost, and access to market at the larger towns and villages, or through the different lines of railway which traverse the country. By means of these, daily communication is had with the cities they connect, or the places along their course. Many localities thus favored, have additional natural advantages, and require but the aid of capital and energy to enable them to rise into importance as centres of manufacturing or commercial business,

The land which is still wild, is either the property of the Crown, the British American Land Company, or of private individuals who have become possessed of it by purchase or heirship. Millions of acres of surveyed lands are always in the market in Canada, and the prices are affixed at which settlers can acquire them upon application to agents in different localities.

The class of settlers best adapted to this country in its present state, are those known at home as small farmers; men who do their own work or a part of it; whose wives are also accustomed to the work of the house or dairy, and think it no hardship to get up at four o'clock of a summer morning and proportionally early in winter, to see that each department of the housework is properly attended to. Such men are sure to succeed unless under very exceptional circumstances.

Energy, self-command, and strength to labor, are the essential elements of success in a new country; a want of these must involve failure, and exaggerated expectations must invariably end in disappointment. An emigrant coming to this country with little capital, would act wisely if before purchasing land, he placed his money in some savings bank and worked for wages a year, thus acquiring a necessary knowledge and experience of the country. Such a course is not deemed degrading in Canada, and is sure to result in ultimate good. It must be borne in mind that all emigrants whether possessed of one hundred or one thousand pounds, will fail unless they come determined to labor themselves ; and it may be asserted without fear of contradiction, that a man who pursues this plan, will in a few years be in advance of him—no matter what his capital may be—who has not taken to the axe and hoe. A determination to work, carried out with spirit, will in time bring with it a degree of prosperity not to be surpassed in any other part of America ; and will insure comfort if not independence to every prudent, sober man.

Experiences in the past have shown that those who came to the country entertaining romantic ideas of " Life in the woods," were most unfortunate : all such were victims here, and need not have expected ultimate success : while profiting by their mistakes and sufferings, those who have applied themselves to labor, by energetic industry have secured independent positions ; and the path by which they have risen through all the intermediate stages from poverty to wealth, is still open to others.

It will doubtless be news to many of our readers, that an internal emigration from front to back settlements should be constantly taking place ; yet such is the fact. The forest in perspective has no terrors for such men as comprised a large part of our early population. There is an excitement, a species of fascination about bush life, and a charm in the idea of winning more wealth from the wilderness, which a certain minded class of men never gets over. The working of new land requires less labor, less capital, and less knowledge of the science of farming, than the subsequent cultivation of the cleared farm.

Many of our early settlers were content to sow and reap, and take what the native richness of the soil would give them. They knew little or nothing of farming as a science. The modern improvements of husbandry by which the average yield of land has been doubled, were to them hidden mysteries. All they looked for was immediate success, as they knew that when their present farms failed them, the forest was still open, and they well understood the process of its subjugation.

It is to replace this hardy and adventurous class of primitive settlers, that we require the tenant farmers of the old world. We want them to take these partially improved farms and cultivate them with skill and energy. Such lands can always be had, and are usually well worth the money asked for them. The buildings on such properties are generally poor, but they are a beginning; and there is too often around them a store of wealth in neglected fertilizing substances which, when properly applied, will go far toward renovating the land. Situations convenient to mills, markets, schools, churches, &c., can often be secured at a moderate outlay and on easy terms.* The

---

* Many of the foregoing items of information were originally published in the *Emigration Gazette, Canadian Farmer*, &c., from which they have been condensed and prepared as they now appear.

subjoined extracts from Dr. W. H. Russell's work on Canada, have been found to contain so much that is true to the life, and also so applicable to the subject under consideration, that they are introduced nearly *verbatim*.

" The traveller in Canada has been struck with the peculiarly cheerless, dreary, and desolate appearance of the settler's log hut. With only a small patch of clearing, apparently in the midst of a densely wooded tract, the aspect is lonely beyond description. For weeks and perhaps months he sees no strange face, but the same still wild meets his view, at morning, noon, and night ; and his only hope is inh is good right arm and the axe he so sturdily swings over his shoulder. The first fruits of his efforts are seen in the few slender blades of corn or the few hills of vegetables that spring up about his hut, which seem to struggle for very existence against the weeds and briers that refuse to be rooted out to give them place. Tall trees with blackened trunks stand out to give prominence to the desolation of the scene, while the surrounding forest,— dense, dark and still,—seems reared between him and the world.   *   *   *   *   *   *   *

A few years later, the same traveller passes the same way, and perhaps but a few miles from the town or city, stands a heat frame dwelling painted white ; and near it, the identical log hut, now, however, used as an outbuilding. The clearing has encroached on the forest till what was counted by yards, now measures acres in extent, and the stumps which were then so numerous as to afford little room for the corn and vegetables, have almost entirely disappeared. A plentifully filled frame barn stands on one side, and on the other is a garden full of luxuriant vegetables. * * * A *parterre* bright with autumnal-flowers, immediately fronts the house, while at the rear is an orchard in which the trees are loaded with ripening fruits. See the man on his farm and perhaps you will discover little else than the color on his cheek to distinguish him from an inhabitant of the neighboring town. * * * All this may be and has been accomplished by the resolute and persevering industry of man. The settler can say honestly that his own right arm has won him the battle, and can enjoy the fruit of his labor in feeling that though the struggle has been hard and long, the home he has earned well repays his toil. He had not yielded to the despondency of the hour of trial, nor given way to those feelings of discouragement which have induced some to throw away what has been gained and give up the struggle as if the difficulties were insurmountable, but has persevered till the end was gained.

He who nobly pushes back the wilderness and hews out a home for himself upon the conquered territory, has necessarily but a bony hand and rough exterior to present to advancing civilization. His children too, are timid, wild and uncouth. But a stranger comes in ; buys the little improvement on the lot next him ; has a wife with refined tastes, and children who are educated. The necessities of the new comers soon bring about an acquaintance with the pioneer, and their families are brought into contact. They are timid and awkward enough perhaps at first, but children know nothing of the conventionalities of society and are governed by innocence in their friendships. So they play together ; go to school in company ; and thus imperceptibly to themselves are the tastes and manners of the educated in some degree imparted to the uncultivated, and in like proportion the energy and fortitude of the latter, infused into their more effeminate companions.

Manly but ill-tutored success is thus taught how to enjoy its gains, while respectable poverty is instructed how to better its condition. That pride occasionally puts itself to inconveniences to prevent these pleasant results, must be admitted ; and that the jealousy and vanity of mere success sometimes views with unkindness the manner and habit of reduced respectability, —never perhaps more sensitive and exacting than when it is poorest,—must also be acknowledged. But that the great law of progress and the influence of free institutions have a tendency to break down and obliterate these exceptional feelings and prejudices, is patent to every observer of society in this country. Where the educated and refined undergo the changes incident to laborious occupation, and where rude industry is also changed by the success which gives it the benefit of education, it is impossible for the two classes not to meet. As the one goes down—at least in its occupations—it meets the other coming up by reason of its successes, and both eventually occupy the same pedestal. This social problem has been often wrought out in Canadian society. *Pride must stoop to conquer, and industry is sure to rise.*"

CHAPTER XI.

MINERAL RESOURCES AND THEIR DEVELOPMENT.—GOLD MINING.
—SILVER AND LEAD.—COPPER.—IRON.—IRON PYRITES.—
CHROMIUM. — TITANIUM.—ANTIMONY. —ASBESTOS. —BUILD-
ING STONES.—LIMESTONES.—QUARTZ, OCHRE, &C.—MARBLES.
—SERPENTINES.—ROOFING SLATES.—BRICK CLAY.—PEAT.—
SOAP STONE.

To be wholly independent and self reliant, a country must contain within itself the elements of an enduring prosperity. Neither favorable climate, productive soil, commercial advantages, nor yet all these combined, have been so powerful to attract an extensive influx of population to any country, as its mineral wealth. To a great extent, England owes her proud position at the present day, to her coal and iron mines.

However much may have been written or said respecting Canadian minerals and the best manner of bringing them into notice, as yet there is no well conceived or matured plan for effecting this object. The copper mines that have been opened, unless with few exceptions, have been worked with but varying success; and while local causes might have induced the abandonment of some, the merely speculative element may have entered too largely into the business generally. Yet the history of mining in all ages and all countries shows that it has ever born the same characteristics, and has been attended with the same or even more marked results than among us. Evidently mining in the Eastern Townships is yet in its infancy; and though the success which has attended it in some parts cannot be said to have justified the investments made, it is by no means the proprietors of lands who have been the losers in these transactions; for as a general thing much more money has been brought into the country and left here, than has been taken from it. If, as a result of the mistakes that have been made, more of the real earnest working element succeeds to what is but imaginative and speculative, the work which has been but too superficial in places, will be changed in character, and if not profitable to both proprietors and workers, it will be abandoned and the land revert to its rightful owners.

The principal economic minerals, such as metals and their ores, are found in many sections of the townships; and there is little doubt that with a larger general experience and knowledge of their value, more of them might be found to ensure fair returns to the employment of capital and skilled labor. Sulphur and sulphuric acid, super-phosphate of lime, and other productions for which there is abundant material, must attract very early attention.*

Gold has been shown to exist over a large extent of the Eastern Townships, from near the boundary line as far as Quebec, and probably farther to the north-east, along the mountainous belt which stretches to the extremity of the Province. It is from the breaking down of the rocks of this *Notre Dame Range*, that have been derived the sands, clays, and gravel, which make the soil of this belt of hills, and of the regions to the east and south of them. Gold has often been found in these rocks, but most attempts made to work the precious metal hitherto, have been by washing the superficial sands and gravels. This has been done with such marked success in some parts, that those regions are attracting skilled labor and capital, which may meet with profitable returns.

Copper. The ores of copper are widely disseminated in the Eastern Townships for the most part in the form of irregular beds and interstratified masses.

Though many of the workings have scarcely proved remunerative, there are exceptions, and from the wide diffusion of the metal in the rocks of the district, and from the richness of some that have been opened, there is reason to expect that many of them may become sources of profit. Capitalists from New York and Bos-

---

*Much of this chapter has been extracted and condensed from the pamphlet before referred to, as having been published by authority of the " Bureau of Agriculture."

ton have invested considerably in mining lands in this region.

Lead and Silver. Small quantities of lead ore, rich in silver, have also been found here.

Iron. Extensive beds of good iron ore occur in the Eastern Townships. They are iron slates consisting in a large part of red hematite, and under favorable circumstances, might be smelted with advantage. Hitherto the ore has been taken to Vermont for smelting.

Iron Pyrites. This is abundant and is a material of value for the manufacture of copperas, and as a source of sulphur for the fabrication of sulphuric acid, or oil of vitriol. This latter substance is one of great importance to the manufacturing industry of a country, for it forms the starting point in the ordinary processes for the production of chlorine, bleaching powder, and soda-ash. Of these, the latter is an indispensable material for the manufacture of soap and of glass. Sulphuric acid is moreover largely consumed in making superphosphate of lime, and for the refining of petroleum.

Chromium in the form of chromic iron ore, is another substance which is found in considerable quantities in some parts, and is valuable as the only source of chromate of potash, an article now extensively used in the arts for the manufacture of several pigments, and in various processes of coloring an dcalico printing.

Titanium. This substance which has within a few years attracted the attention of iron manufacturers for its supposed beneficial influence upon iron, and has also been prepared for several other uses in the arts, is likewise found here.

Antimony, a metal of a grayish or silvery white, is used as an ingredient in mirrors, giving them a finer texture. It renders the sound of bells more clear, tin is made more white, hard, and sonorous by it, and printing types, are made more firm and smooth by its use. It is also necessary in the fusion of metals, and the casting of cannon balls. In its crude state it is harmless to the human constitution, but many of its preparations act violently as emetics and cathartics. It is found in some sections of the Eastern Townships.

Asbestos, a stony fibrous substance found in the earth, is usually of a white or grayish hue, but sometimes has a greenish or reddish shade. The finer varieties have been wrought into gloves and cloth which are incombustible. The cloth made of this material was formerly used as shrouds for dead bodies, and has been recommended for firemen's clothes. Asbestos is also used in the manufacture of iron safes and for lamp-wicks. This substance is also common here.

Building Stones. East of the *Notre Dame Range* are quantities of granite of a superior quality for building purposes; but as this material is both more costly to work than the abundant limestones and sand stones, and generally more remote from the centres of consumption, it is yet scarcely made use of.

Limestones fitted for burning, are found in great abundance in some parts. The use of lime as a fertilizer for many soils is well known, and for this purpose the greater part of the limes in Canada are well fitted, on account of their freedom from Magnesia. Many of the limestones in the townships are susceptible of a good polish, and present pleasing variations of color; but though well suited for internal decoration, are yet scarcely known.

Quartz, Ochres, &c. Quartz of the purity required for glass making, and materials used for millstones, are also found in the Province. Ochres of a great variety of colors are likewise found; also the sulphur of barytes which is largely used by painters.

Marbles. The hills of the Eastern Townships afford many marbles of considerable beauty; white, colored, and variegated; but little has as yet been done to bring them into use.

Serpentines are also found here, generally of dark green veined with lighter green and white; much resembling the famous *verd antique* or serpentines of Corsica and Cornwall; though none of these materials have been cut, except for exhibition.

Roofing Slates. Extensive quarries of roofing slates of a superior quality have been opened in the Eastern Townships. Plates of large size are readily obtained.

Brick Clay is found in abundance in almost every section of the country, and bricks are now coming into very general use for building.

Peat. Extensive bogs of this material are found in some sections of the townships, though on account of the abundance and cheapness of wood, no systematic attempts have been made to turn it to use as a fuel. In the future, however, it may be of more account.

Soap-stone used for lining furnaces, and in some parts for the construction of stoves; white sand-stone for the hearths of furnaces, fire clay, and moulding sand, are common in many places.

Phosphate of lime. This material is abundant in the country; but in order to convert it into super-phosphate, large quantities of sulphuric acid are required; which latter material is not made in Canada, and is imported only at considerable expense. As yet the value of super-phosphate as a fertilizing agent is little understood; but farmers are beginning to learn its importance; and as there is abundant material in the country for the manufacture of these articles, it is desirable that they should be turned to account.

EASTERN TOWNSHIPS. 251

Part Third.

CHAPTER I.

BEDFORD DISTRICT. — LOCATION OF PUBLIC OFFICES. — COURTS. — PHYSICAL FEATURES OF THE DISTRICT.—YAMASKA RIVER.— BROME COUNTY. — BROME. — BOLTON. — EAST FARNHAM. — POTTON.—SUTTON.

THE District of Bedford, constituted such by act of Provincial Parliament in the year 1857, includes the counties of Brome, Missisquoi, Shefford, Iberville and Rouville, the two latter of which lie entirely within the French seigniories. The Court house, Jail, and Public Offices for the District, are located at Nelsonville in the township of Dunham.

The Court of Queen's Bench for the district of Bedford, is held at Nelsonville on the 21st of the months of February and October; continuing till the business of the term is finished. The district of Bedford cases of appeal and error, are heard and determined at Montreal.

The terms of the Superior Court for the district of Bedford, are held at Nelsonville, from the 13th to the 19th of the months of February, May, and October.

The district of Bedford Circuit Court is held at Nelsonville, from the 7th to the 12th of the months of February, May, and October.

Many of the more common physical features of the district receive the requisite attention in the sketches of each township respectively; but as the Yamaska river drains the greater part of the section as a whole, a notice of it has been thought proper in this connection. The main branches that form this river have their sources within the limits of Brome and Shefford counties : the streams that unite to form the north branch, come from Brome and Waterloo lakes; the smaller rivulets that make up the south branch, come from south Brome and north Sutton; while those which form the Black river, mostly have their head waters in the northern townships of the district, and unite with the main branch in Ely or Roxton, when the stream takes a north-west course into Acton. It then turns to the west and south-west through the northwest part of Milton into the seigniories, and joins the Yamaska at a point between the parishes of St. Damase and St. Pie, about 22 miles below the village of West Farnham.

The north and south branches of the Yamaska meet within the limits of West Farnham, when the river continuing west through the village of that name, turns

EASTERN TOWNSHIPS. 253

north into the seigniories, and after being enlarged by the waters of Black river, receives occasional tributaries along its way, till it enters the St. Lawrence about nine miles below Sorel. With the exception of those waters which find their way by the north branch of the Missisquoi river through northern Vermont into lake Champlain, and those which discharge into the same lake through Pike river, very nearly all the surplus waters of the district are carried through the Yamaska to the St. Lawrence.

BROME COUNTY.

This county includes the townships of Brome, Bolton, East Farnham, Potton, and Sutton. Knowlton in the township of Brome, is its *chef-lieu*.

The county circuit is held there, from the 26th to the 30th of the months of January, April, and September. The county Agricultural shows are also held at Knowlton.

BROME.

A tract of land lying within the district of Montreal, bounded north by Shefford, east by Bolton, south by Sutton, and west by Dunham and Farnham, containing 58,460 acres and the usual allowance for highways, was surveyed, divided, subdivided, erected into a township named Brome, and granted August 15th 1797, to Asa Porter and his associates, viz, William

Porter, Henry Collins, Ezekiel Lewis, Thaddeus Hall, Benjamin Crocker, Cyrus Cleveland, Samuel Gott, Jonathan Ayres, Joseph Wilson, Jonas Joslin, Nicholas Hall, Silas Westover, Asahel Dunning, Reuben Moore, Joseph Wilson junior, William Douglas, Brewer Dodge, Asa Warner, Billy Porter, Daniel Eames, Thomas Tennant, Ephraim Stone, Eliphalet Perrin, Aaron Porter, John Hubbell, Lewis Hoyk, Andrew Truck, John Solomon, Allen Davis, Benjamin Spencer, Elias Truax, and Hezekiah Weed.

It appears however, that through some defection, the associates of Porter could obtain no satisfactory titles to their lands for a long period; which fact operated very materially in retarding the influx of a desirable class of settlers. It was not till the year 1827, that arrangements were finally effected by which satisfactory titles could be secured to the occupants of lands.

The first permanent locations were made in this township, during the later years of the eighteenth century; but for a long period all the difficulties and embarrassments common to the early settlements of the country were felt in their full force and had their usual effect. Wheeled vehicles were introduced about the year 1807, but the roads were hardly passable for them till a much later date, and it was only by the hardest labor that the poor people could procure the necessaries of life from the older settlements.

The brothers Henry and Ebenezer Collins who came

from the United States at a very early period, may be considered the first settlers in the township, and located in what is known as *West Brome*. In 1798, Isaiah Sweet from the State of New York, came to the same place. The first grist mill in the township was built near this in 1802. The location is on the south branch of the Yamaska river, near the south-western corner of the township; it being a thickly settled farming section rather than a village. Beside the diffusely scattered dwellings, it contains a house of worship belonging to the New Connection Methodists, which was built in 1857; a post office opened in 1852; two stores, a tannery, woollen factory, and mills. Commissioner's Courts are held here and at Knowlton alternately. The improvement of the place has not been rapid.

Brome Corners.—The name by which this locality is known owes its origin to lines of road which intersect at this point. The first settlements were made here in 1799, by Ephraim Stone and Valentine Smith; and in 1804, the first saw-mill built in Brome was erected here. A public house was opened in 1805, a store in 1808; a school house was built in 1810; and a post office was opened in 1831. A Congregational church society was organized here in 1843, and a church edifice subsequently erected by them.

A Church of England mission was established here in 1855, and a church edifice in connection with it, was built in 1859. The Methodists have also a society in the vicinity. There are now two stores and a public house in the place, and for many years, much of the township business was done here.

Knowlton.—Settlements were commenced in the near vicinity and around this place, as early as 1800 and the few succeeding years ; but no locations were made upon the site of the village till about the year 1815. A saw-mill was built here in 1821, and a school house in 1822, but the settlement could be hardly considered as successfully begun till 1834, when Col. P. H. Knowlton took up his residence here. A store was opened about that time, a grist-mill erected soon after, and the saw-mill rebuilt. A public house and post office were opened about the year 1851.

Religious services had occasionally been held here by the Rev. Messrs. Cotton of Dunham, and Whitwell of Shefford, both clergymen of the Church of England ; and in 1840, the Rev. W. Bond, travelling missionary, visited the place. From this an interest was awakened and an earnest effort made toward establishing a mission and building a church edifice in Knowlton, which was finally successful, and in 1842, the Rev. W. Cusack came here as resident missionary. During the year the church building was finished, and opened for divine service. Mr. Cusack was succeeded by the Rev. J. Scott who remained till 1849, and after, by the Rev. Robert Lindsay, present Incumbent.

A Wesleyan Methodist society was formed here in 1852, by the Rev. R. A Flanders, and a house of worship belonging to these people was erected some time subsequently.

The late Col. Knowlton was largely instrumental in establishing the English Church in this place; in founding the high school in 1854; and in various other local improvements tending to promote the interests of the community; beside giving his influence and efforts towards such as were designed to benefit the public generally, as the opening of roads, &c., and laboring earnestly in behalf of judicial decentralization when that question was before the country.

Knowlton as the seat of business for Brome county, contains a county house in which are court and council rooms, registry office, &c. A company of volunteers are under organization here, and a battalion drill shed has also been erected.

Lines of telegraph from different points on the frontier, viz, Mansonville in Potton, Abercorn in Sutton, and Frelighsburg, in St. Armand, the latter of which passes through Dunham and Nelsonville, centre in Knowlton, where they connect with the line running to Waterloo, and thence to St. Johns and Montreal.

The village is situated in the east part of the township, about one half mile south-east from the lake, on a small stream coming from Bolton called Cold Brook, and is about three miles from Brome Corners. Beside the buildings already mentioned, there are several stores, many mechanics' shops, and a large number of private dwellings, many of which are substantial and

R

some even tasteful. Owing to the uneven surface of the land on which Knowlton is located, there is less regularity and uniformity in its general appearance than might otherwise have been the case ; the ascent from the stream to the vicinity of the court house, seeming almost too abrupt for convenience.

Fulford is the name given to a settlement in the north part of the township, about midway between its eastern and western limits, which was commenced about the year 1830. A saw-mill was built here in 1857 ; a tannery in 1858 ; a grist-mill in 1863; and a post office was opened in 1864; besides which are a store, some mechanics' shops, and a small collection of dwellings. A Church of England mission was established and a church building erected here in 1864. A house of worship has also been erected by the Methodists recently, who have a society here.

As early as 1803 or thereabout, some scattered settlements were formed near the outlet of Brome lake, but notwithstanding the advantages of the location, they were not improved by the erection of mills till 1832. A post office opened here in 1858, is called Bromere. West of the lake is a large tract of land which has received the name of *Brome Woods*, where the scattered settlements were commenced at a much later period than in many other parts of the township. For a long time the settlers in this locality formed an isolated community, obtaining their supplies mostly from the older settlements west and south-west. A society of Baptists was formed here in 1840 ; a school house was built in 1845 ; and a post office called "*Iron Hill*" was opened in 1853.

Clergymen of the English Church had paid occasional missionary visits to the locality, when in 1863, the building of a house of worship was resolved on, ground given for a site, and in 1864, the church edifice was erected. The mission here in connection with that at Fulford, is in charge of the Rev. T. W. Fyles.

The land in Brome is generally broken and hilly, and is even mountainous in the western and north-western parts. It is best adapted to grazing, stock raising and dairy produce being the most important interests of the farmer. The census of 1861, gives the municipality a population of 3,136 inhabitants, of whom 212 are of French origin. There are 23 elementary schools in operation in the township. The nominal valuation of real estate in Brome is $509,605 ; the number of legal voters 563.

Bog iron ore has been found in various sections, and in many places there are surface indications of copper. The largest body of water is Brome lake, which lies within the north-eastern quarter of the township ; beside which is Brome pond, a smaller body near the Farnham line. The principal streams are the outlet of this lake, which drains the northern and north-western parts of the township, as it takes a north-western course into Shefford, and the south branch of Yamaska river which drains the southern and south-western portion, as it passes into Dunham. Brome lake covers a space of 2,642 acres. Its general form is circular, though bays project inland at several points. It has mostly a bold, rocky, and in some places a densely wooded shore, but openings in the forest and glimpses of cultivated fields meet the eye at different points, and give variety to the prospect. Two islands,— the one a small barren rock, the other containing several acres of low woodland,—named respectively *Rock Island* and *Land Island*, lie within it. Its largest inlets are Cold Brook which enters it at the south about one mile from Knowlton, and the *Big Inlet* which comes from South Stukely through a corner of Bolton into Brome, and enters the lake on the north-east. The stage road between Waterloo and Knowlton, crosses this inlet, and for some distance winds around the east side of the lake, on a naturally elevated strip of land of sufficient width for a road, which divides the waters of the lake on the one hand from low marshy ground on the other. This natural ridge of land has been an object of curiosity and remark to the traveller.

A "South-east counties junction Railway" has been projected, which is designed to connect with the Waterloo line at some point in the west, and passing through Farnham, a part of Dunham, Brome, South Bolton and Potton, join the Passumpsic extension at the head of Lake Memphremagog.

BOLTON.

A tract of land lying within the district of Montreal,

bounded north by Stukely, east by Lake Memphremagog, south by Potton, and west by Brome, containing 87,670 acres, was erected into a township named Bolton, and granted August 18th 1797, to Nicholas Austin and his associates, viz, Silas Peaslee, Mark Randall, Joel Frazer, Jacob Place, Joshua Peevy, Peter Dils, Simon D. Wadleigh, Alexander Thompson, James Taylor, Joseph Buzzell, Jeremiah Page, Jeremiah Page junior, John Eastman, Joseph Chandler, Samuel Page, Jonathan F. Kelly, Jonathan Griffith, Andrew Clow, John Moore, Nicholas Austin junior, Wilder Page, Jacob Rosenburgh, Staffle Katsbatch, Helmas Strauling, Ezra Freeman, Henry Grout, John Brill, Caleb Grout, David Grout, Joseph Brill, John Grout, William Grout, John Hunt, Joseph Rickart, George Hayner, David Brill, Benjamin Brill, William Brill, Peter Yates, Robert Manson, William Manson, Henry Barhurt, Ernest Kisman, Peter Rosenburgh junior, Bamsby Lord, Richard Adams, Benjamin Page, David Brill, Peter Weare, Thomas Shepherd, Daniel Taylor, Moses Copp, and Roger Hibbard.

Owing to some unfortunate oversight in the arrangements respecting the division of these lands, disputes arose and resort was had to litigation which threw the matter into inextricable confusion ; and as it appeared impossible to effect any definite and satisfactory partition, such of the associates as acting in good faith had moved on to the ground, located themselves on such lots as suited their convenience. Others sold their rights for what they could get, merely defining them as such portions of land lying in common, or such a part of the five sevenths of the township; consequently much of the land fell into the hands of absent speculators.

The first location in Bolton was made in the east part o f the township, by Nicholas Austin who came from Newhampshire with his family and several hired men in 1795, and settled on the western shore of the lake, where he had previously made some preparation for their reception. During the few succeeding years, others chose locations in the same vicinity, it being more readily accessible than parts farther into the interior. Among these, were Jeremiah Page and Simon D. Wadleigh, the latter of whom kept a ferry for many years over the lake for the accommodation of such as travelled that route.

At that time the settlements in north-eastern Vermont were few and far between, and in consequence, most of the difficulties and obstacles to be overcome by the emigrants, lay in their way before they reached the lake, which afforded a comparatively easy way of access, either by boats in summer or on the ice in winter. The head of the lake once gained, the worst was over, unless in very exceptional cases.

Mark Randall and others settled near a locality known as Peaslee's Corners, as early as 1797; a short distance from which, Alexander Thompson built mills. Daniel Taylor from Danville Vt., also settled near this, at an early period. James Taylor who had come originally from Scotland, and landed at Newburyport in Massachusetts, came to Canada about the year 1797. His business being that of a master millwright, he was employed in putting up mills in different sections of the country, his family meantime remaining in Bolton. On one occasion after having built a mill at Shipton, he started to follow a *spotted line* through the woods from that township to Magog Outlet, to avoid the usual circuitous route. Thinking to get through in a day and not wishing to burden himself unnecessarily, he started with only food for that time, and without the accustomed fire materials. A gently falling rain had turned to snow which stuck and froze to the wet trees completely hiding the marks by which the way was indicated; when becoming bewildered, he strayed from the right course, wandered about, and spent three nights in the woods without fire or food; or without even knowing where he was or whither going. Fortunately however, he came upon the Magog river some distance below the lake, and followed up the stream till he came to a cabin. No one was within but the ashes on the hearth were warm, and these he thoughtlessly drew over and around his feet, the coverings of which were frozen too stiff to be removed. In consequence of this imprudent act, he was hardly able to reach the nearest point where help could be obtained; from which he was taken to his home. A severe illness, during part of which his life was despaired of, followed this exposure, and only after long and intense suffering he recovered so as to walk with a staff. He died at his residence in Bolton in 1846, and was buried on the farm where he first settled.

Richard Adams of Irish birth, came from Henniker, Newhampshire, at a very early period in the history of Bolton. He was an intelligent, cultivated, and kind hearted man, and during the period of his active life, filled the office of civil magistrate, acceptably performing its duties. There being no ordained clergy in the country at the time, Mr. Adams was frequently called upon to marry parties, which marriages, with others performed under like circumstances, were subsequently legalized by the government. By a severe cold and exposure while on a journey over the then wretched roads to Montreal, Mr. Adams contracted disease which after a time so disabled him that he could only move about with crutches; and in the end even that liberty was denied him, and he was obliged to remain a close prisoner. Yet while suffering this deprivation, instead of giving himself up to useless complaints and repinings, he at once reconciled himself to the best possible use of his remaining physical powers, and received the affliction as a discipline. Still anxious to benefit his fellow creatures, he commenced teaching such of the children of the scattered inhabitants as could assemble at his house; and during intervals of leisure from this, though his hands often shook like those of a paralytic, he busied himself in carving articles from wood, and painting them with various devices, showing both a remarkable skill and taste. By nature religiously disposed and susceptible of deep and tender feeling, he joined hinself with the early Methodists in Bolton, their preachers ever finding a home and welcome beneath his roof. During the later years of his life he was kindly cared for by a daughter, an only child who had married a person named Thompson, and died at Bolton in 1830, aged nearly 76 years.

Another person prominent and active among the early men of Bolton, was Mark Spinney, a native of Portland, Maine. Losing his father at a very early age, his youthful life was one of change and vicissitude. At the age of fourteen, he went to sea ; a sailor's life appearing congenial to his daring and adventurous spirit ; but after various shifts of fortune and many unpleasant experiences, he tired of the life and abandoned it, resolving to try his fortunes in Canada. With him to decide was to act ; when with a sack containing provision and clothing, and an axe slung over his shoulder, he started one of a company of ten, to seek a home here. The agent for Bolton was known to some of the party, and this determined them to seek him. At the last settlement on their line of travel, they supplied themselves with such provisions as could be had, and proceeded on their way with the intention of crossing the Barton river, and following down the west side of the lake.

Finding the river too high to be forded, they came down to a point opposite the site of Newport, in search of a crossing; but as is always the case in the spring, the ice had gone for some distance from either bank, and even in the middle of the lake were large openings, which made them fearful of attempting the passage. In this dilemma, some were for returning the way they had come; but young Spinney, though secretly sharing their fears, put a bold face upon the matter, and assuming a cheerfulness and courage for the occasion, proceeded to form a temporary bridge of such timbers and branches as could be collected on which to cross the first opening, which materials were to be taken forward to the second. They found the ice on the middle of the lake so worn and thin from the action of the current underneath, that they feared to cross in company lest their added weight should cause all to sink together. But the alternative before them was either starvation in the wilderness or possible death by drowning. Their last biscuit had long before been eaten, and there was hope of relief if they could succeed in crossing, as they could see the smoke of a cabin fire on the opposite shore. It was therefore arranged that they should cross singly and each take a pole to try the ice before venturing upon it. Spinney loosed the straps of his sack, that he might throw it off if obliged to swim, cheered on the others with words of hope and comfort, and while hiding the sore misgivings of his own heart, bravely led on and reached the opposite shore. The others came on in succession safely till the last, who broke through into the water over head, but was rescued by his companions; when all together repaired to the cabin in sight, where on opening the door, the first object that met their famished gaze, was a large fish that had that morning been taken. After refreshment and rest, they proceeded on their way.

In time Spinney became a proprietor; and being of vigorous physical constitution, as well as of fearless, open, independent character, and withal possessing presence of mind, quickness of perception, and readiness of action, he was looked upon as an efficient helper in case of emergency. He finally married and settled in Bolton, where he remained till his death in 1831.

John Brill, Jonathan Duboyce, David Blunt, and others settled in *West Bolton* as early as 1800. A post office has of late been opened in this vicinity for the convenience of the inhabitants.

In *South Bolton*, settlement were not commenced till about the year 1815, when Brooks Davis first located here. He was followed at different periods by others. Nathan Hanson opened a public house on the road leading west through the mountain pass; which house is still kept by his son-in-law and successor. Simon D. Wadleigh had been for some years a resident of East Bolton, but removed to the southern section of the township. Joshua Peevy was also one of the associates and first settled in East Bolton, but finally changed his ocation to South Bolton.

Richard Holland was another prominent man among the early settlers of this section of the township. He was a native of Cape Ann, Massachusetts, and being an orphan, was subjected to vicissitude and change. In 1810 he came to Canada, and for several years kept a public house on the site of the "*Camperdown*" in Georgeville; but in 1814, removed to the west shore of the lake where he kept both a public house, and a ferry from Bolton to Stanstead. While in this place he was greatly instrumental in opening the roads coming from different sections of the country, all of which led to the ferry. In 1817, he removed to South Bolton and built both grist and saw mills on the north branch of the Missisquoi river, which mills did good service for the early settlers in this region. He died in June 1851, aged 76 years.

The first school house built in South Bolton, was at a point known as Rexford's Corners. A post office was opened near in 1852.

Three miles north of this place is a locality known as Willard's mills, near which, Joseph Buzzell settled in 1808, where he built a saw-mill. The property has since passed through different hands, and some improvements have been made. There are now a store, public house, post office, grist and saw mills, tub factory, and a small collection of dwellings in the place. It is called *Bolton Centre* as it is about midway between the eastern and western limits of the township, although it is south of the *real* centre.

The north and north-east parts of Bolton were not generally settled till a much later period, but the copper mines recently opened in that section have given an impetus to the work. Saw mills have been built in the vicinity, and in 1865, a post office was opened named "*Bolton Forest.*" From present indications the belief is but reasonable that improvements here will be more rapid in the future.

The progress of Bolton in the years that are past, was no doubt greatly retarded by uncertainties respecting the validity of titles to the lands which were occupied. From time to time attempts were made by interested parties to ascertain their rights and secure a division ; but nothing effective was accomplished till 1857, when the government purchased the rights of those absent proprietors, and appointed a commission to examine and adjust the claims of all concerned ; so that after much annoying delay, the complications that had grown out of these intricate and vexed questions were ended and the whole set at rest.

Some idea may be gathered of the embarrassed and unsettled state of feeling in the community, from the fact that though settlements were begun in East Bolton as early as 1795, no school-house was built there till 1826. A store was opened in that section in 1841, and a post office in 1852.

The first religious teachers in Bolton were Baptists, but the early Methodist preachers visited the place and formed societies here at an early day. In 1825 a house of worship belonging to the Wesleyan Methodists, was built near Thompson's mills.

At present there are two church buildings at Peaslee's Corners, both of which were erected in 1865. One of them is owned by the Church of England which has a mission in that locality ; the other by the New Connection Methodists who also have a society there. A small French church is located in the north part of the township ; where they have also dissentient schools.

Till about the year 1820, the road leading west between the mountains, was not considered passable for wheeled vehicles, but was travelled on horseback and on foot, it being the only route by which the inhabitants could have intercourse with the townships west of them. During severe cold or stormy weather, it was particularly difficult and even dangerous to attempt passing through, and on one occasion at least, when a traveller insisted on making the attempt against the advice of those who better understood the risk, his life paid the price of his temerity.

In 1826, a united effort was made to improve the " Magog road " then coming from Stanstead across the lake, through South Bolton, Brome, parts of Dunham and Farnham, and thence west to Montreal, and a subscription of $1,100 was raised and worked out upon it. In 1830 a government grant was made by which it was so improved that waggons could pass tolerably well over it.

Numerous small lakes or ponds are found in the

northern and north-eastern section of this township, the best known of which is "*Mountain pond*" or as more recently called " *Orford lake*," a small body of water which will be remembered by the traveller who has visited this section, as it lies at the base of Orford mountain, and the stage road from Waterloo to Magog, winds around its southern shore. The next is " *Lake Dillon*" better known as "*Long pond.*" Another called the " *Enchanted pond*," situated in a wild and unfrequented part of the township, is difficult of access, and owes its name to the fact that some who had visited the locality and thought themselves able to find and identify it at once, were obliged to confess themselves bewildered and utterly unable to recognize it as the same. Still another, is called *Trousers leg* pond, from a fancied resemblance in shape, to that garment spread out. These are a few of the many ponds which are found within the limits of Bolton, some of which lie in a section seldom frequented except by hunters.

The principal stream of water is the north branch of the Missisquoi river, which has its extreme source in a small pond lying partly in South Stukely; and as it takes a southern course through Bolton, receiving the waters of many small streams in its way, it may be said to drain nearly the entire township; there being very few which find their way east into the lake, or west into Brome. Bolton is an independent municipality, with a population of 2,520 souls. Its assessable property is valued at $304,973. There are 20 elementary schools under control of the commissioners, for the support of which, the sum of $1400 is raised by yearly assessment.

Notwithstanding the reputation Bolton has acquired as a rough out-of-the-way place, it contains within itself the elements of an enduring prosperity. Many fine farms lie embosomed among its hills, or are extended on its elevated plains; and if the progress of its people has been slow in years past, a gradual but effectual awakening to their true interests, gives hope and confidence for the future.

EAST FARNHAM.

The warrant of survey for a tract of land lying within the district of Montreal, bounded north by Granby, east by Brome, south by Dunham and Stanbridge, and west by the seigniories, was issued August 27th, 1798. The tract was erected into a township named Farnham and granted in part to Samuel Gale, Oliver Wells, Samuel Wells, Robert Wells, Richard Wells, Micah Townsend, Ephraim Nash, Nathaniel Church, David Wells, Rueben Church, Abraham Cuyler, Cornelius Cuyler, Jacob Glen Cuyler, John Jones, James Sutherland, Alexander Schut, John Goudy jun., John Mebris, Amaziah Howe, William Mathews, William Sutherland, John Steele and Charles St. Ours. Active among the class of persons known as U. E. Loyalists was Col. Samuel Wells of Brattleborough, Vt.

He was of English origin, though a native of Deerfield in the Province of Massachusetts, and removed to Brattleborough then in the Province of Newhampshire, while yet the population of those grants was very sparse. Being a person of decided character and considerable means, his position enabled him to exercise a good degree of influence so long as the authority under which he acted as judge, justice of the peace, and chief militia officer of the section, was recognized by the people; and when policy which governs the conduct of many men, would have dictated an opposite course of action, Col. Wells evinced a most uncompromising loyalty. Though strongly opposed to the popular cause, he had yet sufficient skill and influence to avert the confiscation of his property; yet it was not always possible to escape the odium attached to the name of a loyalist, or the punishments often meted out to such. Col. Wells' principles were firmly maintained till the last of his life, and the opening sentence in his will shows conclusively that his submission to the ruling powers, was absolute necessity. He never acknowledged the newly constituted government, but passed his time in retirement till after the peace, of '83 when his mortal career ended at his residence in Brattleborough, in the 55th year of his age. He died deeply insolvent, as the firmness with which he had adhered to the cause of his Royal Master during the revolutionary struggle, had subjected him to repeated and severe losses.

s

After the close of the war, the British government granted portions of the Crown lands in Canada, to reward the services and remunerate the losses of those subjects who had been faithful to their allegiance; when on application, the children of Colonel Wells received each a grant of 1200 acres. These lands were located in the township of Farnham, Lower Canada, and Ephraim Nash, a son-in-law of Colonel Wells and a land surveyor, was employed to measure out so much of the eastern part of the township as was required for the Wells family and thirteen additional associates.

The exploring and surveying party consisted of Ephraim Nash, Oliver Wells, Richard Wells, Robert Wells, Nathaniel Church, and Samuel Wells Townsend; three of whom were sons, two sons-in-law, and the last named, a grandson of Col. Wells. Several of them chose locations on the line of road running north through the eastern section of the township, which had been followed by the early men of Shefford, and made preparations for a removal thither; and in the few succeeding years, most of Col. Wells' heirs left Brattleborough to settle on their newly-acquired lands.

Samuel Gale, from Hampshire, England, was engaged in the British service, and was ordered to America about the year 1770. Abundant evidence exists that he was both a talented and educated person, and it is also certain that he possessed a thorough practical knowledge of surveying. In June 1773, he married

Rebecca, the eldest daughter of Col. Samuel Wells of Brattleborough, and soon after left the army to enter upon the life and duties of a civilian. But at this period, turbulence and discontent were rife among the Colonies.

Being warmly attached to the royal cause and zealous in behalf of what he deemed the right, he perhaps outstepped the bounds of a calculating prudence, and in his efforts in behalf of his party, drew upon himself the hatred and distrust of leaders in the opposition. He was repeatedly arrested and imprisoned, and part of the time subjected to close confinement and personal discomforts if not actual suffering; but through the intervention of friends, an application made to the provincial Congress was so far successful that he was released on parole of honor, and after a critical examination of his case by the authorities, he was relieved from his parole and restored to liberty. Being anxious to avoid a repetition of scenes which to him and his had been fraught with sorrow and distress, he prudently removed with his family to Quebec, where he was favorably received, given honorable employment, and in the capacity of secretary, subsequently accompanied governor Prescott on his return to England. While in that position, it is more than probable that his influence and efforts greatly facilitated those arrangements by which the heirs of Col. Wells received remuneration for the losses their father had sustained through his loyalty. Mr. Gale subsequently rejoined his family in Canada where he lived in retirement, and died at his country residence in Farnham, on the 27th of June, 1826. He left a daughter since deceased, and a son who became an eminent lawyer and judge of King's Bench at Montreal, where he died in the spring of 1865. The family mansion and property in Farnham are still owned by the heirs of Judge Gale, though occupied by strangers.

Micah Townsend, another of the associates of Farnham, was born on Long Island, May 13th, 1749, and after a preparatory course of study, at the early age of fourteen years, entered college at Nassau Hall, Princeton, New Jersey. Graduating from there, he immediately commenced the study of law in the city of New York. This was continued for a term of four years, when he was admitted to the practice of the law by a commission under the hand and seal of the Hon. Cadwallader Colden, British governor of the colony of New York. Soon after his admission to the bar, he established himself in his profession at " *White Plains*," where he remained till the commencement of the revolutionary struggle, when he sought in the interior of the country a residence less exposed to the disturbances of that exciting period; and finally settled in Brattleborough, Vt., where in 1778, he married Mary, third daughter of Col. Samuel Wells. Being no political partisan, he here continued the practice of his profession successfully and profitably for twenty-four years, comprising that most eventful period of American history.

Mr. Townsend was less distinguished as an *eloquent advocate*, than esteemed for his *strict integrity, elevated views, and the soundness of his legal judgment and attainments.* His superior education and ability in drafting judicial and legislative documents, were reasons why he was chosen to fill various important offices where such qualifications were essential ; and his official life was characterized by habits of promptitude and regularity, which were highly appreciated and readily acknowledged.

Having resigned his office as secretary of the State of Vermont, and retired from all public business, he continued to reside in Brattleborough till the year 1801, when he disposed of his estate in that place, and in the spring of 1802, removed to settle upon his lands in Farnham, Lower Canada, where his interests had been represented by his eldest son, Samuel Wells Townsend. The father located upon lots No. 16 and 17, first range.

In this new home, subjected to the untried experiences of backwoods life, and to many uncongenial associations, he remained till 1816, when he removed to St. George, (Clarenceville,) to reside with his third and youngest son, the Rev. Micajah Townsend, rector of that parish, where he died April 23rd, 1832, aged about 83 years.

After his retirement from public business, his thoughts had been turned more to the consideration of his spiritual concerns; and for the last thirty years of his life, his daily practice had been to retire an hour at twilight for secret meditation and prayer; and yet his personal piety which was thus sustained, and was further evinced by a constant attendance on public worship and communion in the Episcopal church, of which he had been from his youth a member, was of that meek, chastened and unobtrusive character which commends itself more by deeds than words.

Richard Wells, Charles Kathan, Gideon Bull, Oliver Wells, Samuel Wells Townsend, and others, first located along the line of road running north. Capt. Clark Hall came to Canada in 1807, and settled on a newly opened line of road leading west toward the locality known as Allen's Corners. A son retains the old homestead, and several others reside in the near vicinity.

Allen's Corners. This place is situated at the point where the road running west, intersects that leading north from Cowansville to Granby, and is about three miles north of the former place. Josiah Allen made the first opening here about the year 1820; and next in the vicinity was Henry Jewell, who settled about the year 1821. John Hoskins, Abner Bede, Seth Barnum, Levi Vincent and others, located near the place about the same time. The village contains a post-office, two stores, a union chapel where the Methodists and Freewill Baptists worship alternately; a carriage manufactory; wheelwright and furniture shop; sash and blind factory, with other smaller mechanical works, and some twenty or thirty private dwellings.

The only society of *Friends* in the Province, have a meeting house about a mile from the Corners. A few of these people were among the settlers who came in from Newhampshire and Vermont during the earlier years of the present century; their numbers gradually increasing till 1815, during which time meetings were occasionally held among them by travelling *Friends*. Their first house of worship was built in 1823, and in 1826 regular meetings were established among them. In March 1831, their meeting house was unfortunately burned, but the present place of worship, a plain, substantial unpainted building, was erected near the same location in 1835.

Adamsville, on the road to Granby, three miles north of Allen's Corners, has mostly grown up since the year 1849. It has an academy; a post office, which was opened in 1859; two stores; a large tannery, mills, and tub factory, with about twenty dwellings.

Brigham a small place on the road leading to West Farnham, three and a half miles from Allen's Corners, has a post office which was opened in 1860, a large tannery, mills, and a small collection of dwellings.

Farnham Centre, one and a half mile south of Brigham, is on the road from Cowansville to West Farnham. The Presbyterians and Wesleyan Methodists have each a house of worship here; beside which are a post office, two stores, some mechanical works, and a number of scattered dwellings.

Nashwood, is the name of a post office which was

opened some years since in the north-east part of the township, on the road leading to Shefford.

The land in East Farnham is well adapted to agricultural purposes, there being tracts of the different qualities suited to each department. Corn and other grains grow well, and large quantities of dairy produce are taken to market annually. Hops are also cultivated to some extent. The Rock Maple grows here in its native abundance, and many of the farmers have extensive groves of the *second growth*, from which much good sugar is made every spring. The township is watered by the main branches of the Yamaska River, which pass through it. In 1855, it was separated into two distinct municipalities, for the better arrangement of the local affairs of either section. The nominal value of assessable property, in the eastern part, for the year ending in 1866, was $352,000; the number of registered voters 350; $360 was raised by the yearly assessment for schools, aside from that apportioned to dissenters. The yearly government grant, was 217,74. Beside the academy are ·nine elementary schools under the control of commissioners. Three cheese factories are in operation. Population given as 1,925.

POTTON.

A tract of land lying within the district of Montreal, bounded north by Bolton, east by Lake Memphremagog, south by the Province line, and west by Sutton, after the necessary forms, was erected into a township named Potton; of which, a part containing 8,400 acres was granted October 31st, 1797, to Laughland McLean, Captain in the eighty-fourth regiment. (reduced.) On the 7th of July 1803, further grants were made to Henry Able, Edward Brewer, Jeremiah Brewer, Eleanor Brevort, Bethuel Brumley, Joseph Burton, Garret Barron, James Brunson, Martin Brunson, Daniel Brunson, Leslie Bryant, Isaac Bryant, William Brisbaine, Samuel Brisbaine, Henry Church, John Church, Reuben Garlick, Henry Hogle, John Hogle, Duncan Cameron, Duncan McGregor, Henry Ruiter the elder, Philip Ruiter, John Ruiter, Jacob Ruiter, Henry Ruiter the younger, Abraham Savage, Edmund Simpson, James Hughes, Margaret Walker, Joseph James Walker, and fifty-eight others.

The first permanent location was made in Potton by Moses Eldridge who came from Peacham, Vt., sometime during the later years of the eighteenth century. He was soon after followed by others, many of whom had suffered either voluntary or compulsory exile, and had been engaged in the British service. Prominent among this class, was Col. Henry Ruiter, a U. E. Loyalist from the province of New York, who had served in the army during the revolution, and at its close, made a temporary stay in the seigniory of Foucault, near the outlet of Lake Champlain. Land being granted to him in Potton, he removed there in 1799, and within the few following years, built both grist and saw-mills in the south-western part, which were the first erected in the township. As early as 1798, settlements were commenced by Jacob Garland and Jonathan Heath, in a locality now know as Meigs' Corners.

Col. Ruiter originally owned the land where Mansonville now stands, and sold it to Joseph Chandler and John Lewis. In 1803, a saw-mill was erected here, and during the several successive years, others located in the place. In 1809, a building was erected which long served the triple purpose of meeting, school, and court house; and was for many years the only school house in Potton.

In 1811, Robert Manson purchased the property, and at once built a grist mill at the place which from him, took the name of *Mansonville;* but the war of 1812 put a stop to further improvements.

It may well be imagined that on the re-awakening of the passions and prejudices which had begun to slumber, there was little to encourage religion or education, and for years there was an utter destitution of all moral or religious influences here. Those who know what human nature is when left to its own devices and desires, can well conceive what must have been the case in such a community, without the restraints of divine precept or human law.

At an early period a winter road was opened through to the northern section of the township; but for a long time it was a dreary solitude which could only be passed by sleds, on horseback, or on foot. In 1814, to the horror and consternation of the few inhabitants, the body of a murdered traveller was found in the woods near this road. It was that of a stranger, and who he was, whither from, where going, or how he came by his death, were tales which nothing that remained could tell; secrets known only to Him who will bring to light the hidden things of darkness.

It was not till about the year 1830, that this road was so improved that wheeled vehicles could pass comfortably over it. The northern section of the township has been settled at a much later date than parts farther south and west; some of the earlier locations being made about the year 1819. The first post office in Potton, was opened at a point in the north-east part, now known as Knowlton's landing, after which it was removed to South Potton, but in 1845, was permanently located at Mansonville.

Various religious societies have been formed from time to time during the progress of settlements, both the Congregationalists and Baptists organizing bodies here; which however, were considered but branches of those respective churches in Troy, Vt.; till in 1835, the Baptists in Potton became a separate organization with the Rev. T. Merriman as pastor.

In 1831, the New Connection Methodists were introduced here, and have now a numerous society. In 1856, the Rev. J. Godden, clergyman of the church of England, was sent as missionary to Potton and the townships adjoining; at which time few in the section were acquainted with this church and its institutions. Subsequently the Baptist church edifice was purchased and appropriated for their use in Mansonville ; and in 1860, a new church building was erected in North Potton. A customs house was established at Mansonville in 1844. There is also a house of worship here belonging to the Methodists, several stores, public houses, mechanics' shops, and some forty or fifty private dwellings.

Some years since, a medicinal spring was discovered in the north part of the township, near the Bolton line, which is usually known as the " Bolton Spring." It has obtained considerable *local celebrity*, its waters being thought beneficial to certain classes of invalids.

Much of the surface of Potton is uneven and hilly, though there are tracts of intervale along the margin of the Missisquoi river ; more especially in the southern and south-western parts of the township. The land is generally better suited to grazing then graingrowing. The forest timber is a mixture of hard and soft. The " Green Mountain Range," enters from Sutton, and passes diagonally through the north-west part into Bolton. In the east part near the lake, are also several prominent elevations, the highest of which, are the " Owl's head" and " Sugar loaf" mountains. At the foot of the latter is Sugar loaf pond, a frequent resort for fishing parties. From the summit of Owl's head, those who choose to climb the ascent, have opened out before them a varied and interesting view. At their feet lies Lake Memphremagog in its tranquil beauty; in verdant foliage and dress of varied green appear the small islands of the lake; while on the eastern shore are cultivated fields, clustered farm buildings, and green pastures, interspersed with reaches of wood land, and occasionally a mansion with its outbuildings and ornamental grounds.

Further in the distant view, appear stretches of wooded plain interspersed with an occasional opening in the forest, a stream or pond, and a mountain prominence.

In the west and south, the prospect is bounded to some extent by the Green Mountain Range; but through occasional openings are caught glimpses of more distant hills, while in the extreme back-ground the pale blue outlines of the mountains of Vermont and New York, seem to meet the horizon; and perhaps in the intervening space the eye may catch sight of a glittering spire.

The assessable property of Potton is valued at $352,605. It has 425 voters. The school rates for the year ending 1866, were $1,000, and the government grant for the same period $224. There are eighteen elementary schools under control of the commissioners.

Indications of copper and lead are found in different localities; and soap-stone is also abundant, though at the present no mines or quarries are worked. The population is given as 1,194.

SUTTON.

The warrant of survey for a tract of land lying within the district of Montreal, bounded north by Brome, east by Potton, south by the Province line, and west by St. Armand and Dunham, was issued March 29th, 1802, by Robert Shore Milnes, Baronet, Lieutenant Governor of the Province of Lower Canada; when after the usual preliminary steps, it was erected into a township named Sutton, and subsequently granted to a company of U. E. Loyalists, 170 in number. Most of these grantees having served in the British army during the revolutionary contest, had found a temporary refuge in some part of Canada, but settled upon the lands granted, or as was often the case, sold their claims to other parties, early in the 19th century.

The first locations were made in Sutton by Thomas Spencer and Alexander Griggs, who in 1792, with their families and such a stock of household goods as could be carried on horseback, found their way into these wilds, reared a cabin, and commenced a clearing in the vicinity of the present site of *Abercorn*.

In 1799, Thomas Shepherd from Newhampshire came to Sutton for the purpose of building mills. Improvements were by no means rapid in those early times, as no school houses were built in the township till 1808. The first store at Abercorn was opened in 1820. In 1845, a customs house was established at the place; and in 1848, a post office was opened. There is a brick church edifice here belonging to the Church of England, the mission being connected with another in the township. A company of volunteer infantry was organized here in consequence of the border troubles. Abercorn is also connected by telegraph with Knowlton, and thence by way of Waterloo with St. Johns and Montreal. The village is situated on a branch of the Missisquoi river, somewhat over a mile north of the boundary line, and some five miles south from *Sutton Flats.*

A settlement was commenced near the latter named place about the year 1797, by a Baptist minister named William Marsh. He was born in Shaftsbury, Vt., in 1767, and lost his father in the British service sometime during the revolutionary war, by which calamity the widow who was a person of education and refinement, had been reduced from a station of comfort and respectability to poverty and dependance; and what was still more wounding and aggravating, her situation as the widow of a deceased loyalist failed of securing to her and her helpless children, the interest and sympathy usually accorded to those in her condition of life. They remained in their old home however, amidst neglect and persecution, till after the close of the war, when William who was the eldest son, advised and encouraged by his mother, went to Caldwell's Manor where he provided a new home for the family.

From that place, he came to Sutton in 1797. William Huntington also located here about the same time and subsequently built mills in the vicinity. The first religious body formed in Sutton was a Baptist Church, organized by Mr. Marsh. In 1799 Lorenzo Dow and other Methodist preachers visited the place, and formed societies which through the changes of time, have remained to the present. There are also New Connection Methodists and Adventists in Sutton. In 1845, a union meeting house was commenced, but not finished for several years.

A Church of England mission was opened here by Archdeacon Scott in 1844, at which time he held service in a school-house. In 1846, a site was given and steps were taken toward erecting a church edifice. In 1850, the Rev. R. Lindsay was appointed to the mission, when the work received a new impulse, and a substantial stone church was built; since which it has been successively in charge of the Rev. Messrs. Montgomery, Sykes, and Smith; the latter of whom remains to the present.

The first store opened here was in 1827; the first public house in 1841; a grist mill was built in 1846; and a town house erected in 1849, the upper story of which was fitted up for the High school opened in 1854.

Sutton Flats are on a level tract from which the land rises gradually toward the north and west, but more abruptly toward the mountainous east. A stream of water coming from the hills on the north-east, though of inconsiderable size, forms a power that is improved by the erection of machinery.

North Sutton. William Sowles who came from Rhode Island, like many others mentioned in this work, was driven into Canada by the political persecutions so rife in the colonies at a certain period. After the close of hostilities, he and others settled on a section of land which, as was supposed, belonged to Caldwell's Manor, but which proved to be a part of Alburgh, Vt. On being convinced of this mistake, some of them left their improvements to retire within the limits of Canada. Joseph, son of William Sowles, came to Sutton in the year 1799, and first located in the northwestern part of the township, but subsequently removed farther east. John Smith, another pioneer of Sutton, had come from Scotland before the revolutionary war as paymaster in the British army, and was among the number who afterwards settled in Alburgh, Vt., by a mistake which was not discovered till the parellel of 45° was accurately defined; when with others he removed to Sutton.

Glen Sutton. This settlement which lies on the east side of the mountains, was commenced by James Miller, who in 1799, made his way up the Missisquoi river from Richford, Vt., a route followed by the Indians who then frequented the country. A person named Jones married a daughter of Miller and settled near the Potton line, and during the scarcity which followed the cold seasons of 1815–16, these isolated families suffered extreme destitution. As in time

T

the settlement increased, the early Methodist preachers found their way here and formed a large society.

In former years Glen Sutton has acquired—whether justly or not—the unenviable reputation of being a sort of hiding place for refugees from justice. Persons of questionable antecedents and doubtful pursuits were known to make this their abode for a length of time, much to the annoyance of the respectable inhabitants; while its isolated situation near the boundary line, gave a seeming probability to the unfavorable impressions and rumors which were prevalent concerning it. More recently however, a change for the better has taken place, morally, socially, and intellectually, and the unpleasant incubus of an evil name, is being effectually removed.

The first school house was built here in 1823; the first public house opened in 1836; and a post office was established in 1861. Until the year 1846, there was little more than a footpath across the mountains between the sections of the township; when a grant of $3,500 was obtained from government and expended in the construction of a road. The work was considerably advanced, but found to be of such magnitude that another grant was necessary to complete it.

The surface of the land in Sutton is greatly varied by mountain and plain, hill and vale. The highest elevation is called "Round Top," near which, but on another mountain peak, is a pond or small lake covering an area of three or four acres, which is fed wholly by springs, and is supposed to be of great depth.

The streams are the north branch of the Missisquoi and its small tributaries in the south and south-eastern sections; and in the north and north-western parts of the township, such rivulets as running north into Brome help to form the head waters of the south branch of Yamaska river.

During the last twenty or thirty years, the material improvement in Sutton has been great. The soil of the township is best adapted to grazing, and stock raising with the produce of the dairy are the chief sources of income to the farmer. The assessable property is valued at $485,000. The yearly assessment for educational purposes, is $2,135; the yearly government grant $356. There are eighteen elementary schools under the control of the commissioners. Two volunteer companies are under organization here. There are 625 legal voters in Sutton; four church edifices : four post offices; ten stores; two grist mills; a door, sash and blind factory; two tub factories; two planing mills; a shingle machine, some smaller mechanical works, and twelve saw mills, three of which have circular, and nine have upright saws. The census of 1861 gives it a population of 3,151 inhabitants.*

---

* Several items respecting the early settlement of this township have been drawn from Thomas' Contributions to the "History of the Eastern Townships."

CHAPTER II.

MISSISQUOI COUNTY.—DUNHAM.—FARNHAM WEST.—STANBRIDGE.
—ST. ARMAND.—FOUCAULT AND NOYAN.

MISSISQUOI county includes the townships of Dunham, Farnham West, Stanbridge, and the seignories of St. Armand, Foucault, and Noyan. Its *chef-lieu* is Bedford in the township of Stanbridge. The Missisquoi County circuit court is held at Bedford from the 2nd to the 5th of the months of February, May, and October. The county Agricultural Shows are also held at Bedford.

DUNHAM.

A tract of land lying within the district of Montreal, containing 57,252 acres, 3 roods, and 30 perches, bounded north by Farnham, east by Brome and Sutton, south by St. Armand, and west by Stanbridge, was erected into a township named Dunham. The petition for this grant was dated April 28th, 1795; the warrant of survey issued August 27th of the same year; and in 1796, the township was granted to

EASTERN TOWNSHIPS. 293

Thomas Dunn and his associates, viz., Joseph Buck, John Heliker, Jacob Heliker, George Saxe, Mathew Hall, William Ferrand, David Ferrand, Joshua Chambers, Amos Woodard, David Reychart, John Clark, Thomas Best, Daniel Mills, Jeremiah Reychart, Daniel Trevor, Alexander McDougall, Thomas Pell, Andrew Ten Eyck, Henry Ten Eyck, Archibald Henderson, Henry Hall, Elisha Dickinson, Jacob Best sen., George Waymore, Abraham Lampman, John Mills, Stephen Jenner, Jacob Best jun., Adam Deal, Frederick Streit, Samuel Mills, Philip Ruiter, and Jacob Ruiter.

It is said that Dunham was the first township erected in Lower Canada. Among the earliest inhabitants if not the very first to locate within its limits, was Andrew Ten Eyck from New Jersey, who settled in the south-western part of the tract, in 1793. He was a U. E. Loyalist, and came to Canada as the forerunner of a numerous influx of the same class of settlers. Johnathan Hart located in the south part of the township in 1795.

Among the earliest families in Dunham, was that of Joseph Baker, who with his wife and several young children came from Petersham, Mass., in 1799. They came as far as Georgia, Vt., in a large canvass covered waggon drawn by four oxen; when on account of the distance between houses in some stages of their journey, they were obliged to pass the night in their movable tent, while the oxen were turned loose. At Georgia, they were obliged to change their waggon for a sled, which manner of travelling from that place to Dunham, occupied three days. In March 1799, George Shufelt and Henry Church settled in Dunham, and about the same time Capt. Jacob Ruiter, John Church and Isaac Gleason, located here.

The first settlers on the site of the village of Dunham, were Jacob Helliker, Amos Hawley, Gideon Hawley, Lemuel Hawley, Abraham Lampman, and John Wagner; all of whom located here about the year 1795. Mills were built on the south branch of the Yamaska river, in the north-eastern section of the township, within the few succeeding years; and in 1804, a winter road was opened through to the French seigniories by way of West Farnham, which was finally extended past Mount Johnson to the Chambly river. Ox-carts were first used here about the year 1802.

The township which is partly hilly and partly level, is situated in the section where the mountainous regions seem to descend to a comparative level with the plains in the vicinity of the St. Lawrence. The different qualities of land are found here in all their variety, as parts are excellent for grain, while other sections are better suited to grazing and for dairy produce.

The largest collective body of water is Selby lake, so called from a resident near its shore, but better known as Dunham pond, which covers about 600 acres. The largest stream is the south branch of Yamaska river which enters the north-east part of the township from Brome; beside which, are others of smaller size running different ways into other townships.

The earliest religious teachers here were American Methodists. Their first preachers were Hezekiah Wooster and Lorenzo Dow. Societies were formed, and in 1813, a chapel was built by these people on lot number 13 in the sixth range.

The Rev. C. C. Cotton of the Church of England, was the first clergyman who settled in the township, and continued to reside here for a period of more than forty years. He was a native of England, and when in his 25th year was ordained and subsequently sent out as a missionary to Canada. In 1821, a church edifice was built and opened for Divine service, and in the same year Dunham was erected into a Protestant parish. In consequence of failing health Mr. Cotton was assisted for a short period by the Rev. H. Evans. He was soon removed by death however, and in 1846, the Rev. J. Scott then incumbent of Brome, commenced holding service in Dunham each alternate Sunday, about which time steps were taken for the erection of a more suitable and convenient church edifice which was finished and opened for Divine service in 1849. Mr. Cotton died in 1846, aged 73 years, and was succeeded in the incumbency by Mr. J. Scott.

Joseph Scott, D.D., archdeacon of the diocese of Montreal, was a native of Yorkshire, England, and with his father's family emigrated to the United States in 1817. He was educated at Burlington, Vt., and in 1840, came to Canada. Three years afterwards he was ordained and sent to Brome, where he resided till he succeeded to the rectorship of Dunham. He remained here till his death in August 1865. The Rev. J. Godden has succeeded to the incumbency. The church in Dunham has of late undergone repairs, having been greatly improved and beautified by the addition of a stained glass chancel window.

In 1842 the Roman Catholic Bishop of Montreal while on a visit to Dunham, marked out the site of a church which was built in 1843, and named the church of the Holy Cross.

Within a few years the Methodist chapel in the sixth range, has been superseded by a more substantial building in a more convenient location.

A stone building for an academy was erected in 1840. A company of volunteer infantry was organized in 1866. The telegraph line from Frelighsburg to Knowlton, and thence to Montreal, passes through Dunham.

The village long known as Dunham Flat, incorporated January 1st, 1867, as Dunham, includes the half of lots No. 10, 11, and 12, in the sixth range, and the corresponding number of half lots in the seventh range. Its location in the midst of a rich farming section of country, is favorable to its material growth and prosperity. It lies a little south of the centre of the township, the principal street running north and south. The assessable property of the village is valued at $72,000. It has fifty voters. Within the corporation are two churches, an academy, post office, five stores, two tanneries, two public houses, many mechanics' shops, and some fifty or more private dwellings.

Outside the village corporation, the assessable property of the township is valued at $828,800. There are also 568 voters. Two grist mills, eight saw mills, and several cheese factories are in operation within the township. The amount of tax levied for educational purposes, township and village included, is $1,257.50; and the government grant is $406.16. There are twenty-five districts where schools are in operation eight months in the year.

Nelsonville. Capt. Jacob Ruiter settled in this part of Dunham, late in the eighteenth century, and built the mills on the south branch of the Yamaska, which were long known as Ruiter's mills, though in the changes of time, they have given place to others owned by different proprietors. Being an enthusiastic admirer of the hero of Trafalgar, Capt. Ruiter gave the name of Nelsonville to the settlement he had founded; but for some cause, when in 1839 a post office was established here, it received the name of Cowansville.

In 1852, a Congregational society was organized

here by the Rev. Mr. Connor, and a meeting-house was erected soon after. His successors in the pastorate have been the Rev. Messrs. Miles, Rathay, and for a period the pulpit was supplied by a theological student from Canada West. In October, 1856, the Rev. A. Duff became pastor of the churches at Cowansville and Brome, remaining such for a period of years. He was succeeded by the Rev. J. A. Farrer, who remained till 1866, when the pulpit was again temporarily supplied by a student of the Congregational College of British North America. In May, 1866, the Rev. C. P. Watson, formerly of London, C.W., became pastor, and divides his services between Cowansville, Brome and Dunham.

About the year 1854, the Rev. J. C. Davidson became a resident of the place, and the Missisquoi High School opened under his supervision, was located at a point between the extremes of Nelsonville. In 1860, Trinity Church was consecrated, and about the same period a brick building was erected for the use of the Female Academy. A Wesleyan Methodist church edifice was dedicated here in 1865. Thus the part of Nelsonville called Cowansville, contains three church buildings, a female academy, post office, several stores, public houses, mills, a woollen factory and other mechanical works, beside some thirty or more private dwellings. There is also an extensive tannery at a locality called Freeport, one and a half mile below Cowansville.

The small village upon the same stream nearly two miles above, was formerly called Churchville from John Church who at an early day opened a store and public house at that point; but as the property changed hands, the place in time came to be called Sweetsburg, and in 1854, a post-office was opened here under that name.

Nelsonville being the *chef-lieu* for the district of Bedford, the Court House, Jail, and Public Offices are located in Sweetsburg, by which means many professional gentlemen and other inhabitants are drawn to the vicinity. The board for the examination of teachers and the granting of diplomas for elementary schools, meets here and at Waterloo alternately. An English church edifice stands a little below the court house, beside which, are the post-office, several stores, a printing office from which issues a weekly paper, two public houses, several mechanics' shops, and some twenty-five or thirty private dwellings.

The two villages of Cowansville and Sweetsburg are of necessity merged in the common name of Nelsonville in all legal documents; and the probabilities are that at no distant day the space intervening between them will be taken up in sites for dwellings and public buildings, and the sections form one town.

East Dunham. Settlements were commenced in this part of the township as early as 1797, when Solomon Squire chose a location here, and others soon settled around him.

In 1824, the New Connection Methodists formed a society here, and in 1857, the Wesleyan Methodists built a house of worship in the vicinity. Two steam saw mills are in operation here, and in 1862, a post office named East Dunham, was opened. Many substantial farmers reside in this section of the township, among whom the modern improvements in agriculture are being generally introduced. A cheese factory has of late gone into operation among them. The population of Dunham is given as 3,903.

FARNHAM WEST.

The warrant of survey for Farnham was issued August 27th, 1798, soon after which the tract was erected into a township, and in part granted to the heirs of Col. Samuel Wells and thirteen additional associates. These grants lay in the eastern part of the township, and many openings were made there, while yet the tract now known as West Farnham remained an unbroken wilderness. An extensive grant of this wild land was made to George Allsopp, Esq., for government service; but years elapsed before it was claimed by the heirs of the grantee; and in the meantime several families of settlers had located upon different parts of it; mostly however, in the vicinity of the Yamaska river which here affords many valuable mill sites.

William Cook, from Rhode Island, built a saw mill here in 1817; and nearly the same time, Isaac Gibbs located about one mile east of the present site of the village. J. Higgins settled on what is now known as Higgins' hill, and Capt. Buck chose a location near the forks of Yamaska river. The fact that these lands were owned for a series of years by non-resident proprietors, operated very unfavorably toward their permanent settlement; as in consequence of there being no one to look after the interests of the real owners, much valuable timber was taken from the premises by irresponsible parties.

These lands were first occupied by the heirs, in the persons of three grandsons of George Allsopp, viz., George Carleton Allsopp, John Bonfield Allsopp, and John Charles Allsopp. They did not locate here permanently however, till after the year 1840, since which, the land has been mostly sold to other proprietors.

In January 1827, John Bowker, a young man from St. Armand, located upon the site of the present village, at which time there were but three log houses on the premises, and few indications of settlement for a distance of seven miles toward St. Cesaire. At first, these settlers were obliged to carry their grain to Stanbridge for grinding, till in 1834, a run of stones was placed in the saw-mill for this purpose; the first grist mill being built about the year 1840.

The first public road through the place was the continuation of the Stanstead line which was finally carried past Mt. Johnson to the Chambly river, whence there were frequented routes to Montreal. For many years nearly all the travel on this line was done in the winter, as on account of the peculiar nature of the soil, travel in summer over the imperfectly constructed road, was particularly difficult, not to say dangerous or impracticable. In 1830, however, a government grant was obtained and expended in such improvements as made it more passable. In 1855, the township was separated into two municipalities.

The surface of the land is decidedly level, much of the timber originally standing being pine. The most valuable of this however, had been taken off while yet there was no one to look after the interests of the absent proprietors. Here as well as in many other parts of the section, the soil requires a peculiar system of culture, including drainage, &c; and is better suited to the production of grain and vegetables, than for grazing. In the south-west part, are still considerable tracts of unsettled land, which has been purchased by individuals for the hemlock timber standing upon it.

The one great advantage of West Farnham lies in its extensive and valuable water power. Outside the village corporation, the assessable property is valued at $164,947; there are also 270 voters. For the support of six Protestant dissentient schools in the village and township, the sum of $400 is raised by assessment; beside the government grant which varies from $70 to $80.

The village was incorporated January 1st, 1862. It is about one and a half mile in length from east to west, by about three fourths of a mile from north to south. There are fully sixty feet of fall in the river in its course through the corporation. Its assessable property is valued at $69,025; it contains 225 legal voters and not less than 200 heads of families. There are three churches, some dozen stores, a post office, railway station, several public houses, three grist and three saw-mills, a woollen factory, two furniture shops, a manufactory for musical instruments, two cooper factories, many small mechanics' shops, and some 300 dwellings, most of which are small. The great majority of inhabitants in West Farnham are French Canadians.

The municipality of West Farnham and a portion of East Farnham have been erected into a parish for ecclesiastical and educational purposes, under the name of St. Romuald de Farnham, which includes six French schools, viz : one superior school for both boys and girls, which is located at the village of West Farnham ; and five elementary schools in different parts of the parish. The Roman Catholics have a large church built of stone and covered with tin, standing in a prominent location on the north side of the river. The Rev. E. Springer, Curé, has an assistant.

The Church of England mission was opened in this place, in occasional services performed by the Rev. T. Johnson, and the Rev. J. Jones. The latter undertook a very successful collecting tour in England where he raised funds for the erection of a church and parsonage, and to found a partial endowment of about £600, which is the oldest endowment fund in the Diocese. In January 1847, the land on which the church and parsonage stand, was deeded to the church by James Allsopp, Esquire, son of the original grantee.

In September 1848, the Hon. A. T. Galt, representing the British American Land Company, presented fifty acres. of land to the mission. The first resident clergyman here, was the Rev. William Jones, who commenced his ministry in 1847, and remained ten years, when he was succeeded by the Rev. A. C. Scarth who remained but two years. In 1859, the Rev. T. W. Mussen who is present incumbent, commenced his duties here, since which time various improvements have been made in the buildings and grounds. The church edifice which is of wood painted white, now has a fine bell of 700 lbs. weight; a costly Harmonium ; and in the chancel, a rich stained glass window has recently been placed to the memory of the late John C. Allsopp, Esquire.

The first Wesleyan Methodist society was formed here in 1842, by the Rev. Mr. Hutchinson, and soon after, the present house of worship was erected. The station has been successively connected with the Dunham and St. Armand circuits, but is now an independent mission. The Presbyterians hold occasional services in the school house here. The population of West Farnham is given as 2,530.

STANBRIDGE.

Under the hand and seal of Sir Robert Shore Milnes, a warrant was issued for the survey of a tract of land in the district of Montreal, bounded north by Farnham, east by Dunham, south by St. Armand, and west by the seigniories, bearing date of May 7th, 1801 ; when after the preliminary forms it was erected into a township named Stanbridge, September 1st of the same year, and granted to Hugh Finlay and his associates, viz, John Cutting, Hannah Kellar, Clark Reynolds, Edward Martindale, Solomon Dunham, Adam Schoolcraft, John Bockus, Willard Smith, David Partolo, Caleb Tree, James Martindale, Mathew Kemble, John Bomhower, Luke Hitchcock, Jacob Bomhower, Griffin Reynolds, Benjamin Reynolds, Frederick Whaler, Thomas Wrightman, Mathew Saxe, Joseph Smith, John Ruiter the younger, Stephen Lampman, Adam Clapper the elder, Moses Westover the elder, Peter Cutler, Peter Rosenburgh, Adam Clapper the younger, Henry Clapper, Peter Krans, Michael Lampman, Christopher Cartright, John Hogle the elder, Philip Kruller, John Ferguson the younger, Frederick Kemmerman, Almond Cartright and Thos. Douglas.

From what has transpired respecting the proprietorship of land in Stanbridge, it would appear that comparatively few of these grantees made "Actual settlement" upon the lands drawn; and that consequently many tracts reverted to the Crown.

The first locations in this township were made as early as 1797, when Nathan Andrews came in from Rhode Island and settled here. The same year Caleb Tree with his family came from Williamstown, Mass. These two pioneers settled near the site of Stanbridge village. The latter left a large family, some of whom retain the old homestead. About the year 1800, William Wilson from Waterbury, Vt., became owner of the lot on which is situated the mill privilege and where the main part of the village now stands, when he built both grist and saw-mills, and put up the frame of a building which was long kept as a public house. The first country store was opened here by Ebenezer Hart, about the year 1810. Ebenezer Martin built the first tannery here in 1808. In March 1820, John Baker from Barre, Vt., started the wool carding and cloth dressing business ; and being a skillful mechanic, not only made the machinery required in his own works, but also for other establishments of the same kind ; no small undertaking when considered in connection with the fact that then it was exceedingly difficult to obtain the necessary materials and tools for such work.

The early settlers of Stanbridge had their share of the difficulties incident to pioneer life ; particularly during cold and unproductive seasons. Some who are now living, remember that as boys they used to be sent on horseback to Saxe's mills in Highgate, Vt., for

Virginia corn (brought there by boats on the lake) for which they had to pay three and a half or four dollars per bushel; and then to convey it through the woods over wretched roads, one bushel at a time.

Before reaching Stanbridge, the mountain range which comes from the south into Canada, seems to have "*melted into a plain,*" as the land in the township is level, generally soft timbered, some portions low and marshy, and altogether better suited to the production of grain and vegetables than for grazing. The most considerable stream of water is Pike river, which enters at the south-east from St. Armand. This stream is so called from the kind of fish found most plentiful in its waters; and it appears that the Indian and Frenchman as well as the English speaking settler, had each a name for it significant of this fact. Frequent rapids occur in its circuitous course through the township, which afford numerous mill sites, many of which have been improved by the erection of machinery. Grout Creek coming north from St. Armand, falls into Pike river at Bedford.

The assessable property of Stanbridge is valued at $1,066,920. This may appear a high figure compared with the valuation of property in other townships; but can no doubt be satisfactorily explained to the inquirer. One fact which will of itself throw light upon this point has already been mentioned; viz: the existence of numerous valuable mill privileges along the course of Pike river. The number of legal voters is 787. An assessment of two mills on the dollar is levied on the rateable property for the support of schools. The government grant averages from $400 to $425 per year. Beside two academies, are twenty-one elementary schools under control of the commissioners, and also several dissentient schools, as a proportion of the inhabitants are French Canadians. A Roman Catholic parish named "*Notre Dame des Anges*" has been formed in Stanbridge for ecclesiastical purposes. There are in all eight post offices in the township, which will be indicated in their respective localities; also five grist mills, five tanneries, and fifteen or more saw-mills.

Bedford. Before the war of 1812, little had been accomplished toward effecting the general settlement of this part of the township; yet some few openings had been made in the wilderness, and a grist-mill built on Pike river at this place. This however, was carried off by a flood, and was not rebuilt till 1815. At that early day the standing forests in Stanbridge were valuable or would have been so, had there been a market available for the timber. In 1820, a large tract was destroyed by a fire which had been accidentally ignited, and spread north from St. Armand.

The village of Bedford is by no means compactly built, the buildings being scattered principally along the left bank of the stream which is here quite rapid.

As Bedford is the *chef-lieu* of Missisquoi County,

the building containing court and council rooms, registry office, &c., is located here. There is an English church which was erected about the year 1832. The first missionary here was the Rev. Mr. Robertson; two others subsequently officiating for a short period each; when in 1842, the Rev. James Jones took charge and continued to reside here till 1864, at which time he was succeeded by the Rev. G. Slack, present incumbent.

A post office, several stores, an academy, public houses, mills, tanneries, a number and variety of manufacturing establishments, and some eighty dwellings, help to make up the village.

Taking Bedford as a centre, about four miles to the east is *Stanbridge village*, near which the first locations in the township were made. In December 1834, a weekly Newspaper called the "*Missisquoi Post*" was started here and published three or four years, and a post office was opened in 1836. The Wesleyan Methodists have a society and house of worship here, which was built in 1861. A two story brick building for an academy was erected in 1854, since which the school has been in successful operation.

The first Episcopal church which was built here in 1829, was taken down in 1860, to be rebuilt, enlarged and improved; and when entirely completed, will present both externally and internally, a fine specimen of church architecture. The Rev. John Constantine is incumbent. Stanbridge village also contains a banking and exchange office, three stores, two public houses, a tannery, grist-mill, the never-failing smaller mechanics' shops, and some forty inhabited dwellings.

Riceburg is a small but thriving place, one and a half mile down the stream from Stanbridge village, and about three miles a little north of east from Bedford. The first opening in the forest was made here in 1799, by Jacob Seagel, many of whose descendants are now living in the township. About the year 1814, George Saxe built the first saw-mill in the place; and the first oat-mill in Lower Canada, was built here in 1827. A foundry was established here about thirty years ago by H. W. Rice, which has been in successful operation since, and more recently important additions have been made to the works by Messrs. M. & C. A. Rice. The Messrs. Lambkins have extensive shops and the best of machinery for preparing house-building materials, and are also largely engaged in the manufacture of furniture of every variety of style and finish. There are also mills and a cooper-factory in the place. A post office was opened here some years since.

Two miles west of Bedford is *Mystic*, or *Stanbridge Centre;* and five miles a little to the east of north, is *North Stanbridge*.

Stanbridge Station is situated two miles west of Bedford, in the midst of an open and cultivated section of country, its general appearance indicating a village in its incipient stages. Beside the railway station, it has a post office, several stores, a public house, and some ten or twelve dwellings.

Malmaison. Large tracts of land in Stanbridge were at one time owned by F. A. Des Rivières, Esquire, (a French gentleman, as the name indicates) from whom it descended to his sons, Messrs. F. W. and Henri Des Rivières, who were natives of Canada, and came to reside on their property in the western part of the township in 1841. The first saw-mill was built here in 1842, and a grist-mill the year succeeding. A Roman Catholic church was erected near the place in 1845. The location is on a rapid on Pike river, and beside the family mansion which stands a little apart from the other buildings, the church and mills, is a collection of laborers' cottages. At a short distance is a station of the Junction railway between St. Johns and the Vermont Central, known generally as Des Rivières station, in which building a post office named Malmaison was opened in 1863.

Pike River Villaye is located on the western boundary of the township, where settlements were commenced as early as 1816, by persons named Larkins, Tilley, and Blakesly. The village now contains a Wesleyan Methodist church edifice, built in 1848; a post office opened in 1836; two school-houses (French and English), a grist-mill built in 1858; a saw-mill put up in 1836; several stores and mechanics' shops, and some sixty or more dwellings, most of which are small. Large quantities of grain, lumber, &c., are collected and taken from this place, as vessels of 300 tons can come up from the lake. From this point the river flows south into Missisquoi Bay, an arm of Lake Champlain. The population of Stanbridge is given as 5,277.

ST. ARMAND.

A tract of land six leagues in length, along the Missisquoi River and Lake Champlain, by three leagues in width from north to south, was granted " In fief and seigniory, with all the rights and perquisites appertaining," by the French governor La Gallisonière and the Intendent Bigot, to the Sieur Nicholas René Lavesseur, Sept. 23rd, 1748, which grant was ratified by the king of France in 1749.

After the conquest of Canada by the English, this seignoiry by purchase or otherwise, came into the possession of the Hon. Thomas Dunn, sometime president of the council, and as such, for a short period acting administrator of the government; after which he became a Judge of the Court of King's Bench at Quebec.

From him the tract was called "Dunn's Patent," and long known as such. The lands in this seigniory were disposed of in lots by deeds, the parties coming into possession agreeing to pay a certain sum with interest within a specified time, and also a yearly rent of one shilling for every hundred acres; by which arrangement, the lands were released from every other seigniorial claim. However, on the definite settlement of the boundary question by taking the 45° of latitude as the line of separation, it was found hat nearly two-thirds of the original grant lay south of that parallel, and consequently within the territory of the United States. Subsequently a tract four miles square was annexed to the east end of the seigniory, the lots in which were ceded to purchasers in the same manner.

The first permanent settlement made in St. Armand was in the autumn of 1784 ; when a party of United Empire Loyalists, most of whom had been in the British service during the revolutionary war, chose locations near Missisquoi Bay. Many of them were of German origin, and had left their homes on the Hudson or elsewhere, to share the fortunes of the Royal cause. Their land was purchased of Mr. Dunn on very favorable terms. The distance to St. Johns was twenty miles through the wilderness, or over fifty miles around by the lake and river ; and before they could raise enough grain for their families, they had often to go this distance, or to Burlington, Vt., for the necessaries of life.

The names of the first party of settlers were, John Ruiter, Alexander Taylor, Christjohn Wehr, Harmonas Best, Adam Deal, Lewis Streit, Christjohn Hayner, Conrad Best, Alexander Hyatt, Gilbert Hyatt, John Saxe, Jacob Barr, John Mock, Philip Luke, Joseph Smith, Garret Sixby, James Anderson, Frederick Hayner, and Peter Miller.* Several of these

---

* For this and several other items respecting the early settlement of St. Armand, we are indebted to Thomas' " Contributions to the History of the Eastern Townships."

men afterwards removed to other sections of the townships, becoming agents or associates.

Many of them however, located permanently near the Bay, at which point the settlement increased rapidly. The locality soon assumed the appearance and characteristics of a village, while the aspect of the surrounding country was fast changing from a solitary wilderness to cultivated fields and green pastures.

The first religious meetings here, were held by the eccentric Lorenzo Dow, about the year 1787.

In 1804, the Rev. C. C. Cotton, of the Church of England, came to reside here and remained four years. In 1808, the Rev. Dr. Stewart was sent out to the mission by the Society for the propogation of the Gospel in Foreign Parts, and located at St. Armand East. He was of a noble family but gave up the advantages and enjoyments of birth, station, and wealth, to become a pioneer of the church among the early settlers of these townships. Upon his arrival at the field of his newly assumed labors, services were held in a school-house till a church building could be erected. Here he remained useful, respected, and beloved, till in 1815, he returned to England. His visit to that country was but temporary however, as within a few years from that time, he came back to Canada ; in 1826 he was consecrated Bishop of Quebec, and died in 1837.

All accounts agree in bearing testimony to the exalted character of this good man who has been deservedly called " the model of a Christian gentleman." Our respect and reverence are greatly increased when we consider the social and worldly advantages he voluntarily relinquished, and the nature of the duties as willingly assumed; as well as other sacrifices he made for the permanent establishment of the church of his affections, and the amount of his public and private charities.— " The memory of the Just is blessed."

In 1811, a church edifice was erected about one mile north-east from Missisquoi Bay, in order to accommodate the settlement which was rapidly extending in that quarter. This mission with that in the eastern part of the seigniory, was for many years in charge of Dr. Stewart, and subsequently of his successor Mr. Reid, till in 1834, the seigniory was divided into two ecclesiastical parishes, known respectively as St. Armand East, and St. Armand West, when the Rev. R. Whitwell was appointed rector of the latter named parish.

Methodist societies were formed in St. Armand West at an early day, and a house of worship was built by them at the Bay in 1819. These people have since become numerous.

Many of the early inhabitants of St. Armand were of that class who had suffered exile for their loyalty, and later events have gone to show satisfactorily, that a large infusion of the old element still exists among their descendants.

ST. ARMAND WEST.

As already stated, the first locations were made in

this section of the seigniory, and for many years the village springing up on the north-east shore of the Bay, was a centre of trade and business for the settlements forming around, as supplies could be brought here by boats on the lake. The first store was opened in 1800. John Ruiter and Alexander Taylor, two of the company of U. E. Loyalists before mentioned, were the first proprietors of the land on which the village was built.

This place has been from time to time the scene of considerable excitement from border troubles, in consequence of its proximity to the frontier. During the war of 1812, an attack was made on it by a body of armed Americans, when a number of prisoners were taken by them. Much excitement and apprehension were also felt at the time of the rebellion of '37 and '38, when a company of volunteers were stationed here. The fears of the people were not realized however, to any great extent.

The Rev. R. Whitwell, first rector of St. Armand West, was of English birth, and came to Canada in 1821. He was first appointed to the new mission at Shefford, where he remained till 1826, when he removed to St. Armand West, and continued in charge till, in 1855, increasing bodily infirmities obliged him to resign. In 1856, he was succeeded by the Rev. C. A. Wetherall, and two years later by the Rev. H. Montgomery, present incumbent of the parish. Mr. Whitwell died in 1864, in the 78th year of his age.

This village was incorporated in 1846, as *Philipsburg*, so named in honor of Col. Philip Ruiter. At different periods two weekly newspapers have been published here, named respectively the " *Gleaner*," and the "*Missisquoi News*," the latter of which is still continued in St. Johns, with the title somewhat changed. Of the recent invasion of our frontier by the " *Army of Ireland*," all our readers have heard; on which occasion, though this village escaped a *visitation*, the minds of the people were intensely excited.

St. Armand Station, on the St. Johns and Vermont Junction Railway, was formerly known as Moore's Corners. It is situated but a short distance from Philipsburg, and was made memorable in the rebellion by a night skirmish between a company of volunteer militia, and a party of rebels and sympathisers, in which the rebels retreated across the Province line, leaving one dead, two wounded, and three prisoners in the hands of the victors.

Though small at present, the place will increase in size, as the railway necessarily brings in considerable business. A post office was opened here in 1865.

Pigeon Hill is the name given to a locality in St. Armand West, near which George Titemore settled in 1788; soon after which, Henry Grout settled in the near vicinity. In 1791, Adam Sager located here, soon after and was joined by his father and three brothers, who purchased the lots on which the village now stands. The place was long known as Sagersfield, but in consequence of the numbers of pigeons frequenting it, the name was changed to *Pigeon Hill*, which difference can hardly be termed an improvement. A school-house was built here in 1803, a public house opened about the same time, and in 1804, a Methodist society was formed by the Rev. Thomas Best of Highgate, Vt. A store was opened in 1810 ; a house of worship erected by the Methodists in 1823 ; and a post office established in 1851.

While Mr. Whitwell was rector of the parish, he held frequent services in this place, but no church edifice was erected during his ministrations. Subsequently however, one has been built, in which weekly services are held. A society of Adventists have also a meeting house here.

In the summer of 1866, Pigeon Hill received a visit from the "*Army of Ireland,*" and suffered from its depredations in common with several neighboring localities. The population of St. Armand West is given as 1,328.

ST. ARMAND EAST.

We learn that as early as 1789, Simpson Jenne who had served in the British army during the revolutionary war, settled on land about two miles east of the site of Frelighsburg. This family were then seven miles from other inhabitants, and for months saw no human faces but those of each other. Jeremiah Spencer settled on an adjoining lot, and among other early settlers, were William Ayer, and Daniel Chandler. In 1790, John Gibson built a log dwelling near the present site of the mill, soon after which a person named Owens built a grist-mill. This he sold to individuals named Conroy and Yumans, by whom the mill was enlarged and improved, and a saw-mill built adjoining. These parties sold the premises to Abram Freligh who also purchased a considerable tract of land in the vicinity, and from this proprietor the village has derived its name. A public house was opened in 1797, and a store in 1801. Elijah Kemp who located here in 1797, was a prominent man among the early settlers.

In 1808, the Rev. Dr. Stewart came as missionary to St. Armand, and soon after a church edifice was erected in this place. On his return to England in 1815, he was succeeded by the Rev. James Reid, who in a great degree, partook of the character of his predecessor, and, like him had a deep hold upon the confidence and respect ef the people. Religious meetings were also held in those early times by both Methodists and Baptists in the place. The registry office for the county of Missisquoi, was located here for several years, and in 1838, a weekly paper called the " *Missisquoi Standard*," was commenced and continued for several years.

Several designations have at different periods been given to this locality, First it was called " Conroy's Mills ;" then the derisive appellation of " *Slab City*" seemed to cling to it for a long time ; but the name by which it was incorporated January 1st, 1867, is *Frelighsburg*. The corporation includes over 372 acres of land, and beside the parish church, it contains a parish hall, customs-house, academy, post office, five general stores, a public house, mechanics' shops, and some fifty or more inhabited houses.

Abbott's Corners. The earliest settlements were made here about the year 1797, by the Rev. Jedediah Hibbard, Dr. James Abbott, and others. In 1799, a Baptist society was organized, of which Mr. Hibbard was pastor, and a house of worship was erected, but every vestige of this has long since disappeared; the Baptist church edifice now standing, having been built in 1841. Mr. Hibbard's successors have been the Rev. Messrs. Galusha and Smith. As early as 1800, a Methodist society was formed here, which also has a house of worship built in 1841. A post office was opened here in 1852. The place which was formerly of more local importance than at present, is situated about two miles south-east of Frelighsburg, on an airy and pleasant elevation. The inhabitants are generally able and substantial farmers.

St. Armand Centre. This place was formerly known as "Cook's Corners," so called from an early settler of that name. John Titemore settled a short distance south of this in 1788, and two years after, a person named Perry located in the near vicinity. In 1792, John Toof and four sons from the state of New York, came to the place, from which the tide of emigration flowed steadily in. A public house was opened here in 1811. Properly speaking, this is a thickly settled farming locality rather than a village, with a few mechanics' shops and dwellings situated around a point where roads from different parts of the country intersect. Fine farms abound here on which are extensive groves of the sugar maple.

Lagrange, is a collection of buildings on Pike river, about one and a half mile north-west from Frelighsburg. The first proprietor of the place, was Philip Luke, who at the opening of the revolutionary war, left his home in Albany and went to New York, where he enlisted in the British army and was commissioned a lieutenant. At the close of the war he came to Canada, and was one of the company who first settled at Missisquoi Bay, but afterward purchased the land on which these mills now stand. In 1796, Abraham Lagrange purchased the property of Luke and built mills here, since which, other works have been added. In 1865, a post office was opened here for the convenience of the inhabitants. This place also received a visit from a detachment of the "Brotherhood of Fenians," which was attended with the usual demonstrations.

North Pinnacle. In 1796, a settlement was commenced north of the Pinnacle, a prominent elevation in the eastern part of the parish. The first settler here was Reuben Dodge ; the second, a person named Holiday who built a saw-mill, and during the earlier years of the present century, several others located here. This portion of the seigniory lying nearest the township of Sutton, is considerably broken and hilly. A post office was opened here in 1865.

In the parish of St. Armand East, the asssessable property is valued at $547,340. It has 259 voters. The amount of asssesment for educational purposes is $756.22 ; the annual government grant $216,32. There are ten school districts within the parish, beside the High school at Frelighsburg. The local assessment with the government grant, form a fund sufficient for the support of the schools in the more populous districts during the scholastic year of eight months ; and in the smaller districts a monthly fee or scholar tax covers deficiencies.

There are in all four church edifices in the parish ; four post offices; two grist mills and four saw-mills. A volunteer infantry company is under organization here. Frelighsburg received a prolonged visit from the "Army of Ireland" in the summer of 1866, and remained six days in the hands of the invaders, during which time the hotel and store keepers were the principal sufferers. Private loss has, however, been made up from the public chest.

The interests of the people in this seigniory are essentially agricultural, and modern improvements respecting tillage, stock raising, and dairy conveniences are being generally adopted. The western parts are level and in some sections even swampy; in which districts the cedar was formerly abundant. So much of the land has been improved that comparatively little of the original forest is left standing, unless it is the soft timber on swampy grounds, or the sugar orchards which abound in St. Armand East.

The well known Pinnacle in the extreme east is the highest land, from the top of which is an extended prospect. Near and around it are formed the head waters of Pike river which receives the waters of many small rivulets in its course through the eastern parish, among which is the outlet of Dunham pond. Pike river in the east, and Grout Creek in the west are the largest streams in the seigniory. The population of St. Armand East is given as 1,825, of whom 279 are of French origin.

FOUCAULT AND NOYAN.

The seigniory of Foucault as originally granted by M. de Beauharnois, April 3rd, 1733, to the Sieur Foucault, fronted on the Chambly river (now Richelieu,) and extended from the boundary of the seigniory of Noyan, two leagues along the river and lake, and in depth just to Missisquoi Bay. The grant from the French governor was subsequently ratified by the King of France. It appears however, that nothing had been effected toward the settlement of this tract, up to the conquest of Canada by the English, after which it became the property of General John Caldwell, and from him was named Caldwell's Manor.

During the revolutionary war, numbers of the class of persons known as U. E. Loyalists, found a temporary refuge in Canada, and at its close, many settled on lands known to have been included in the original grant of the seigniory. But when the boundary limits were clearly defined, part of the tract thus granted, was found to lie south of the 45th parallel, and according to the terms of the treaty, within United States territory; and consequently many who had settled there, sought other locations. At present Foucault consists of a strip of land about three miles in width, extending along the boundary line from the Richelieu river on the west, to Missisquoi Bay on the east, in which the lands are held by the seigniorial tenure.

Noyan was granted by M. de Beauharnois, April 2nd, 1733, to the Sieur Chavoy de Noyan, captain of a company of marines in the country; and extended in front two leagues along the Chambly river, by three leagues in depth; and included the islands in its vicinity. The ratification of this grant bears date of July 8th, 1743. After the conquest it became the property of Gabriel Christie, Esquire, and from him was called Christie's Manor. At present Noyan is bounded north by other seigniories, east by Stanbridge, south by Foucault, and west by the Richelieu river. The southern part of the seigniory in common with Foucault, was settled mostly by families of English, Scotch, Irish, or German origin, who had been driven from their homes by the political persecutions then so rife in the colonies. Isaac Salls who came in before the Declaration of Independence, settled near the site of the English Church in Clarenceville. Peter Hawley settled in a locality now known as Beech Ridge ; and farther west was the place chosen by Colonel Henry Ruiter, afterward a pioneer settler in Potton. There were also the Derricks, the Youngs, and others, the descendants of whom still occupy the same lands. In those early times, the country was covered with a vigorous growth of forest timber, which included a mixture of hard and soft wood, and the land when cleared was extremely productive. Large crops of grain and vegetables were raised, as the cultivation of the soil was almost the sole occupation of the people. The reputation of the land for fertility had been the chief reason why the section was so rapidly settled. Its surface is generally level, what little is waste lying in swamps.

It may well be imagined that among those who had then so lately been subjected to all the hardening and demoralizing influences such a war as that of the revolution must inevitably bring in its train, a low standard of morals and piety would prevail; and whatever religious sympathies these people had, were from early association, in favor of a Presbyterian form of worship and church government. In 1810, some of the most religiously disposed among them, resolved on erecting a house of worship on Caldwell's Manor, and obtaining the services of a resident minister of the Presbyterian order. The next year a wooden frame was put up and covered, but further work on it was suspended by the war of 1812. After peace was assured, a deputation was sent to the Presbytery at Albany, to learn the terms on which a minister could be obtained, but the conditions were considered too hard, and further negotiations ceased.

The Episcopal Church was then but little known in the northern part of the United States, and up to the year 1809, only two of its clergy had visited these seigniories; but after the arrival of Dr. Stewart as missionary at St. Armand, he occasionally visited and instructed these destitute people. By his singularly earnest, consistent, and self-denying efforts to benefit his fellow creatures, he won their respect and confidence, thus obtaining a strong influence over them.

On the failure of their attempts to procure a Presbyterian minister, he promised to see them supplied with a clergyman on conditions within their reach; which proposal was considered and accepted; and in May 1815, the Rev. Micajah Townsend was ordained and licensed to administer the Gospel; and having been accepted a missionary by the Society for the Propagation of the Gospel in Foreign Parts, was appointed to exercise his sacred calling in Caldwell's and Christie's Manors.

On the 11th of June, 1815, he entered on his new duties, and held his first morning service in a school house at Christie's Manor (Clarenceville), and his first evening service at Caldwell's Manor (St. Thomas). In 1820, a new church was built at Christie's Manor; and in 1822, the two seigniories of Foucault and Noyan were erected by Letters Patent into two ecclesiastical parishes, named respectively St. George and St. Thomas; the division between them being quite independent of the seigniorial limits. Subsequently the parish of St. George was separated into the parishes of St. George de Henryville, which comprises the northern part and is principally settled by French Canadians, and St. George de Clarenceville, which includes the southern part, where the inhabitants are mostly English-speaking Protestants. Each of these parishes regulates its own municipal affairs.

In 1843, a new brick church building was commenced at the village of Henryville, in the most northern of these parishes, for the accommodation of the Protestant inhabitants there and in the vicinity, but was not finished and consecrated till 1851, when it received the name of St. Mark's Church.

The old parish church in St. Thomas having become too dilapidated for use, a new brick edifice was erected in 1858, two miles farther north.

With occasional help, Mr. Townsend has officiated in both these parishes, and even held services at stated periods in Henryville; but within a few years the infirmities of age and failing health have rendered the help of a permanent assistant necessary. June 11th, 1865, he completed the 50th year of his ministry, at which time the church in Clarenceville was re-opened after a thorough repairing ; when he preached the same sermon he had delivered on his first arrival among the people.

This unusual event was further celebrated on the following Wednesday, by a *fête* in the rectory grounds, when in addition to a pic-nic, luncheon, and other appropriate festivities, was added the formal presentation of an elegant and costly testimonial to the rector from his parishioners, commemorative of his services among them for a period of fifty years. The articles presented were a beautiful silver *Epergne* and *Plateau;* on the latter of which, were engraved appropriate inscriptions. The rector in returning his acknowledgments to the donors, and reverting to the more prominent events of their fifty years of intimate intercourse, stated that during his ministrations in the parishes, there had been 2,266 baptisms, 320 marriages, 751 burials, 730 confirmations, and notwithstanding deaths and removals, there remained 120 communicants.

At a very early day in the history of these seigniories, American Methodist preachers from the northern conference crossed the line into Canada, and occasionally visited these parts, where they met with some success in forming societies ; and when in 1821, they were entirely superseded by the English Wesleyan missionaries, this section of country was included in the first formed circuits. The Methodists are now numerous here, and have a neat brick church edifice in Clarenceville, which name has been given to an independent station.

In the course of time the forests here have been gradually receding, until most of the timber left standing is in the swampy districts. The land has justified its reputation for productiveness, but of late years the farmers are becoming convinced that soil which has been so long under cultivation as to become exhausted, requires not only the application of fertilizing agencies, but calls for a radical change in farming operations generally ; consequently more stock is kept, and less extent of ground sowed to grain than was formerly the case. A cheese factory has been recently built about one mile from the village of Clarenceville.

Beside the English and Wesleyan church edifices, an academy, customs house, post office, stores, a public house, mechanics' shops, and some thirty or forty inhabited dwellings comprise the village. There are also post offices at St. Thomas, and at the locality known as Nutt's Corners. The streams of water in these seigniories are very insignificant. The population of St. George is given at 1,761 ; and that of St. Thomas as 811.

CHAPTER III.

SHEFFORD COUNTY.—ELY.—GRANBY.—MILTON.—ROXTON.—SHEF-
FORD —STUKELY.

SHEFFORD County includes the townships óf Ely, Granby, Milton, Roxton, Shefford and Stukely. Waterloo, in the township of Shefford, is its *chef-lieu*. The Circuit Court for this county is held at Waterloo from the 21st to the 25th of the months of January, April, and September. The county agricultural shows are also held here.

ELY.

Under the hand and seal of Sir Robert Shore Milnes, lieutenant governor, &c., a warrant was issued for the survey of a tract of land lying within the district of Montreal, bounded north by Acton, north-east by Melbourne, east by Brompton, south by Stukely, and west by Roxton; which after the usual preliminaries and subdivision into 296 lots, was erected November 13th, 1802, into a township named Ely; one fourth part of which was granted to Amos Lay the younger and his associates, viz, Peter Brewer, Ozro Hamilton, Enoch Hoskins, Amos Lay the elder, Timothy Mills, John Strong the younger, Chauncy Smith, Ella Smith, and Timothy Woodford.

The first locations in Ely were made some time about the commencement of the 19th century; but owing to certain local causes, the settlement failed of making that rapid advancement which characterized many localities. Of the names prominent among the early settlers of this township are those of Amos Lay, agent, Nathan Darby, Silas Woodard, William Woodard, Daniel Oliver, Jewett Putney, Isaac Westover, and persons named Wright, Wales, and Collins.

At one time during the earlier days of Ely, a party consisting of five persons, viz, Peter Cramer, Andrew Auringer, a man named Trenholme, and two of Cramer's sons who were then but boys, were out on a surveying tour in the township. Having given up work for the night, some of them thoughtlessly set fire to a dry pine tree which stood near the camping ground, after which they all laid themselves down and went to sleep. The tree continued burning and as the trunk proved to be hollow, it gave way and fell upon the prostrate forms of the men, in such a manner that Trenholme was instantly killed, the elder Cramer mortally hurt, and Auringer badly bruised and disabled. The two boys escaped unharmed, but had to go five miles before they could obtain help. Their father was still alive on their return to the scene of disaster, but died soon after being taken to his home. Auringer had no bones broken, and recovered in time.

The surface of the land in Ely is generally level or nearly so; the soil being considered of good quality for farming purposes; whatever is unfit for cultivation lying mostly in swamps. The woodland contains a mixture of hard and soft timber; much of the former being the rock maple, from which quantities of sugar are made each spring.

The principal streams of water are the east branch of Black river which comes from North Stukely, and the tributaries it receives in its course north, then west into Roxton. Some smaller streams flow north into Melbourne. In 1861, the northern and southern parts of the township were separated for school purposes; and in 1864, for local municipal convenience.

South Ely. Most, if not all of the early settlers of the township, located in the southern section, in which is now a fast increasing majority of French Canadian inhabitants. It has three post offices, viz, Valcourt, South Ely, and Boscobel. A Catholic church is located at Valcourt; a Church of England mission was established at Boscobel in 1863, and steps have been taken for the erection of a church edifice. Different sects of Protestants meet for worship in the various schoolhouses. There are mills in South Ely, and minera indications abound, but no mines are worked at present.

North Ely. In 1830, Ira Bartlett came from Bethel, Vt., and located his family at North Ely, where for three years they lived at a distance of ten miles from neighbors, during which time they were subjected to almost inconceivable inconveniences and privations. The next settlers in the locality were Irish emigrants; a class of inhabitants since become quite numerous.

The taxable property in North Ely is $72,460; the number of legal voters 163. The yearly assessment of $400 raised for schools, with the government grant of $78.00, and the usual scholar fee, amount to about $800.00 yearly, for the support of eight elementary schools. The post office at which a mail arrives twice per week, is called Bethel, and is situated about five miles from the Grand Trunk Railway station in Durham.

The land in North Ely is of good settling quality; roads are opening up and improving rapidly. There is one church here; also three stores; and three saw-mills are in operation in the settlement. The population of Ely altogether is given as 1,784.

GRANBY.

The tract of land in the district of Montreal, bounded north by Milton, east by Shefford, south by Farnham, and west by the French seigniories, containing 261 lots with the usual allowance for highways, was erected into a township named Granby, by Letters Patent, bearing date of January 8th, 1803; and finally granted to the officers and privates of Canadian militia, and the widows and orphans of such as were deceased. The grantees were ninety-five in number.

Some few locations had been made in Granby previous to the war of 1812, as we find that Roswell Spalding, son of John Spalding one of the associates of Shefford who had settled near the mountain, came to Granby in 1809, and fixed his habitation about two miles east from the site of the village. Simon Door located nearly the same time about one mile from that point, in the same direction. Several families from Vermont, named Horner, settled upon the site of the village. Jonathan Herrick settled near that place about the year 1812.

After the close of that war, parts of the wild land in the township were given to soldiers who had been discharged from the British service ; and while some few may have settled upon their grants, and others disposed of their claims for a reasonable consideration, the great majority sold them for some paltry price, and thus certain parties accumulated large tracts.

Richard Frost who had come to Canada from Newhampshire early in the 19th century and settled at Shefford, was engaged in the government service during the war, at which time he resided in Sorel. In 1818 he returned to Shefford and opened a public house and store at Frost Village. In the meantime, he received a grant of five hundred acres of land in Granby, and purchased from the agent of an absent proprietor named McWaters, the tract on which the village of Granby now stands. At the time of this purchase, the only frame building on the premises was a barn, which with three log dwellings, a grist-mill the stones of which were taken from the neighboring mountain, and a saw-mill constructed in the most primitive manner, included the extent of improvements within the limits of the present corporation.

In 1825, Mr. Frost came to reside in Granby, and in 1826, a post office was opened here on the direct line of weekly mails sent from Chambly to Stanstead. About the year 1830, a person named Douglas purchased a site and built a mill on the premises.

Of the timber originally standing, pine and tamarac were the most valuable for exportation, and in the early days of settlement, so soon as roads could be made passable, large quantities of lumber were taken to the river at St. Pie, and thence down the Yamaska and St. Lawrence to the Quebec market; yet such was the time and expense involved in this labor, that little profit remained to the settler after all his toil.

The stream on which the village of Granby is located, comes from Shefford in the east, and on entering the corporation commences a series of rapids by a gradual descent into a valley, in the course of which there occur some sixty or seventy feet of fall, affording numerous sites for industrial works. The railway station is located upon the left bank of the stream, which is crossed by three bridges at different points, as the principal street is situated on the right side, and is considerably elevated above the water.

The lower or more northerly section of the village,

is chiefly inhabited by French Canadians, and here stands the Roman Catholic church, the first house of worship erected in the place. As a great improvement upon country villages generally, the principal street here is macadamized. Both the French and English languages are necessarily spoken to some extent.

Within the corporation are four church buildings, a' distributing post office, a printing office whence issues a weekly newspaper, ten or twelve stores, an academy, a hall for courts, lectures, and public meetings, two grist-mills, four saw-mills, three tanneries, two carriage shops, two furniture shops, many smaller mechanical works, three public houses, and some hundred and twenty-five private dwellings. The assessable property of the village is valued at $113,140. There are two common schools (one French and one English) in the place.

The Church of England mission in Granby was established in 1843, and the church edifice erected about the same time. The first resident missionary was the Rev. G. Slack, who was succeeded in turn by the Rev. T. Machin, and the Rev. W. Jones, present incumbent.

The mission includes a part of North Shefford, where a substantial stone edifice called St. Peter's Church was erected some few years since, and also the south part of the township of Roxton.

The Congregational church in Granby, was organized in March, 1833. The first minister was the Rev.,

James Dougherty, who has been succeeded in turn by the Rev. Messrs. Glede, Chapin, Fox, Gibb, Lancashire, McLeod, Bucher, and Howell, the latter of whom is present pastor.

Wesleyan Methodism was introduced into Granby in 1822, by the Rev. Thomas Catterick, who formed a small class, and till the year 1857, it continued to form a part of Shefford Circuit; but at that period through the efforts of the Rev. R. A. Flanders, a church edifice was erected, and in 1864, a parsonage was purchased, and all claim renounced to the mission fund; since which, Granby has been an independent circuit. The number of church members is 124. The stationed minister is assisted occasionally by the Rev. E. S. Ingalls, retired Wesleyan missionary, residing in the place. Weekly services are held in the church at Granby village, and semi-monthly services in several other localities. Increasing congregations require the erection of additional houses of worship to accommodate the inhabitants of the different sections, and steps have been taken to meet that want.

The surface of the land in Granby is usually level, and whatever is unfit for cultivation, lies mostly in swamps and morasses. Its agricultural capabilities and products, are similar to those of West Farnham and Stanbridge. Some tracts were hard timbered, and those parts where the rock maple grew most abundant, were generally chosen by the early settlers for location, in preference to the soft-wooded portions.

Since the construction of the railway, the timber left standing, which is mostly hemlock, finds an easy avenue to market, and a ready sale.

The most considerable stream of water in Granby is that on which the village is situated, viz, the outlet of Waterloo pond, which enters the township from Shefford, and after passing through the village, turns to the south-west into Farnham. There is also the outlet of Roxton pond, which enters the north-eastern section of the township, and after several turnings, re-enters Milton, and passes west into the seigniories.— The small village of Mawcook, in the north of Granby, is located on this stream at a point where about the year 1833, John Darrel built mills and commenced business. The place now has a post office named Mawcook, a store, grist-mill, five saw-mills, and a collection of dwellings.

There are two slate quarries within the township, one of which is situated three miles west of the village of Granby; the company to which it belongs having been incorporated in the summer of 1867. It has complete machinery for marbleizing the slate, and also for preparing it for flooring. The other quarry is three miles south of the village. This slate is for roofing. The company has been but recently organized, and therefore their works are not in as complete operation; but their prospects are fair, and the slate appears of superior quality.

In a good farming district in the south of Granby,

a store and post office have been opened, and public worship is held each Sabbath.

The S. S. & C. R. R. enters the township from the seigniories, and approaches the village from the south-west, after which it diverges to the south-east, and passing around Shefford Mountain, has its terminus at Waterloo.

Outside the village corporation, the amount of assessable property in Granby is $288,219; the number of legal voters 309. For the year ending in June 1866, $1,014.78 were raised for schools, aside from the government grant of $185. Beside several French dissentient schools, there are thirteen English elementary schools in operation. The census of 1861, gives Granby a population of 2,511 inhabitants, 996 of whom are French Canadians.

MILTON.

The tract of land lying within the district of Montreal, bounded north and west by the seigniories, east by Roxton, and south by Granby, surveyed, divided into ranges, and subdivided into two hundred and four lots, was erected by Letters Patent into a township named Milton, January 29th, 1803; and subsequently granted to officers and privates of Canadian militia, and the widows and orphans of such as were deceased.— These grantees were eighty-one in number.

With the exception of the locality known as Milton Corners, where is a considerable settlement of English-speaking Protestants, most of the inhabitants of the township are French Canadians ; and for local convenience it has been separated into two distinct municipalities, named respectively, St. Cecile de Milton, and St. Valerian de Milton.

In surface of land, quality of forest timber, agricultural capabilities, products, &c., Milton much resembles Granby, Stanbridge, and the seigniories near. The largest stream is Black river, which flows through the north-west part into the seigniories. In the south is the outlet of Roxton pond, which after passing into Granby, re-enters Milton, whence it flows west.

A Church of England mission was established at Milton Corners in June 1843, by the Rev. G. Slack, at that time residing in Granby, and was connected with the mission at that place, till in the spring of 1851, Mr. Slack removed to Milton, where he remained in charge till 1864. The mission was subsequently served by the Rev. F. Robinson of Abbottsford, till the appointment of the Rev. A. O. Taylor, who is in charge at the present time. There are also English schools and a post office in this section.

In St. Cecile de Milton, $692,28 altogether, were raised for educational purposes in 1866 ; the yearly grant for the same period, being $250,86. In St. Valerain, the amount raised by assessment was $379,10; the government grant being $106,40. The population of Milton altogether is given as 2,790.

ROXTON.

Under the hand and seal of Robert Shore Milnes, Baronet, lieutenant-governor, &c., a warrant was issued for the survey of a tract of land lying within the district of Montreal, bounded north by Acton, east by Ely, south by Shefford, and west by Milton, which being subdivided into three hundred and twenty-eight lots, was erected into a township named Roxton, by Letters Patent dated January 8th, 1803, and in part granted to Elizabeth Ruiter widow of the late John Ruiter, Philip Ruiter, Hannah Ruiter, Jacob Ruiter, John Ruiter, Hermanicus Ruiter, Catherine Ruiter, all children of the late John Ruiter; John Kobatch, Eliza Ross Conroy, Jean Shirley Conroy, Cornelia Conroy, Mary Ann Conroy, Margaret Pell, James Kerr, Margaret Kerr, James Hastings Kerr, Jane Helen Kerr, Margaret Kerr the younger, Magdalen Kerr, Christian Wehr the younger, Sarah Morris, Anne Morris wife of Samuel Sansum, Robert Hunter Morris, Lewis Genevray, David Alexander Grant, Duncan Fisher, Etienne Dechambault, Gilbert Miller, Mary Platt, John Platt, George Platt, Anne Platt, and John Robb.

Notwithstanding this grant, few permanent settlements were made in the township before the year 1834, when James Savage, Alanson Ball, Benjamin Kilborne, Rufus Kempton, and A. Sanborne, located in the southern part; since which the settlement has greatly increased. The post office in this section receives a tri-weekly mail.

Most of the inhabitants of the more northerly parts are French Canadians.

The incorporated village of Roxton Falls on the Black river in the north-eastern part of the township, is six miles from the Grand Trunk station at Acton, and receives a daily mail from that point, with which it is connected by stage. There is a Roman Catholic church in the place; also a large and convenient school-house where the Protestant community meet for worship; and several stores, mills, two large tanneries, public-houses, and mechanics' shops, beside a large number of dwellings. Considerable lumber is manufactured here.

In many parts of Roxton the land is uneven and rough, yet there are no very prominent elevations. Roxton pond, in the south-east corner, is the largest body of water, and discharges through a stream running south-west. The main branch of Black river which enters Roxton from Ely, may be considered the chief stream, and runs in a general north west-course, receiving several tributaries coming from different parts of the township.

The agricultural capabilities of Roxton are about on an equality with other townships around, as when well cultivated the land produces abundantly. The French Canadian population is multiplying rapidly, and already forms a large majority. During the year 1866, the sum of $1,102,80 altogether, was levied for educational purposes, aside from the government grant of $360,94. The census of 1861, gives Roxton a population of 3,438 inhabitants.

SHEFFORD.

A tract within the district of Montreal, bounded north by Roxton, east by Stukely, south by Brome, and west by Granby, after the usual form, was erected into a township named Shefford, by Letters Patent dated February 10th, 1801, and in part granted to John Savage and his associates, viz, John Savage the younger, Hezekiah Wood, John Allen, Simon Griggs, Richard Powers, John Savage the son of Edward Savage, Peter Savage, Ezekiel Lewis, Henry Hardie, Anthony Cutler, Isaac Kinneson, Solomon Kinneson, Malcolm McFarland, Peter Hayes, Edward Graves, Henry Powers, Alexander Douglas, Silas Lewis, John Lockhart Wiseman, James Bell, John Mock, Timothy Hoskins, William Moffit, Thaddeus Tuttle, Isaac Lawrence, Isaac Lawrence the younger, Elijah Lawrence, James Berry, Abraham Kinneson, John Spalding, John Katchback, John Mock the younger, Joseph Mock, William Bell, John Bell, and Samuel Bell.

Most, if not all of the above named associates became *bona fide* settlers in the township, and many of them left numerous descendants here. The first permanent resident of the tract was Capt. John Savage, himself the agent of the associates, and as such personally interested in carrying out the conditions on which the grant was to be made. In the spring of 1793, he pioneered the way with compass and axe—the former to indicate the right course, the latter to mark the trees,—and was followed by men who cleared away the forest underwood, in order to admit the passage of ox-sleds on which were brought the household goods and provisions, while the family came on behind. They settled in the south-western portion of the tract. The second inhabitant was a person named Towner, who however, remained but a short time.

The third on the ground was Isaac Lawrence, who came in from Hinesburg, Vt., in the winter of 1794. He had previously chosen a location farther into the interior of the tract, near the body of water since known as Waterloo pond; but on his arrival with his family, shared the shelter of Towner, till a cabin of his own could be prepared. Two of his elder sons were among the associates of Shefford, and a third followed them to Canada soon after; three younger were still at home, and eventually the whole six settled permanently in Shefford, Stukely and Brome. Several of this family lived to an advanced age and left numerous descendants, now however, widely scattered.

The associates of the township mostly located on their lands during the later years of the 18th century, but improvements were slow: In 1797, a winter road was opened from Shefford through Granby to the Black river at St. Pie ; and by October of the next year, streams were bridged and causeways constructed so that ox-sleds could pass to that point in summer.

At an early period several families named Frost settled in the south-east part of the township, from whom the settlement in that locality received the name of " *Frost Village.*"

When the settlements were so far advanced as to make it necessary that a way of communication should be opened between Montreal and the townships east,and a route was chosen from Magog Outlet, through Stukely, Shefford, Granby, &c., to Chambly, Frost Village became a sort of centre for the retail trade of the sec tion, and several business and professional men located here.

Prominent among these was Dr. Stephen Sewell Foster, born at Oakham, Mass., November 22nd, 1791. February 7th, 1813, he married Sally Belknap of Dummerston, Vt., and in 1817, settled to the practice of his profession in Newfane, Vt., where he remained till in 1822 he came to Canada with his wife and four children. His first location was at Frost Village, but after a residence here of one year, he removed to the locality where is now situated the thriving village of Waterloo, at the time when there were but two dwellings in the place, one of which is still standing and in use for a printing and other offices. There were also mills, cloth-dressing works, and a blacksmith's shop. After a short residence there however, the Doctor returned to Frost Village, and settled upon the farm, until recently occupied by his second son the Hon. Asa Belknap Foster.

His license to practice his profession, had been received from the Vermont Medical Society, but after coming to this country he attended lectures at Quebec, and obtained license to practice in Canada. Under the Earl of Dalhousie, he was appointed surgeon to Col. Jones' battalion. After the establishment of McGill college he attended lectures there for a period, and on the formation of the College of Physicions and Surgeons, was elected one of its governors, which position he held till in 1866, failing health obliged him to resign. He also held the office of justice of the peace and commissioner for the trial of small causes, when there was no other court in the Eastern Townships. In 1841, he was elected to the Provincial Parliament from Shefford County, and being re-elected, was a member of that body for seven years.

At the time Dr. Foster settled in Frost Village, there was no other physician for many miles around, his practice extending from Yamaska Mountain to Missisquoi Bay; and it was no uncommon thing for him to be called to attend patients in Stanstead, or even in Derby and Coventry, Vt. At such times he went by bridle paths through the forest to the outlet of Lake Memphremagog, (six miles intervening between dwellings at places on the way;) and thence up the lake in a log canoe. On other occasions he was guided by nothing more definite than marked trees; sometimes seeing the wolves cross the path before him, and often hearing them howl in the woods on either hand.

In the practice of his profession under such circumstances, he was often brought in contact with scenes which excited his warmest sympathies, and had frequent occasion for the exercise of a benevolent and kindly feeling, which was manifested in ways peculiar to himself, and which won upon the hearts of the people among whom he lived and practised so long, and established a claim upon their lasting esteem and gratitude. In October 1857, he removed to Knowlton in Brome, with the double view of retiring from the active practice of his profession, and of being near his eldest son Capt. Hiram S. Foster, of that place.

It must have been a source of extreme satisfaction to Dr. and Mrs. Foster in their declining years, to witness their success in rearing a family, several of whom occupy high official positions in the country. Still more must they have found their happiness in the filial love and attention manifested toward themselves, and in the fraternal and sisterly affection existing among their children—traits of character both ennobling and refining—strengthened and cultivated by frequent meetings and annual family gatherings.

On the evening of February 7th, 1863, the " *Golden Wedding* " or FIFTIETH ANNIVERSARY of their marriage was celebrated at the residence of their son Samuel W. Foster Esq., advocate, at Knowlton Brome.

Feburay 7th, 1813, they were married at Brattleborough, Vt. Their decendants now living are eleven children, all married, and twenty-five grand-children.

At seven o'clock on the evening in question, family relatives and intimate friends assembled, and after prayer by the Rev. Robert Lindsay, at eight o'clock the company sat down to an elegantly prepared dinner. The repast ended, brief addresses were made by C. Dunkin, Esq., M.P.P., the Rev. R. Lindsay, and Dr. Barber, congratulating the venerable couple who were the honored guests of the occasion, on their safe arrival at that hour and place, after a long and prosperous journey, with so few marks of age ; also upon their success in life, and above all, upon the multiplied evidences of filial affection with which they were surrounded in their declining years. The speakers also congratulated the children and grand-children on the heritage they had received in the teachings, examples and good name of their parents.

S. W. Foster then addressed a few words to the friends assembled ; when on behalf of all present and absent, he responded in suitable acknowledgments to the above named addresses and congratulations.

In the course of the evening, presents of gold and silver had passed from the hands of children and grand-children to the venerable pair, and the wish was oft repeated that they might live long to enjoy the affectionate esteem of their friends, and the health and happiness which follows a life of sobriety and usefulness.

Though subjected to the increasing infirmities of age, and gradually yielding to their power, Dr. Foster lived till in the fall of 1868, a more rapid decay of the vital forces indicated that the end was near, and after a confinement to his room for five weeks, during which time, though suffering severely, he was soothed by the affectionate attentions of his children, all of whom were with him more or less, he died at his residence in Knowlton, December 29th, 1868, and was buried January 1st, 1869.

Sometime between the years 1821 and 1825, through the efforts of Richard Frost, Samuel Willard, and David Wood of Frost Village, and John Wetherbee of Magog Outlet, a weekly post was established between Chambly and Stanstead, which was carried on horseback in summer, and usually in a single sleigh in winter; about which time the post office was opened at this point. Previously, the nearest post had been either at Stanstead, Missisquoi Bay, or at Chambly. Owing to local causes the Frost Village of the present is not thriving as formerly; its prosperity seeming to have become generally absorbed in that of Waterloo. The academy and public offices formerly located here, have been transferred to that place, and most of the prominent inhabitants have left for other localities. A small but neat stone church edifice belonging to the Church of England, built in 1852 and consecrated early the next year; a Methodist chapel, one or two stores, a post office, public house, tannery, some few mechanics' shops and a number of dwellings now comprise the village; but among many of the buildings the work of decay is going rapidly on.

West Shefford, otherwise called Shefford plain, is in the south-west part of the township where the first locations were made in 1793. For a time, inhabitants increased here rapidly, the situation being pleasant and favorable. It lies on a main branch of the Yamaska river, a few miles below the point where the stream issues from Brome lake. A church edifice belonging to the Church of England, built about the year 1821; a Roman Catholic church quite new; a public hall built in 1863; two stores, a post office, some few mechanics' shops, and a considerable number of private dwellings, comprise the village. Progress here has been slow.

The body of water long known as Waterloo pond received its name while yet the bustling, thriving village now situated near its bank and along its outlet, was in its incipient stages; and imagination must furnish reasons *why* the name of a world-renowned European battlefield which decided the fate of an empire, should have been chosen to designate a then obscure locality in the midst of a wild and uncultivated region of country. .

It appears that the first mills were built on the outlet of this pond by a person named Lewis; and that subsequently they passed through different hands, till about the year 1822 the premises were purchased by

Hezekiah Robinson, machinery introduced and put in operation, and a business commenced which, conducted by energy and perseverance laid the foundation of a permanent prosperity.

Within the few succeeding years, several other families located in the vicinity, among whom were those of Adolphus Bennet, Samuel Brown, Calvin Richardson, Daniel Taylor, Dr. Sewell Foster, and the Rev. R. Whitwell. Messrs. Lyman and Child opened the first store in the place. In 1825, Charles Allen commenced work here as a blacksmith, and a few years later began making iron-castings; which business was conducted on a small scale at first, but has been enlarged at various times, and has gradually grown to its present extensive proportions.

Waterloo which is now the principal village in Shefford, and the *chef-lieu* of the county, was incorporated January 1st, 1867. The corporation covers several lots and parts of lots in the third and fourth ranges of the township, and contains within its limits four church buildings; an academy; a county house; a post office opened in 1836; a branch of the Eastern Township's Bank; a registry office; ten or more general stores; a printing office whence issues a weekly newspaper; four public houses; two clothing stores; a hardware store and tin shop; two furniture shops; extensive iron works; a large tannery giving employment to many hands; a door, sash, and blind factory; two planing mills; a wholesale and several retail groceries; two jewellers' shops; a drug store; numerous smaller trading establishments; many mechanics' shops; and 300 or more inhabited dwellings. Among these are found the usual representatives of the various professions.

The post office, court house, bank, printing office, registry office, mills, many private offices, and several of the principal business establishments and important industrial works, are located at the older or *lower* section of the village; also many convenient and tasteful private residences. Yet Waterloo owes its more recent rapid growth and to a great extent its business importance, to its situation as the terminus of the S.S. & C. R.R. The *upper* section of the village where are located the railway station and offices, has literally sprung into existence within the last few years as the direct effect of railway enterprize; and in consequence, the buildings in the immediate vicinity are all new or nearly so: that locality wearing the air of bustling activity pertaining to such generally. Many comfortable and substantial private dwellings have also been built around the square, while on the rising grounds at a short distance, are still more in which elegance and convenience are combined, while some display superior wealth and taste.

These two sections are connected by two principal thoroughfares, the sites on which are being rapidly taken up for public buildings, private dwellings, or mechanics' shops. The academy is located on one of them, about midway between the two extremes.

The place has daily communication by railway with Montreal and the intermediate points; by stage with Knowlton in Brome, and during the season of summer travel, with the steamboat terminus at Magog. Also, tri-weekly connection by stage with Stanstead and other places on the east; Melbourne and others north; Nelsonville, &c., south; beside which, it is the centre point of a perfect net work of roads by which it is connected with the neighboring localities. A telegraph line connects it by way of Knowlton with several points on the frontier, and in another direction with St. Johns.

The Church of England Mission in Shefford was opened about the year 1821, through the influence and efforts of the Rev. Dr. Stewart, who, true to his calling as pioneer and patron of the church in these townships, contributed generously toward its establishment. The Rev. R. Whitwell was appointed to the charge, and divided his services between East and West Shefford. His successors here have been in turn the Rev. Messrs. Salmon, Balfour, Whitten and Lindsay; the latter of whom is present incumbent of Waterloo and Frost Village; West Shefford being now a separate mission in charge of the Rev. A. Whitten.

Since the construction of the railway and the consequent increase of population in Waterloo, the place of worship hitherto in use here, has been found entirely too small to accommodate the congregations assembling on Sundays; beside which, it is located quite apart from what is now a central point of the village. Preparations have therefore been made for the erection of an edifice that shall combine the modern improvements in church architecture with more comfortable dimensions, more convenient arrangements, and a more suitable location. The work on the new church has already progressed to some extent, and is to be finished the ensuing season.

A convenient church building nearly new, belonging to the Wesleyan Methodists, was unfortunately burned here in the winter of 1868, but has been rebuilt on an enlarged and improved plan.

The Adventists have also a house of worship in Waterloo, but have at present no settled minister here. The Roman Catholic church here was built in 1864.

It may not be improper in this connection to speak of the probable future of Waterloo, considered in reference to its advantages in being located at a point which may eventually prove to be of more interest and importance than is now apparent; but which will be clearly seen when improvements that have been projected and are already in contemplation, shall have been carried to a successful completion.

About two miles a little east of north from Waterloo, is a locality named Warden, which was settled to some extent, at a very early period in the history of the township. It was at first known as Mock's mills, from John Mock, one of the associates of Shefford, who commenced the erection of a grist mill here in the fall of 1795; it being the first mill of the kind built in the township. The place has since been known as Knowlton's Falls, but more recently as Warden. A neat brick church building belonging to the Wesleyan Methodists, occupies a conspicuous location here; beside which, are two stores, a post office, public house, mechanics' shops, mills, and a collection of inhabited dwellings.

The surface of the land in Shefford is broken and hilly in sections, though the only prominent elevation is the well known Shefford Mountain in the western part. Most of the grains grow well here; vegetables produce luxuriantly; and many parts afford excellent facilities for the raising of stock and for the produce of the dairy.

Waterloo pond or lake as it is more recently termed, is the largest body of water in the township, and the most considerable stream running any length in it, is the outlet of that pond. This at first takes a northerly course, then turning west, passes into Granby. The outlet of Brome lake enters the south-west corner of Shefford, when crossing a point of Granby, it passes into Farnham. The S.S. & C.R.R. enters from Granby, and passing around south of the mountain, has its terminus at Waterloo, though freight trains occasionally pass up as far as Frost village, the track being laid thus far. Two companies of volunteer infantry are under organization in Shefford.

There are altogether ten church buildings, an academy, a model school, and twenty-four school districts in the township. The total amount levied for educational purposes in 1866, was $2,392,61; the government grant for the same year being $419,64. The nominal value of assessable property is $515,000; the number of legal voters 659. The census of 1861 gives a population of 3,712.

STUKELY.

Under the hand and seal of Robert Shore Milnes, Esquire, Lieutenant Governor, &c., a warrant dated May 10th, 1800, was issued for the survey of a tract of land lying within the district of Montreal, bounded north by Ely, east by Orford, south by Bolton, and west by Shefford. As originally surveyed, the tract contained 62,914 superficial acres of land, which was erected into a township named Stukely, by Letters Patent bearing date of November 3rd, 1800, and in part granted to Samuel Willard and his associates, viz, Josiah Arms, Houghton Dickinson, Luke Knowlton the younger, Jonathan Deming, Frederick Hawes, Henry Lawrence, Thomas King, Reuben Partridge, David Partridge, Joseph Gleason, James Bacon, Silas Knowlton, John Morse, John Rutter, Erastus Lawrence, Joel Dickinson, Luke B. Osgoode, Artemas Stevens, Lemuel Stevens, Luther Sargent, John Arms, Roswell Sargent, John Osgoode, John Holbrook, and Samuel Page.

Samuel Willard, agent for these associates was born in Petersham, colony of Mass., in December 1766.

He belonged to a family of distinction in that section, being the son of Major Josiah Willard, and nephew of Col. Abijah Willard of the Provincial Service ; the latter of whom was conspicuous during the French and Indian wars, as a sagacious, brave and efficient officer.

Major Willard was a zealous adherent of his King during the exciting period of the American revolution, and at an early age Samuel exhibited an intelligence and strength of character that recommended him to the confidence of their political friends.

When of proper age, he established himself in business at Newfane, Vt., where he married and remained for a time, but came to reside permanently in Canada, somewhere about the year 1800. Here he entered into active life as agent for the associates of Stukely, and after a residence of more than thirty years in the country, most of which time he was an efficient public servant, died at his farm in this township, October 29th, 1833.

In 1796, several persons from Southern Vermont, visited this tract for the purpose of choosing locations, and in the autumn of that year, Silas Knowlton and John Whitney came on as pioneer settlers. They were soon afterward followed by others who all located in the southern part of the tract.

At an early day, a line of road was laid out through the forest to Magog outlet, leading around the north side of Mountain pond (Orford lake), up a narrow and dangerous ascent between a ridge of Orford mountain and the deep water at its base. Notwithstanding the government aid that has been received and expended, and the improvements made from time to time upon this road, it was found impossible to overcome the natural obstructions presented, or prevent the serious and even fatal accidents that occurred there. Many years since, a person named Wadleigh who was travelling east from Hatley, lost his life at this pass, and more recently others have lost their teams over the precipice. To avoid the dangers of this route, another line of road has since been opened, which leads around the south side of the pond, and is now the main travelled line from Waterloo east, the old road having been abandoned except by people living along its course.

In 1836, Henry Lawrence who had been one of the associates and early settlers of Stukely, left his location in the southern part of the township, and purchased a tract of land containing a water power, in the northern and unsettled portion, situated on the east branch of Black river. Here he built a saw mill and factory for cooper ware, for which the forest around afforded an abundant supply of material; and from this may be reckoned the commencement of settlements in North Stukely, which have since increased rapidly; most of the inhabitants being French Canadians.

A few years since, for the better regulation of their internal affairs, the township was divided into two distinct municipalities known as North Stukely and South Stukely.

South Stukely. Most of the settlers of this section being of English origin, the majority of its inhabitants are English-speaking Protestants. The interests of the people are essentially agricultural, the raising of horses, cattle, and sheep, being their principal sources of income. The surface of the land is very uneven, yet the only mountainous elevations are a part of the Orford range in the south-east. There are strong indications of mineral deposits in different parts, and mining work has been commenced in some few places, yet hitherto without any very marked results. A superior quality of limestone which is abundant here, bears a fine polish, and has been pronounced by competent judges to be suitable for internal decorations. Material for the manufacture of lime is also plenty. Asbestos, soap-stone, &c., are found likewise.

The nearest approach to a village within the municipality, is at *Stukely Mills* on the small stream running south-west, where a saw mill is in operation. There are also some few mechanics' shops near; likewise a public house, post office, and store, at a point where the roads running different ways intersect each other. A stone church, and a school house stand on the rising ground at no great distance, but the dwellings are very diffusely scattered around.

A Church of England Mission which was opened here some years since, is now in charge of the Rev. C. P. Abbott. The Wesleyan Methodists have also societies here, which meet for worship in the school houses in different localities.

There is no large stream of water in South Stukely, the most considerable being formed by small rivulets coming from swamps, or such as are the outlets of small ponds. One of these streams finds its way into Brome lake under the name of the *Big Inlet ;* another passes through Frost Village and discharges into Waterloo lake. The northern branch of Missisquoi river has also its extreme source in a small pond which lies partly in Stukely.

The assessable property in South Stukely amounts to $132,093. There are 142 legal voters. In the year 1866, the total amount levied for educational purposes was $463,60 ; the government grant for the same year being $80,94.

North Stukely. In the small village called Lawrenceville from its original founder and proprietor, are now a post office, two stores, excellent mills, several mechanics' shops, and some eighteen or twenty inhabited dwellings ; also an English dissentient school. In other sections of the municipality where the inhabitants are exclusively French Canadian, are small settlements or *villages* where are found the invariable *eglise, magazin,* and *auberge.* For the year 1866, the amount levied for educational purposes in North Stukely, in all amounted to $1,778 ; aside from which was the government grant of $237,86.

A tri-weekly stage passes through this section to Ely and Melbourne, returning next day. Indications of various minerals are found in different parts of the municipality; serpentines, slates, &c., also abound. The land in this section of the township though somewhat rough and stoney, is yet free from mountaineous elevations; and though the labor of clearing a farm is considerable, when once the work is effected, the land is very productive. The eastern or main branch of Black river, has its extreme sources in small streams in this vicinity, which uniting in one, passes into Ely.

The population of the township of Stukely altogether, is given by the census cf 1861, as 2,320 inhabitants.

CHAPTER IV.

ST. FRANCIS DISTRICT.—COURTS OF THE DISTRICT.—LAKE ST. FRANCIS.—RIVER ST. FRANCIS.—TOWN OF SHERBROOKE.

IN the third year of George IV, the " Inferior District" of St. Francis was established. In the third of William IV, this was called the District of St. Francis. As at present constituted, this district comprises the counties of Compton, Richmond, Stanstead, and Wolfe. The Court House, Jail, and Public Offices for the District are located at the town of Sherbrooke.

The Queen's Bench meets on the first of the months of April and October.

The terms of the Superior Court are held from the 20th to the 26th of the months of February, May, and October ; and from the 21st to the 26th of December.

Superior *Enquêtes*, from the 28th to the end of the months of January, February, March, April, May, June, September, October, November, and December.

The Circuit Court for the District of St. Francis is held from the 10th to the 15th of the month of

February; from the 11th to the 16th of May; and from the 10th to the 16th of the months of October and December.

Enquêtes, Sherbrooke, from the 21st to the 23rd of January; April 9th; June 25th and 26th; and from the 9th to the 11th November.

Lake St. Francis, a body of water some fifteen miles in length, lies between the townships of Price, Adstock, Lambton, and Coleraine, to the north and northeast of the district bearing that name; and about forty miles north-east from Sherbrooke. Its only tributaries are the small streams coming from the townships around. The section of country around this lake and the streams falling into it, have been much frequented by lumbermen; immense numbers of saw logs being every year floated down to be manufactured and sent to market. The St. Francis River issues from the north-western extremity of this lake, and takes a south-western course, flowing rapidly about seven miles, when occurs the Bull Head Fall, over which saw logs and timber are driven, though canoes are taken around. Just below this, the river expands into Lake Aylmer, near which point is the mouth of Black Creek, the head waters of which are but one mile from others which flow in another direction into the Nicolet and Becancour rivers. Lake Aylmer is twelve miles in length including the bays at either end, with a greatly varying breadth. Its southern extremity is called Bull Frog Bay, one mile below which, a dam has been built across the river, by which the water is raised eight feet for the purpose of giving a supply for driving lumber over the rapids below. One mile still lower down, the river again expands into Lake Louise nearly three miles in length by about the same width. From this it continues in a south-west course till about three miles below it is joined by the Salmon river from the south-east. After this commence a series of rapids known as the two mile falls, when the river enters Dudswell, where it is crossed by ferries at two points. Three miles below the "*Basin*," and within the township of Westbury is the mouth of Eaton river, near which are sections of rapids; when passing through a corner of Eaton, the St. Francis enters Ascot, and on approaching the centre of that township and receiving the waters of the Massawippi at Lennoxville, it turns to the north-west and at Sherbrooke is joined by the turbulent Magog. Below this it forms the division between Ascot and Orford, and other townships along its entire course.

Sherbrooke and Lennoxville, or as they were formerly called the *Upper and Lower Forks*, from a very early day were centres of trade for the country around, where the settler could exchange his salts, furs, &c., for the most needful articles ; which trade was carried on under great disadvantages at first ; but after it was found that the St. Francis could be made available to reach market at Three Rivers, a new impetus was given it. The first idea of this was taken from the Indians who frequented these parts on their hunting and fishing expeditions, and for a time their paths and *portages* were followed by the boatmen in their birch bark and log canoes; but the business soon increased to such an extent that larger boats were required. A person named Elim Warner was interested in building the first large boat that descended this river, which was about sixty feet in length, built of pine timbers and planks, and was designed to carry about six tons. The launching of this, was an era in the lives of these backwoodsmen, and created almost as much excitement and interest among them, as the launching of a steamboat does at the present day.

At that time there was only a narrow path around the falls at Brompton, but Warner cut out a road by which the boat was taken around on a sort of truck formed by boring short sections of log to serve as wheels. This boat was the conveyance to Lake St. Peters, when batteaux were used for crossing to market.

In many places, *portages* were unavoidable, and in others where the current was strong and the channel somewhat obstructed, slow progress was made by "*doubling the rapids.*"* For a time it was deemed

---

* This ambiguous phrase in common use among boatmen upon rivers, simply means the landing and leaving part of the freight on shore, thus lightening the boat before descending the current with the remainder, which is then taken out at a point below, when the empty boat is taken back for the rest; and when that also is safely down, all is again taken on board, till the next rapid makes it necessary to repeat the process.

necessary to draw the boat as well as freight around the *portages,* but the men finally risked the descent in many places with the empty boat, leaving the freight to be carried around to the foot of the rapid. On the return voyage, skilful and experienced hands could ascend most of the rapids with empty boats by the aid of setting poles, leaving the freight to be taken up in the usual manner.

During the war of 1812, most of the supplies for the settlers in this region were obtained in this way, as for a certain period no communication was allowed with the neighboring states. By means of boats in summer, and on the ice in winter, this river was a highway as far as the St. Lawrence, when the journey was extended to Montreal, Quebec, or Three Rivers, as the case might be.

Casualties involving loss of life often occured upon this river, and almost every fall or rapid along its course was known by some local appellation given by the boatmen in consequence of such occurrences. Thus a rapid where a Dutchman was accidentally drowned, was afterward known among them as the *Dutchman's chute;* and another where a person named Cony lost his life, was known as *Cony's chute.*

One of the most melancholy and afflictive of these casualties occurred in the year 1815, when two valuable lives were lost at Brompton Falls. Three persons named respectively French, Hurd, and Lebourveau, were on an expedition down the St. Francis.

At the falls the freight was removed, and the three men remained to pass down with the boat. Unfortunately it struck a rock and capsized, when French sunk at once; Hurd was seen to strike out for the shore, and being an expert swimmer, hope was entertained by those on the bank that he might be saved, but from some cause, he too sunk and was drowned. Lebourveau at first sprung upon a rock to which he continued clinging as he saw his companions drowning, but could neither save them, nor yet help himself till a rope was thrown from the shore, which he fastened around his waist, when plunging into the boiling current he at first disappeared, but was finally drawn to land.

At another point where stands a small island in the midst of furious rapids, by the capsizing of a boat above, a young lad had escaped with his life to find himself a solitary prisoner where "none had ever been before," as the island was considered inaccessible. Every expedient that had been devised by his friends and neighbors to get him off, or send him food, had proved unavailing. The days passed on and death from starvation seemed his inevitable fate. His friends were nearly frantic at the thought of his perishing thus before their eyes, yet were powerless to save or help him. This came to the knowledge of a crew of experienced boatmen who were making the *portage*, and on understanding the case, they determined to attempt a rescue. Their large boat was anchored out in the river, some distance above the island ; a light skiff to which were attached ropes, was secured to it by strong cables, and then floated down the current ; when after repeated trials and failures, it was borne within reach of the despairing boy. Securing himself in it by the ropes, he was drawn up through the seething waters to the large boat, and thus restored to his frenzied parents.

When the banks of the St. Francis are full, the river appears large, but during the warm season the water is often so low that parts of its rocky bed become quite dry. At such times navigation is of course out of the question ; and is very dangerous also when the water is too high, for at such times the rocks are covered and hidden from view.

This river may be said to drain nearly the whole district, as with the exception of a very few small streams in the north, which unite to form the head waters of the Nicolet and Becancour rivers ; some few others of little importance which find their way into lake Megantic ; and those few from Hereford which flow south into the Connecticut; all, large and small, fall more or less directly into the St. Francis.

The Salmon river from the south-east, brings the waters of numerous smaller tributaries in its course through several townships, and enters the St. Francis in Weedon. Nearly the same may be said of the Eaton river which falls into the St. Francis in Westbury. Two other streams named respectively the

Salmon and Moe's rivers, have their extreme sources in the far off townships of Hereford and Clifton, and after flowing in a north-west course through Compton into Ascot, unite their waters, which as Salmon river enters the Massawippi a short distance above its mouth. Still farther west, but running nearly parallel with those two last named streams, is the Coaticook, which has its source beyond the boundary line, and passing through Barford and a part of Barnston, enters Compton and flowing through that township into Ascot, joins the Massawippi and contributes to swell the volume of water carried by that stream into the St. Francis at Lennoxville.

Next comes the Magog river, which is the outlet of Lake Memphremagog, a body of water some thirty miles in length, with a varying breadth of from less than one mile to three miles or more. This stream takes a north-east course and discharges into the St. Francis at Sherbrooke. Numerous other smaller tributaries fall into it at different points along its course, till it enters Lake St. Peter about sixty-five miles below Montreal. The Indian Village of St. Francis is situated very near its mouth.

SHERBROOKE.

This place, which was incorporated a town in 1852, is situated at the junction of the St. Francis and Magog rivers, a point long ago known as the "*Lower or Big Forks.*" It lies on the Grand Trunk Railway, 101 miles from Montreal. The limits of the town extend nearly three miles from east to west, by about two and a half miles from north to south. The part which lies on the east side of the Magog, was formerly included in the township of Ascot, while the portion west of that stream was taken from Orford. For electoral purposes these two townships are connected with Sherbrooke; their agricultural shows are also held here and at Lennoxville alternately; but otherwise they are included with Compton County.

Much uncertainty has been expressed respecting the date of the first openings made in the forest at this point; some insisting that locations were made here during the later years of the eighteenth century; others contending that they could not have been made before the year 1803; and others still, affix even a later date for them; yet these differences may be set aside by the fact that David Moe who at an early date located just outside the limits of the present town, built the first frame barn that was put up in the settlement, on a board of which building, the date 1800 was engraved; showing the barn to have been built that year. Such being the case, a saw mill must have been in operation previously.

It appears that the very first location was made in the vicinity by Samuel Terry, at a point opposite the mouth of Magog river. The first grist mill was put up by Gilbert Hyatt on the Ascot side of that stream; near which, the first carding and clothing works were soon after built by Jonathan Parker. The first saw mill in the place was built by Jonathan Ball, on the Orford side of the Magog. The attention of many was drawn to this point by the water power which presented so many advantages for the introduction of labor saving machinery.

C. F. H. Goodhue who became a very prominent man here, conmenced the manufacture of axes, an article then much in demand; his assistants in the business being Jonathan Silsbee and George Alger, the two first blacksmiths in the place. William R. Willard built the first tannery; Albert Burchard was the first shoemaker; Felix Ward opened the first public house; and many who had previously chosen other locations, left them to settle here.

During the first quarter of the 19th century, the settlement at the " Lower Forks" assumed the proportions and characteristics of an active thriving village; many mechanical works having gone into operation here in those years.

In 1833, the British American Land Company obtained their charter from the Imperial Government, when they organized, and went into operation the next year. Their chartered capital was £300,000; a certain portion of which,—perhaps one-third—was reserv-· ed for the colonists, but far the greater part was taken up by capitalists at home. A temporary office was opened at Montreal, after which it was removed to Lennoxville where it remained some time, but was finally changed to Sherbrooke where the head office was permanently established. This company purchased land on the east side of the Magog, from C. F. H. Goodhue, Esq. ; and on the west side, from the Hon. W. B. Felton ; also the water power on that stream along which, in a little more than one half mile, the descent is one hundred and fourteen feet; comprising an almost continuous succession of water privileges, many of which have been sold or leased, while many others are still in the market. Several large and important manufacturing establishments, and a great variety of mechanical works have been erected along the line of this descent, and there is abundant room for others. Among the principal of these, are the woollen factories; a paper mill; an extensive iron foundry; carding and clothing works; axe and scythe factory; wheel wright and carriage shop; furniture shop; grist mill; door, sash, and blind factory; match factory &c.

Like the city of Quebec, Sherbrooke has its *Upper*, and its *Lower* town ; not however, separated as in that ancient capital, by walls and gates: no part is overshadowed by rocky prominences crowned with battlements and bristling with cannon: on the contrary, the surroundings of Sherbrooke are essentially indicative of the peaceful pursuits of industry.

Most of the manufacturing works and many mechanics' shops are situated in the Upper Town; and many of the numerous dwellings in that section have been built for the convenience of operatives and laborers. There are however, a better class of houses which are generally occupied by the families of proprietors and overseers.

The stores, banks, public and private offices, and indeed nearly all the business places, are situated along the main streets of the *Lower Town*. The Court House stands in an elevated position at the head of a cross street, and near it, is the Jail. Another prominent public building is the Town Hall which contains the registry office, council rooms, &c. ; and also the office of the Sherbrooke *Gazette*. The Eastern Townships Bank is located here ; beside which, is an agency of the City Bank of Montreal. Three weekly newspapers are printed here. There are five churches, about thirty stores of all kinds, numerous private offices, seven public houses, three bakeries, and many tradesmen's and mechanics' shops in the town. The two sections are united by two principal thoroughfares, the nature of the ground forbidding regularity in the arrangements of the streets.

St. Peter's Church in Sherbrooke, in connection with the Church of England, was founded in 1823. The first clergyman was the Rev. Mr. Lefevre, sent out as missionary by the S.P.G.F.P. He was followed in succession by the Rev. Messrs. Parkyn, Doolittle, Wait, Hellmuth, and Reid, the latter of whom is present incumbent: The church edifice substantially built of brick, was erected in 1844; and was enlarged in

1864, so as to contain about five hundred sittings. It is well attended by a large and attentive congregation, among whom are upward of one hundred communicants.

The congregational church of Sherbrooke was organized December 27th, 1835. There were 29 original members. The subscription for the old church building, bears date of January 4th, 1837. The Rev. James Robertson originally from Scotland, was installed pastor over this church in 1837, and remained such till his decease in September 1861. Mr. Robertson was a man of eminent piety, and a thorough biblical scholar. He was succeeded by the Rev. A. Duff in 1862, who remains to the present time. The subscription to the present church building bears date of April 21st, 1851. Church members, about one hundred in number.

In October 1864, a body was organized in Sherbrooke by the Rev. Joseph Evans, as belonging to the Presbyterian church of Canada in connection with the Church of Scotland, (better known as the Kirk,) which has been an important and successful work. A sabbath school has also been established in connection with this branch of Christian worship, and several neglected localities have been visited in addition to the regularly administered church services.

There is also a Wesleyan Methodist society who have a church edifice in Sherbrooke. The Roman Catholic church and nunnery both occupy a prominent situation near the steep descent into the Lower Town.

For the year 1866, the sum of $2,100 in all, was levied in Sherbrooke for educational purposes; the government grant for the same period being $336,20. Beside the nunnery and academy, is a school that has been supported in part by the colonial church society ; also five elementary, and several private schools.

The Grand Trunk Railway Station is a large edifice built of brick, containing the necessary offices : a railway bridge also crosses the Magog near its mouth. A covered bridge spans the St. Francis leading into Ascot. Most of the better class of dwellings are of brick, or of wood painted white ; and while many of them are substantial, comfortable, and convenient, some are even tasteful and elegant.

That the people of Sherbrooke are public spirited and loyal, is evident from the readiness with which several volunteer companies were raised here during the Fenian excitement in the summer of 1866.

As evidence of the healthfulness of the place, it has been asserted that the only cases of contagious disease known here, have been brought from other parts.

From the rising grounds around Sherbrooke, many points are presented which are calculated to attract and interest the lovers of beautiful landscape. Population 5,899.*

---

* A wooden railway connecting some point on the Grand Trunk near Sherbrooke, with the townships to the north-east, has been projected.

CHAPTER V.

COMPTON COUNTY.—ASCOT.—AUCKLAND. — BURY.—COMPTON. —
CLIFTON.—CLINTON.—CHESHAM.—DITTON.— EATON.—HAMP-
DEN.—HEREFORD.—LINGWICK. — MARSTON. — NEWPORT. —
ORFORD.—WHITTON.—WINSLOW.—WESTBURY.—WOBURN.

COMPTON county includes the above named townships and tracts. Cookshire in the township of Eaton is its *chef-lieu*. The annual agricultural shows for this county are held alternately at Compton and Eaton, as the inhabitants of those townships are largely interested in farming operations generally. The Circuit Court for Compton county is held at Cookshire, from the 8th to the 11th of the months of January, June, and November.

ASCOT.

A tract of land in the district of Three Rivers, bounded north by Stoke, east by Eaton, south by Compton, and west by Orford, subdivided into 288 lots of the usual dimensions, was erected into a township named Ascot, March 5th, 1803; parts of which

were granted to Gilbert Hyatt and his associates, viz,
David Moe, John Newton, Benijah Benedict, Moses
Knapp, James Lobdell, Joseph Hyatt, Abraham Hyatt,
Cornelius Hyatt, Jacob Hyatt, Isaac Hyatt, Francis
Wilcox, Abraham Vontine, Thomas Merihew, John
Merihew, Clement Wilcox, Samuel Dorman, John
Wilcox, Joseph Wilcox, Thomas Wilcox, Ebenezer
Dorman, Thomas Lobdell, Ebenezer Lobdell, Elam
Austin Moe, Jonathan Ball, Joseph Moe, Samuel
Peckham, John Ward, Bildad Hubbard, and Israel
Hubbard.

About the year 1796, Gilbert Hyatt with several
brothers who had previously come into Canada from
Arlington, Vt., in consequence of political troubles,
located themselves upon the tract above named, and
took the preliminary steps toward obtaining the grant
of a township ; but in consequence of a failure on their
part of the conditions, only portions were secured.

At this period, parties of Indians frequented the
vicinity, as the section had been included in their hunting and fishing grounds. They were remnants of the
St. Francis and other tribes that had become greatly
reduced in numbers during the wars that preceded the
final conquest of Canada. While the men were away
hunting, the women were making baskets, moccasins,
&c., which they sold to the settlers for provisions or
whatever they could get.

The first pearl ashery built at the *Upper Forks*,
(Lennoxville) was owned by the Messrs. Dorman,

father and son. C. F. H. Goodhue became a prominent man here and an extensive proprietor of lands. John Beman was also one of the early traders; and George Barnard, Jonathan Ball, Benjamin Stone, Calvin Moulton, James Blodget, Ezekiel Elliott, and Elim Warner were among the early men. Dr. Moses Nicolls was a prominent physician here at a very early day.

The surface of this township though somewhat hilly in parts, is yet free from mountainous elevations, and the land is very generally settled. The principal rivers and streams have already been described as the St. Francis, Massawippi, Salmon and Coaticook.

The Grand Trunk Railway passes through the township and has a station at Lennoxville. The value of assessable property in Ascot for the year 1866 was $640,000. The University of Bishop's College is located here, and connected with it is a large and important grammar school. There are also 19 elementary schools under control of the commissioners. In 1866, the sum of $1,097,10 in all, was levied for educational purposes ; aside from the government grant of $248,70. Two volunteer companies are under organization here.

Indications of copper are very plentiful in this region, and mines have been opened in different localities and worked with varying success. Gold has also been found near, both in the rock and in alluvial diggings.

Lennoxville, in the township of Ascot, is situated at

the junction of the St. Francis and Massawippi rivers, both of which are crossed at this point by convenient covered bridges. The village contains an English church edifice built of brick; a Wesleyan Methodist chapel; and religious services are held at stated times in the Town Hall by a minister of the congregational church: also a post office, several stores, a number of private offices, two large public houses, and many mechanics' shops. The most important of the industrial works are those for smelting the copper found in the vicinity. There are also a large number of inhabited dwellings, the better class of which are mostly of brick.

The University of Bishop's College, the buildings of which are also of brick, stands on a beautiful rise of ground overlooking the junction of the St. Francis and Massawippi rivers. It was founded twenty-three years since, and consists of two distinct departments, viz., the college and school, which though situated on the same grounds, are under different management as regards instruction and discipline.

In some respects however, the arrangements are common, as all meals are taken together, and on Sunday, all assemble for worship in the college chapel.

The Rev. Dr. Nicolls of Oxford, is the first principal and presides over the college. There are also professors of Classics, Mathematics, Divinity and French, in all of which it is designed to give a first class education. Many of the clergymen in this country were educated here ; some have gone to England, and some to the United States. The Protestant Bishops of Lower Canada have the principal control of the institution, as they appoint its trustees and the other members of its corporation.

The college building has both a library and museum. The convocation for granting degrees is held in the month of June annually, and is a season of interest to the friends of the college, as it draws many visitors from the cities and country around.

The school is managed by a rector assisted by a sub-rector and three other masters. The first rector was the present Bishop of Quebec, the Right Rev. Dr. Williams, who was succeeded by the Rev. professor Irving M.A., of Cambridge England; but on the sudden decease of that lamented gentleman, the rectorship was temporarily filled by the principal of the college, in addition to his other duties. The school has an extensive patronage, pupils coming from various parts of Canada and the United States; part of whom live in the school boarding house under the care of the sub-rector, assisted by the junior masters and a matron ; the others in private boarding houses in the village, or with their friends.

The instruction in the school comprises a thorough course in classics and mathematics, English, French, and German, ancient and modern history, book-keeping, drawing, singing, &c. There is a drill master and a shed in which the boys are drilled and practiced in gymnastic exercises. The grounds around the college and school, in all some 300 acres, furnish ample playgrounds, and the boys are well practiced in cricket and the manly exercises. Their field sports form no uninteresting part of the annual celebrations connected with the commencement. There is an excellent bathing place in the grounds, and the boys are speedily taught to swim: also a volunteer rifle corps among them officered by the masters, which on different occasions has earned for itself considerable credit.*

Huntingville. This is a small village within the township of Ascot, situated on the Salmon river, a short distance above its mouth. It contains some fifteen or twenty inhabited dwellings, a Universalist house of worship, a store, post office, mills and several mechanics' shops. The name was taken from families named Hunting who settled in the vicinity at an early day.

There is also a post office and a small collection of buildings at Ascot Corners, near the point where the St. Francis enters the township. The population of Ascot is given as 2,200 souls.

AUCKLAND.

A tract within the district of Three Rivers, bounded

---

* The above account of Bishop's College, has been condensed from a historical sketch of that institution, which was prepared by the Rev. Dr. Nicolls.

north by Newport, east by the Province line, south by Hereford, and west by Clifton, containing 61,717 acres of land, was erected into a township named Auckland, and in part granted April 3rd 1806, to Fleury Dechambault, Gilette Dechambault, Joseph Montarville, Louis Dechambault, Charlotte Dechambault, Elizabeth widow of Dr. John Gould, George King and Elizabeth King, children of Godfrey King deceased, Nicholas Andrews, Samuel Andrews, and twenty-five others. It does not appear however, that it was settled to any extent till a more recent date, the lands probably reverting to the Crown.

The northern parts of this township are little settled as yet, though the land there is said to be of good quality. The southern part though somewhat uneven and rough, has been selected as the site of a settlement. The people have already chosen a location for a church ; a burying ground has been consecrated ; a post office opened named St. Malo ; and a saw mill is in operation on a branch of Hall's stream. The choice of this section in preference to the other, was probably made on account of the cheapness of the land, and likewise because it was more readily accessible from Hereford Gore, where was already a settlement of French Canadians. Auckland is connected with Newport, Ditton and Clinton for municipal purposes, and steps have been taken to open schools.

In the northern and western sections, Auckland is watered by small streams which compose the head waters of Eaton and Clifton rivers, both of which take a north-west course; but in the more southerly parts these all flow south-east, and are carried through Hall's stream into Connecticut river.

Though sections of the township are hilly and stoney, there appear no elevations worthy of note. Main lines of road have been opened both from the north and west, which will advance the settlement of the township. The population is given as 403, mostly French Canadians.

BURY.

The tract lying within the district of Three Rivers, bounded north-east by Lingwick, south-east by Hampden, south by Newport, and north-west by Dudswell, was erected into a township named Bury, March 15th, 1803; one fourth of which was granted to Calvin May and his associates, viz., John Abell, Asa Abell, Benjamin Akin, John Leach, Samuel Laflin, Nathan Pratt, Jehiel Smith, James Torrance, and Samuel Whitcomb.

It would appear however, that these grantees had either suffered their lands to revert to the Crown, or disposed of their claims to the British American Land Company, as we find that something over thirty years ago, Bury was the property of that company, and was settled by English emigrants of the poorer classes, who came out under its auspices.

On finding things so different from what they had been accustomed to, and so entirely at variance with all their pre-conceived ideas, many of this class of settlers become utterly disheartened, gave up in despair and left the place in search of other homes. Others, however, possessing more self-reliance and energy of character, remained; and after years of laborious toil and patient waiting, have secured home and comfort as their reward. Many who left their native land as day laborers, and who in remaining there had no hope of ever becoming other than such, are now independent proprietors of farms, with their sons and daughters settled around, like themselves, owners of the soil on which they live.

The British American Land Company did much toward opening up the country and preparing the way for these settlers; encouraging them by building churches, establishing schools, constructing roads, &c., for their convenience; a work which has proved of lasting benefit.

The land in Bury is generally of an excellent quality, and in a state of nature furnishes a sufficiency of both hard and soft timber; the former perhaps prevailing in quantity. In some sections there are hills, a few of which even approach the precipitous; but there are no mountainous elevations, and few if any rocky ledges. Extensive wooded plains are varied with fine pastures, fertile fields, and rich meadows producing abundantly.

Good wheat has been grown here; and excellent horses and cattle are raised. Quantities of maple sugar are also made each spring. No very large dairies are kept as yet, but it is probable that with such a superior quality of land, Bury may yet equal if not outdo her sister townships of elder birth, in this important branch of farming business.

She has contributed her quota to the volunteer force of the country by the organization of an infantry company, and several young men of the township are members of the Cookshire cavalry company.

The total amount levied for educational purposes in 1866, was $875,28; the government grant for the same period being $111,80. Beside the Model school, are five elementary schools. The village of Robinson, which lies in a valley partly encircled with hills and rising grounds, contains a small church or chapel, one of three originally built by the British American Land Company, in as many different sections of the township; but a new church edifice, more in accordance with the needs of a growing community has been more recently erected, and was opened for divine service in July, 1862; the building formerly used as a place of worship being now occupied by the Model school. The clergyman residing here officiates alternately in the different churches. The Wesleyan Methodists have also a church building here. There are likewise a town hall, store, post office, public house, a number of private dwellings and several mechanics' shops. At a short distance from the village, are mills in operation. Accessions which are made to the community in this place from time to time, indicate a steady improvement.

Excellent roads diverge from this point in various directions. A little north of east from Robinson, is the Victoria road leading through Bury and a corner of Lingwick into Hampden. On this road about four miles above Robinson, stands one of the small churches above mentioned. The country around seems tolerably well settled, the land productive, and the farm buildings substantial.

Another principal line leading from Robinson to Lingwick, crosses the small stream on which the mills are located, and further on, takes a north-eastern course through Lingwick to Winslow.

Passing this in another direction, is a small pond or lake formed by an artificial embankment and supplied with water by a small brook. It covers a considerable space of ground, and is said to abound with fish. The waste water finds escape through a sluice in the side. On a rise of ground at the right of this pond stands St. John's church, one of the small wooden structures erected by the British American Land Company. The scenery around is delightful, there being some few farm houses near; just enough to give it signs of life, and yet not enough to detract from its appearance of quiet and repose. The locality is called De Courtnayville, from a former proprietor.

Further on between the tenth and eleventh ranges of the township, a road turns abruptly to the north-east, through a valley in which a fine brook of water runs nearly parallel with the road. The land rises on either side rather abruptly at first, though reaching back is a sort of extended plain which is said to be level and productive. A post office called Brookbury was opened here some years since for the convenience of the inhabitants of the *range*, which local appellation has heretofore been given to the place. Further on, a road turns to the north-west and after passing through a section in which there are few indications of settlement, it enters the township of Dudswell. Population of Bury given in 1861, as 989 souls.

COMPTON.

This tract formerly within the district of Montreal, bounded north by Ascot, east by Clifton, south by Barford and Barnston, and west by Hatley, was erected into a township named Compton and granted August 31st, 1802, to Jesse Pennoyer, Nathaniel Coffin, Joseph Kilborne, and their associates, viz., John McCarty, Ephraim Stone, Addi Vincent, Stephen Vincent, John Lockwood, Isaac Farwell, Oliver Barker, David Jewett, Samuel Woodard, Silas Woodard, Matthew Hall the younger, Page Bull, Abner Eldridge, Samuel Hall, Nathan Lobdell, Ebenezer Smith, Tyler Spafford and Thomas Parker.

Compton has no mountainous elevations. Its chief streams are the Salmon river which crosses the northeast corner; Moe's river which enters it at the south-east ; and the Coaticook which also comes from the south-east. These streams though at a considerable distance from each other, take a north-west direction and run nearly parallel through Compton, though they gradually near each other as they enter Ascot, and the two first named, unite before reaching the Massawippi.

The Coaticook has its sources in two small ponds south of the Province line, the outlets of which unite in the township of Barford, and by other tributaries a considerable volume of water is accumulated. In its course through Barford there are occasional rapids and other impediments ; and just below Coaticook village, is a fall as the stream descends into a deep gorge or chasm. After this, occasional rapids occur ; but as the river passes into Compton, it is marked by a peculiar freedom from those rocky obstructions which form so common a feature in the scenery of this country, yet its channel is remarkably crooked and winding. Considerable intervale lies along its margin, which is easily cultivated and very productive, but subject to sudden and destructive inundations.

Compton is a rich agricultural township, and since the opening of the Grand Trunk Railway through it, has rapidly advanced in its material interests. The traveller through its main lines of road, is impressed with the air of thrift and comfort apparent. The land which appears to be mostly improved, lies rather high, and though originally to a great extent hard timbered, is comparatively free from stones. There are no extensive swamps, and very little waste land. Abundant maple trees indicate that quantities of sugar are manufactured here. A cheese factory is in operation in the township.

The taxable property of Compton is valued at $468,636. An academy is in operation here, and there are also twenty-three elementary schools. For the year 1866, the sum of $2,678,32 was levied for educational purposes; the government grant for the same period being $340,62.

Compton Centre is a pleasant village containing Roman Catholic, English, and Wesleyan Methodist church buildings; an academy, post office, several stores, two public houses, the usual mechanics' shops, and some forty or fifty dwellings, many of which are painted white. The Grand Trunk Railway station is about one mile from the village.

The Rev. Dr. Stewart when missionary at Hatley, was the first Episcopal clergyman who visited Compton; his successors, the Rev. Messrs. Johnson and Jackson officiating there at regular periods Under the superintendence of Mr. Jackson, a church building was commenced, to complete which, the S.P.G.F.P. granted the sum of £125. February 18th 1840, the Rev. C. P. Reid was licensed as missionary to Compton, and entered upon his charge in the month of March following. His successors have been the Rev. Messrs. Allen, Richmond, and Kemp; the latter of whom is present incumbent.

Moe's River Mills. About two miles east from Compton Centre, are Moe's river mills, situated at a point where the channel of the stream is much obstructed by rocks, giving it a rapid and turbulent appearance. Beside the mills here, are a post office, store, mechanics' shops, and some dozen or more dwellings. No church building has yet been erected, but a society of Freewill Baptists meet for worship in the school house. •

Waterville is a small village in the north-west part of Compton, containing an English church building; a Grand Trunk Railway Station; post office, stores, mills, mechanics' shops, and some twenty-five or thirty dwellings. It is situated on the Coaticook river, some seven miles from Lennoxville, and in the vicinity of the newly opened copper mines. The first mills in Compton were built near this place. An extensive iron foundry was unfortunately burned here in 1866. The population of Compton is given as 3,013 souls.

CLIFTON.

A tract of land in the district of Montreal, bounded north by Eaton, east by Auckland, south by Hereford and Barford, and west by Compton, was erected into a township named Clifton, July 13th, 1799; and in part granted July 3rd, 1803, to Charles Blake, Daniel Cameron, Alexander Cameron, Duncan Cameron, John Cross the elder, John Cross the younger, Ann Hall the widow of Conrad Barnet, Mary Barnet the daughter of Conrad Barnet, Isaac Lemington Hall, Mary Catherine Christy Hall, and Ann Blake Hall.

It appears that few if any of these grantees settled upon the lands thus granted, but probably sold them to other parties. The township is as yet sparsely inhabited; the wild lands being mostly the property of non-resident proprietors, or of the British American Land Company. Two ponds named respectively Lindsay's and Sucker pond, each of which covers some 250 acres, lie within its limits; the former being in the south-east part, and the latter, a little south of the centre of Clifton. Around these ponds, the land is wet and marshy, aside from which, the swamps are of no great extent. Though hilly in some sections, it is mostly suitable for cultivation or pasturage.

Lindsay's pond receives the waters of many small streams, and discharges through Salmon river. Other small streams flowing in the same direction help to form Eaton and Moe's rivers. Roads have recently been opened through the unsettled portions of the township.

There are two post offices in Clifton; that at East Clifton being on the road leading through to Hereford, about five and a half miles south from Sawyersville in Eaton. Near this post office, a church building belonging to the Wesleyan Methodists has recently been erected.

The other post office called Martinville is located in the north-western part of the township, where are also mills and a school house. Public worship is held here alternately by the Methodists and Baptists. The land in this section is of much the same quality as in East Clifton. This settlement was formerly reached through Compton on the west, but new lines of road have more recently been opened in the township, bridges built, &c., connecting the different sections. The south-west part of Clifton is principally settled by French Canadians who already have a parish for ecclesiastical purposes; have opened separate schools; and have taken steps to secure to themselves the rights of a distinct municipality.

Five elementary schools are still under the control of the commissioners, and others are required to meet the growing wants of the people. For the year 1866, $390 were levied for educational purposes, and for the same period the government grant was $61,50; in addition to which, $30 have been received annually from the supplementary fund for the aid of poor municipalities.

There are a grist mill and seven saw mills in the township; three of the latter grind provender for animals, and two of them have bolts attached.

Most of the lumber, has been used for local purposes. The population of Clifton is given as 544 souls.

CLINTON.

A tract lying originally within the district of Quebec, bounded north by Marston, Lake Megantic and a part of Spalding, east by some unsettled portion of country, south by the tract called Woburn, and west by the tract known as Chesham; was erected into a township named Clinton, May 21st, 1803 ; and in part granted to Frederick Holland and his associates, viz., Louis Deguise, Augustin Robitaille, Joseph Larue, Louis Joseph Roux the younger, Joseph Martin the elder, Joseph Tapin, Charles Tapin, Joseph Vezina, and Pierre Delisle the younger.

This is a small irregularly shaped township of land, containing but four ranges of unequal length, and is said to be entirely uninhabited. The land which had been granted in former years to associates or private individuals, had either reverted to the Crown, or has been sold for taxes to non-residents by the authorities of Newport, to which municipality Clinton is attached. This land is said to be well timbered and of good quality.

Arnold river coming from Woburn on the south, which enters Lake Megantic in Clinton, is the principal stream of water ; others from the south-west being very inconsiderable.

CHESHAM.

This tract is not yet erected into a township and though the outlines are defined on the map of the district, very little is known of its interior. It has Marston on the north, Clinton and Woburn east, the province line south, and Ditton west. Small streams coming from it fall into the Arnold on the east, while others flow west and help to form the head waters of Salmon river. Saddle mountain is in the south-east part of the tract.

DITTON.

This tract originally lying within the district of Three Rivers, bounded north by Hampden, east by Chesham, south by Emberton Gore, and west by Newport, containing 380 lots of the usual dimensions, was constituted a township named Ditton, in May 1803, and in part granted to Minard Harris Yeomans and his associates, viz, Stephen Bigelow, Anson Bradley, David Bradley, Christopher Babity, Alexander Brimmer, William Chamberlain,—Eastman, Andrew Henry, Obadiah Jones, Edmund Lamb, Joseph Laret, Charles Lewis, David Morrow, Reuben Ross, Thomas Shadruck, and Ziba Tuttle.

Notwithstanding these grants, no settlements were made at the time indicated. We are left to infer that the true reason why so many granted lands in this section were left to revert to the Crown, was on account of their distance from any inhabited section, and the difficulty of access to them. Though the land here is said to be of an excellent quality, it has had till very recently, few if any permanent settlers. The newly opened gold fields in Ditton are investing the township with an exciting interest, and what is of most account is the *reality* that gold has been found in sufficient quantities to yield handsome returns to those employed in mining. The company have experienced hands at work, and saw mills have been erected in the vicinity. The mines are located in the south part of the township on the Ditton river, which stream is formed of two main branches coming from Emberton Gore on the south. United in one, it runs north till it falls into Salmon river near the centre of the township.

This latter named stream is formed of different branches which have their source in Chesham and unite within the limits of Ditton, the most northern of which comes from among and around the Megantic Mountains. The Ditton which is a noisy rapid stream, is much obstructed at its entrance into the Salmon, by driftwood and rubbish; yet the water separating into many channels finds its way through all these intricacies and finally unites in one very crooked and irregular, deep and sluggish stream. At one point it doubles upon itself and comes again so near its own channel as to form a bow or bend of nearly half a mile in length, a tree growing on this narrow isthmus extending its roots to either bank. Before leaving Ditton, the Salmon becomes more straight and rapid, and carries a considerable volume of water through other townships into the St. Francis in Weedon. The Megantic mountains are in the north-east part. Ditton is included in the municipality of Newport, Auckland, &c.

EATON.

This tract which originally lay within the district of

Three Rivers, is bounded north by Westbury, east by Newport, south by Clifton, and west by Ascot, and contains 64,685 acres and three roods in superfices. It was constituted a township named Eaton, December 4th 1800 ; and was in part granted to Josiah Sawyer and his associates, viz, Israel Bailey, Orsemus Bailey, Amos Hawley, Ward Bailey the younger, John Perry, John Cook, Royal Larned, Samuel Hugh, John French, Levi French, Luther French, Timothy Bailey, Abner Osgoode, Waltham Baldwin, Benjamin Bishop, Jesse Cooper, Abner Powis, Samuel Beech, Jabez Baldwin, John Gordon, Charles Cutler, Royal Cutler, James Lucas, Philip Gordon, William McAllister, Abel Bennet, George Kimpel, Calvin Rice, Charles Lathrop, Abthorp Caswell, and Peter Green Sawyer.

Captain Josiah Sawyer, from whom the village of *Sawyersville* in Eaton takes it name, settled in this place at a very early day. It is situated on the Eaton river, at a point where the Eaton, Newport, and Clifton roads meet, and here were erected the first mills. The place also contains a house of worship belonging to the Wesleyan Methodists, a post office, two stores, a public house, several mechanics' shops, and some eighteen or twenty dwellings.

Cookshire, so named from John Cook one of the associates who settled in this vicinity, is a diffuse village or rather thickly settled farming section, lying within the north-east quarter of the township. It contains a church edifice belonging to the English church, which was built some years since, of which the Rev. —— Parkyn is incumbent; also one belonging to the Wesleyan Methodists, opened in 1862; an academy, two stores, a post office, public house, several mechanics' shops, and a goodly number of dwellings.

In summer, the place has a delightfully cool and refreshing appearance, as from the rising grounds may be seen the white farm houses and their clusters of outbuildings, in pleasing contrast with the beautiful green of the trees, pastures, and fields; and occasionally a glittering spire pointing heavenward: while in some directions a back ground is formed to the scene, by prominent mountains. Of these, the Stoke Mountains are on the north-west; the Megantic on the east; the Hereford hills on the south; while still further in the distance, are the pale blue outlines of prominent peaks, beyond the Province line.

Eaton Corners is a small compactly built village, situated nearly midway between Sawyersville and Cookshire. A Congregational church was organized here in 1835, and a meeting house dedicated in Feb. 1844. The Rev. E. G. Sherrill was installed pastor in 1838, which position he still retains. Number of church numbers 75; sabbath school, 80 scholars and ten teachers. There is also a Roman Catholic chapel in the village, an academy, a post office to which a daily mail is brought, several stores, a public house, mechanics' shops, and some twenty-five or thirty dwellings. The village presents a neat appearance, as many of the buildings are painted white. The Eaton river winds its way among the meadows and cultivated grounds within a short distance ; and excellent roads from different parts of the township intersect here, rendering it a sort of centre for a fine farming section.

The land in Eaton is considered of good quality for farming purposes ; and aside from some thousands of acres owned by the B. A. L. Company, and some few wild lots which belong to private individuals, is generally settled upon. There are no mountainous elevations. The principal streams are the Eaton river, entering at the south-east, and the North river coming from the east, which unite above Cookshire.

There are two academies and fifteen elementary schools in the township. For the year 1866, the sum of $1,253,52 altogether, was levied for educational purposes ; the government grant for the same period being $215,36. There are also about 400 voters in Eaton.

Six post offices have been opened in different sections for the convenience of the scattered inhabitants. A daily stage from Sherbrooke and Lennoxville through Cookshire to Bury connects at Birchton with the line running through Eaton Corners to Sawyersville ; from which latter point, a weekly route is open through Clifton to Hereford. The other points where post offices have been established are at localities named Bulwer and Johnsville.

Of the seven church buildings in Eaton, two are at Cookshire; two at Eaton Corners; one at Sawyersville; one belonging to the Wesleyan Methodists at a locality named Bulwer; and a Baptist church is located at a point near Newport called Grove Hill, of which church the Rev. A. Gillis is pastor.

Few of our townships could furnish as many examples of the permanent and successful settler as Eaton; a class that necessarily combined energy, industry, and sobriety. Among the associates was Mr. John French who in 1797 with his two elder sons, penetrated the wilderness on foot, guided by marked trees, for the purpose of choosing a location for settlement. This done, the remainder of the family moved on in time. They had all been raised in habits of industry and made to feel the necessity of accommodating themselves to any emergency that might arise; to which practical and energetic rearing, their success in after life was mainly due. There were also families here named Bailey, Pope, Cook, Hodge, Alger and others, whose descendants remain among the prominent inhabitants of Eaton; and in some cases occupy the same farms on which their fathers first settled.

There are now four regular grist mills, and fourteen saw mills in the township; several of the latter having arrangements for grinding the coarser grains; also a shop where furniture is manufactured; and likewise machinery for making shingles, laths, clap boards, &c.;

most of the lumber made here being used in the vicinity. The census of 1861, gives Eaton a population of 1,905.

HAMPDEN.

This tract of land though considered a township and to some extent inhabited, is not constituted such however, by Letters Patent. It is of irregular shape and has a corner of Whitton on the north-east, Marston east, Ditton south, and parts of Lingwick and Bury on the north-west. The Salmon river flows through it into Lingwick, beside which, are smaller streams tributary to it, chief among which are Otter Brook coming from the west of Marston, and Mountain Brook having its source in the hilly sections of the Megantic mountains. The settlements are mostly in the northern part near Whitton, with which municipality they are connected. The census of 1861, gives it a population of 103 inhabitants.

HEREFORD.

The tract within the district of Three Rivers bounded north by Clifton, east and south by the province line and west by Barford, subdivided into 308 lots, was erected into a township named Hereford, and in part granted Nov. 6th, 1800, to James Rankin and his associates, viz, Adam Kohlop, Samuel Pangbourne, Ephraim Wheeler, Reuben Brunson, Henry Casgrove,

James Liddle, William Taylor, John Vanvliet, Theodore Stevens, Nathaniel Wait, Silas Town, Joseph Weeks, Daniel Tryon, Michael Hyar, Samuel Danford, Zeras White, Richard Dean, Ephraim Wheeler the elder, James Sears, Doderick Fride, Henry Adams and Wm. Johnston.

It appears however, that the first settlers of Hereford were of that class more significantly than elegantly termed *squatters*, who located upon the lands without right or title ; some of them under peculiar and embarrassing circumstances ; though their descendants of the present day are loyal subjects, and many of them the real *owners* of good farms. We are left to infer, therefore, that these original grantees either suffered their claims to lapse, or sold them to the occupants, or other parties perhaps, as large tracts of wild land in the township are now owned by individual non-residents.

Sections of this township are hilly, the most prominent elevations being what are termed the *Hereford Mts.* Hall's Stream on the east, and Leach's Stream in the south, both of which discharge into Connecticut river, drain the southern section of the township. Some of the larger streams flowing north-west into the St. Francis, have their extreme sources in the northern section of Hereford.

Several reasons have hitherto operated to retard the progress of the township, chief among which, is its isolated situation at a distance from the great centres of action and improvment in our own country; the inhabitants being thus thrown into immediate contact with, and in a great measure dependent upon a people whose views, interests, and prejudices, are alike opposed to our government and institutions. The fact that nearly all the trade and general business of the township has been drawn to the other side of the line, has fostered and increased this state of dependence, and at the same time has had a tendency to suppress interest in the affairs of our own country.

Of late, however, there are growing indications of a disposition to break away from the untoward influences which have almost inperceptibly settled upon the inhabitants of Hereford, and signs appear of an awakening to a subject of such vital concern.

The amount of assessable property in Hereford is valued at $128,158,00; there are 148 voters; for the year 1866 the sum of $1,012,82 altogether, were levied for educational purposes; the government grant for the same period being $41,38. There are ten school districts in the township.

What is termed the village of Hereford is in the southern part, near which, a new Episcopal church has been erected. A post office was opened here in 1849, beside which, are a customs house, store, and a number of dwellings; a saw mill is also in operation, to which is attached a run of stones for grinding the coarser grains. At Hall's stream or East Hereford, is a post-office and store, the former of which was opened in 1850 ; also a store on the new government road in West Hereford.

To the north-east of the township, is Hereford Gore, it being what remained of the tract called Drayton, after the boundary line was run.

The commissioners engaged in this work, after leaving Hall's Stream, took as the line of separation, the height of land which divides the waters running north into the tributaries of the St. Lawrence, from those which flow south into the Connecticut river. It seems to have been a treaty stipulation that no water should be crossed till arriving at a certain point ; and it is even said that in some instances where no water was to be seen on the surface of the ground, resort was had to digging in order to decide the matter. This explanation gives us to understand why the boundary line after leaving the 45th parallel, is so crooked and irregular. South of Ditton, is what remained of the tract called Emberton, now known as Emberton Gore.

Hereford Gore has a considerable population of French Canadians, who have there the parish of St. Venan, with a church, post-office and store, at a locality called Paquetteville. For municipal and school purposes they are connected with the township of Hereford.

During the war of 1812, some border difficulties occurred, mostly relating to smuggling, and one man was shot while engaged in the unlawful work. At a later date have been the *Indian Stream* difficulties, which grew out of the disputes concerning the boundary line. At a particular location on Indian Stream one of the head branches of Connecticut river, was a settlement very near the boundary, formed of persons from either side, led there by interest or convenience. Such as came from Canada, still considered themselves as Canadian subjects; while those who had come from the American side, as strenuously insisted on being within the limits of the state of Newhampshire; each party retaining in full their national and social prejudices. Being at such a distance from the courts of law which had nominal jurisdiction on either side, the matter had been in a measure compromised by a sort of tacit understanding that for the time being, the ground was neutral territory. A voluntary association had framed rules regulating their internal affairs, and chosen a prominent person from among their number to act as magistrate or umpire among them. The population of the place came in time to receive large accessions of an ill-regulated and undesirable class of inhabitants, many of whom were counterfeiters or other refugees from justice. This state of things was not to continue. Such an asylum for unscrupulous characters as the settlement had become, could not long be tolerated. The arrest of criminals by officers sent from either side, and their delivery to those claiming them, was the signal for the opposition and rebellion of fiery spirits among the other party; till at length such a state of feeling prevailed as bid defiance to all efforts at control. Prejudices grew into bitter animosities; disputes led to violence and blows; blood was spilt; and the quarrel which became general, was only suppressed by the arrival of an armed force sent by the Newhampshire authorities. Soon after this, the boundary question was finally determined.

The last census gives Hereford a population of 360, no doubt greatly increased since.

LINGWICK.

This tract which was within the district of Three Rivers, is bounded north-east by Stratford and Winslow, south-east by Hampden, south-west by Bury, and north-west by Weedon; and was erected into a township named Lingwick, and in part granted March 7th 1807, to William Vandelvendon, Joseph Anger, Augustin Larue, Pierre Delisle the younger, Antoine Trudelle, Joachim Delisle the younger, Jean Baptiste Vésina the younger, Michel Tapin, Louis Vidal the younger, and Augustin Vésina the younger.

For some cause however, there appear to have been no permanent settlements made here till a more recent date. The unsettled portions of the township belong to the British American Land Company. Salmon river enters Lingwick from Hampden, and flowing through the south and west parts of the township, turns north into Weedon. In the unsettled portions, are two lakes of some size, named respectively Moffatt's and Magill's lakes, and on the north-east boundary is the small lake McIver; besides which are small streams tributary to the Salmon. In another part is a mountainous elevation, near which is an extensive swamp. The greatest part of the land is said to be of good quality, and for pasturage is not excelled in the Eastern Townships.

The adult inhabitants of Lingwick, are nearly all natives of the island of Lewis on the coast of Scotland, the first of whom came to Canada in 1841. They have had accessions to their numbers in 1849, and at subsequent periods.

The assessable property in Lingwick is valued at $95,774,00; the number of voters is 119. For 1866, the sum of $486,16 altogether, was levied for schools; the government grant for the year being $63,76. There are five school districts in the township.

The only post office in Lingwick is at the village of Gould. The Presbyterian (Free) church was built here in 1845. Nine-tenths of the inhabitants of the township worship in this church. Their minister is the Rev. John Milloy.

There is also an Episcopalian church in the vicinity of Gould, built in 1861. They have no resident clergyman here, the incumbent of Bury holding service at stated periods. There are two stores in Gould; a public house, mills, several mechanics' shops, and a collection of dwellings.

The early settlers here had their full share of the privations and inconveniences of pioneer life, as for ten years after the first locations were made, the only road by which the older settlements, some fifteen or twenty miles distant, could be reached and supplies obtained, was through a line that had been simply bushed out. This was every year becoming worse, till at length it was found dangerous to attempt getting through it with horses. Within a few years, however, there has been a wonderful improvement, and now there are excellent roads through Bury, Lingwick, and Winslow, to Lambton on Lake St. Francis, and thence to Quebec.

During the three years of 1848-49-50, many families who first settled here, left their improvements and took land in Winslow, where it could be had on greatly facilitated terms. In consequence of this, the prosperity of Lingwick has been retarded, few emigrants having come into the section since the year 1849.

The census of 1861 gives Lingwick a population of 564 souls.

MARSTON.

This tract though generally considered a township as indicated on the map of the district, is not however, erected such. It has Whitton on the north, Lake Megantic east, Clinton and Chesham south, and Hampden west. The land though somewhat rough, is comparatively level, with the exception of the south-west part, into which the Megantic hills extend.

The principal stream of water is the Megantic river,

which has its source among those hills, and receiving mnay small tributaries by the way, flows north-east into Victoria Bay, on the west side of Lake Megantic. Though not large, this stream would carry such mills as might be built upon it. There are other small streams, some falling directly into the lake, while others in the west and north-west of Marston, which are the outlets of small lakes in that region, find their way to Salmon river in Hampden. The largest of these is Otter Brook which issues from Otter lake in Marston. This tract is connected with Whitton for municipal purposes, the last census giving it 100 inhabitants.

NEWPORT.

Under the hand and seal of Robert Shore Milnes, Baronet, Lieutenant Governor, &c., a warrant was issued for the survey of a tract of land in the district of Three Rivers, bounded north by Bury, east by Ditton, south by Auckland and west by Eaton; which when subdivided into 308 lots beside the allowance for highways, was erected into a township named Newport, July 1st, 1801. One-fourth of this township was granted to Edmund Heard and his associates, viz, Samuel Hurd, Longley Willard, Edmund Heard the younger, Nathaniel Beaman the younger, Peter Trueman, John Squires, William Heard, William Hudson, Elisha Hudson and Caleb Sturtevant.

From records in existence relative to the first settlement of this township, the following has been gleaned. A person named Williams had taken the first steps toward securing to himself and associates the grant of a township of land. In 1793, Edmund Heard one of Williams' associates, with another person named Sawyer, penetrated the wilderness and arrived at a locality in the tract, now known as *Pleasant hill.* Here they chose sites on which to locate, twenty-five miles distant from any inhabitants on the south, and seventy miles from the French settlements on the north. Within the two succeeding years, these two pioneers had moved their families to the new homes they had provided, and were soon after followed by several others of Williams' associates.

That person still failed of making his appearance and in 1797, Edmund Heard petitioned that the grant might be made to himself and his associates, comprising such heads of families as had already located on the tract as Williams' associates. This petition was considered and finally granted; as with the single exception of numbers, terms and conditions were fulfilled to the letter. The community thus thrown together, had at an early day organized themselves into a body which met regularly for the transaction of any business affecting the interests of the settlement. The manner in which the records above referred to were kept up to the year 1814, indicates that the first settlers of Newport were an order-loving and efficient class of men. After the erection of the township, nearly the same system was pursued.

The war of 1812, affected this infant township unfavorably, as many of the settlers left for parts where the *hard times* were felt less than here. With the return of peace, however, many of them came back, but untoward influences seemed to settle upon Newport like an incubus. In 1815, Captain Samuel Hurd who had been one of the most active and public spirited men in the settlement from the first, was unfortunately drowned at Brompton Falls. This melancholy event cast a gloom over the minds of the people of Newport, who now realized how much they had depended on him, and over the prospects of the settlement of which he had been a ruling spirit.

The settlements in this township are principally in the west and south-western parts, though a few families have located in the north, near the Bury line. In the north-eastern quarter, there is a section of swampy land, but most of the other parts are suitable for cultivation. Much of the wild land is the property of the British American Land Company. Roads have been opened quite through to Ditton on the east, and to Auckland on the south.

For the year 1866, $451,27 altogether, were levied for schools, and for the same year, the Government grant was $45,56, beside which, some further assistance is received from the " Supplementary Fund in aid of Poor Municipalities." There are five district schools in the township.

Many of the members of the Baptist Church in Eaton

are residents of Newport; and also those of a Freewill Baptist Church, the members of which worship in the same house each alternate Sabbath. The Wesleyan Methodists hold service in the school houses at stated times. The Eaton river passes through the south-west part of the township, and the North river flows through from Ditton into Eaton. There are other small streams tributary to these. Four saw mills are in operation, in one of which are shingle, lath, and planing machines, and also a run of stones for grinding provender for animals. The population of Newport is given as 403.

ORFORD.

This tract which originally lay in the district of Montreal, is bounded north by Brompton, east by the rivers St. Francis and Magog which separate it from Ascot, south by Magog, and west by Stukely. After being surveyed, divided and subdivided into 379 lots, it was erected into a township named Orford, May 5th 1801, and granted to Luke Knowlton and his associates, viz., Benjamin Searle, Consider Shattuck, Samuel Shattuck, Seth Shattuck, Benjamin Remington, Seth Hoskins, Stephen Kimball, John McNamara, Sylvanus Holbrook, Daniel Cheney, Samuel Dickinson, Calvin Cook, John Stewart, Daniel Frazer and John Plummer the younger.

Orford is a large township divided into eighteen ranges, which from the irregularities of the eastern boundary are of different lengths, and many of the lots are consequently of unequal dimensions.

Much of this tract is rough and hilly, the highest mountain in the townships lying partly in Orford, from the summit of which is an extended and varied prospect. This whole region abounds in small lakes and ponds, numbers of which may be seen from the mountain top. The principal streams are the outlets of these lakes, many of which discharge into Brompton lake, and thence into the St. Francis in Melbourne. Cherry river which has its sources in small ponds in the west of Orford, runs south into Lake Memphremagog.

One main line of road runs directly west through the township, another leads from Sherbrooke to Magog. A slate quarry has been opened about four miles from Sherbrooke. For the year 1866, $413,60 were levied for school purposes, the government grant being $81.96. It is an independent municipality with a population of about 900 souls.

WHITTON.

A tract of land lying within the district of St. Francis, bounded north-east by Gayhurst, east by Spalding, south by Marston, south-west by Hampden, and north-west by Winslow, containing 73,500 acres of land, was erected into a township named Whitton, March 4th, 1863. This township is of very irregular shape. The little Megantic mountains lie in the north part. The principal stream is the Chaudière, which separates it from Spalding on the east, and several tributaries of that river. There are also small lakes within the township, the principal of which are the Three mile, Moose, and Muskrat lakes, the outlets of which discharge into the Chaudière. In the western part are the head waters of the Felton river which flows into Winslow, and thence into Lake St. Francis.

Whitton, Marston, and Hampden are united in one municipality, the inhabitants of which are mostly French Canadians. The population of Whitton is given as 509 souls, the probabilities being that it has largely increased since the census was taken.

WINSLOW.

This tract which lies in the district of St. Francis, is bounded north-east by Price and Aylmer, south-east by Whitton, south-west by Lingwick, and north-west by Stratford, and contains about 73,000 acres of land. It was erected into a township named Winslow, April 19th 1851, and has been subsequently divided into two distinct municipalities, viz., North and South Winslow.

South Winslow. The south-western section of the township was first settled in 1852 by Scotch emigrants, among whom their native Gaelic is much spoken. They have a church of their own persuasion, where service is held in that tongue.

There are 18,130 acres of land assessed in South Winslow ; 180 legal voters ; and for the year 1866, the sum of $270,23 was levied for schools ; the government grant for that period being $102,18. There are here six school districts, one Presbyterian Church, a post office named Stornoway, four stores, two public houses, two grist mills, four saw mills, and one turning mill.

North Winslow. The north-eastern section of the township is inhabited principally by French Canadians who have a settlement and post office here called St. Romaine. In 1866, the sum of $371 was levied here for schools, the government grant being $80,62 for that year.

The Felton river coming from Whitton is the principal stream. Its western tributaries are Mill Brook from McIver lake, and the outlets of Trout lake and other small bodies of water. On the east, the principal branch of the Felton is Indian river, which has its source among the Little Megantic hills in the north of Whitton.

The stage road from Sherbrooke through Eaton, Bury, and Lingwick, is continued into Winslow where it intersects with lines leading to Lambton and other places. The census of 1861 gives Winslow a population of 1,617 souls.

WESTBURY.

This tract of land originally within the district of Three Rivers, is bounded north-east by Bury and Dudswell, south by Eaton, and north-west by Stoke, and contains 16,396 acres of land. It was erected into a township named Westbury and in part granted August 13th, 1804, to Henry Caldwell, his heirs and assigns.

This is a small triangular shaped township, the ranges and lots in which are of unequal length and of irregular dimensions. With the exception of parts in the south-east, the soil is considered of good quality. The St. Francis flows directly through the township, and the Eaton enters that river within its limits; beside which are small streams in which there is sufficient water in spring and fall to carry the saw mills of which there are several. Such of the land as is not settled upon, is now the property of the British American Land Company.

Though there is no village in the township, a post office has been opened at a locality on the Stage road leading from Sherbrooke, to which a tri-weekly mail is brought. There being no churches, the inhabitants meet for worship in the school houses. As there is no way of crossing the St. Francis but by ferry, at seasons of the year it is both difficult and unsafe to make the attempt.

Certain local causes have operated to retard the prosperity of Westbury; one among which is a want of harmony among the people respecting the location of a bridge over the St. Francis, which would go far toward uniting the interests of the two sections. Again, as they are few in number and limited in resources, they feel poorly able to bear unaided the necessary expense of such a construction. Further still, long habit has accustomed them to dependence on their neighbors in other townships, for accommodations wanting in their own. However, among the more energetic of these people, improvements are in contemplation which may to some extent, remedy existing evils.

Though formerly connected with Ascot for municipal purposes, Westbury is now an independent municipality, containing about 70 voters. In 1866, the sum of $329,38 in all, was levied for schools; the government grant for that year, being $33,58. There are five elementary schools within the township.

Indications of copper are found on lots 9 and 10 in the fourth range of Westbury; also a quarry where excellent roofing slate abounds, on lot 9 in the third range. The census of 1861 gives the population as 293 ouls.

WOBURN.

The tract of land indicated on the map of the district of St. Francis by this name, has not yet been erected a township; but is still in a state of nature, with few signs of survey, and none whatever of settlement. It has the Province line as its boundary on three sides; owing its peninsular form to the fact that the waters within its limits flow north through the Arnold river into Lake Megantic. It was by following down this stream to the lake, that Col. Benedict Arnold and his command entered the Province, on occasion of the memorable expedition against Quebec in 1775.

CHAPTER VI.

RICHMOND COUNTY.—BROMPTON.—CLEVELAND.— MELBOURNE.—
SHIPTON.—STOKE.—WINDSOR.

RICHMOND County contains the townships of Brompton, Cleveland, Melbourne, Shipton, Stoke and Windsor. Its *chef-lieu* is Richmond in the township of Cleveland. The circuit court for Richmond county, is held at Richmond from the 1st to the 5th of the months of March, July, and November: also at Danville in the township of Shipton, from the 14th to the 18th of the months of January, April, and September.

BROMPTON.

A tract of land lying within the district of Three Rivers, bounded north by Melbourne, part of which is inserted in it at a right angle, north-east by the St. Francis which separates it from Windsor and Stoke, south by Orford, and west by Ely, was erected a township named Brompton, November 27th, 1801.

Parts of this township were granted to William Barnard and his associates, viz., Samuel Barnard the younger, Samuel Childs, David Arms, Enoch Rice,

Levi Rice, Jonathan Rice, Samuel Hayford, Barnabas Wilcox, Samuel Bishop, Joseph Pierce, Roswell Bartlett, Ephraim Kee, Ephraim Knapp the younger, William Wakefield, Jedediah Caswell, Ira David Hyde, Stewart Kee, Samuel Terry, Miles Dorman, Wyman Wakefield, John Wakefield, David Steele, Elijah Harwood, Oliver Sherman, Lebbeus Sherman, Ozias Caswell, Ebenezer Kee, Nahum Ward, Jairus Bonney, Thomas Bartlett, and Ephraim Knapp.

Settlements were commenced in this tract near the Little Brompton Falls on the St. Francis, as early as 1797, by Ozias Caswell, Samuel Pearce, Samuel Bishop, Jedediah Caswell, and several others. Some year or two after the opening was made on the river, a locality farther into the interior of the tract, since known as Wakefield Hill, was settled by several persons of that name, two men named Harrington, and one named Martin.

Among the early settlers was a widow and her several sons, named Heustin. One of these, a youth of rather a weak mind, was lost in the woods of Brompton, no trace of him being ever found. A person named Wakefield from the interior settlement, was also lost while trying to find his way through the woods to the river during a severe snow storm, and though persevering search was made, nothing could be found to give assurance of his death, or indicate the fate he had met. The probable solution of the mystery concerning him, is, that becoming bewildered by the blinding snow, he wandered to the river, fell through some opening in the ice, and was carried away by the current. In later years, parts of human skeletons have been found in the woods of Brompton, but nothing was left by which the remains could be identified.

Including Brompton gore, this township is a large irregularly shaped tract. There are no very prominent elevations, and though there are hills in some sections, much of the land is level, and some even wet and swampy.

Brompton lake lies partly within its limits and partly in Orford; its outlet being the largest stream in the township through which it flows north into the St. Francis at Melbourne. The next in size is Kee Brook which also comes from some of the numerous lakes in Orford, and enters the St. Francis near the railroad bridge about one mile below Brompton Falls. The only road through from this part of Brompton to Melbourne, is laid out so as to pass the Rockland slate quarry.

The gore or *augmentation* of Brompton, which lies to the south-west of the southern angle of Melbourne, is connected with that township for municipal and school purposes, such an arrangement being more convenient for the inhabitants, on account of the distance between the two sections.

Brompton Falls on the St. Francis, are six miles below Sherbrooke. Here is located the largest lumbering establishment in this region, giving employment to many hands. The main building which contains several mills, is 333 feet in length, by about 73 feet in width, and is painted white. In the sawing department there are three separate gangs; one of which contains 26 saws and cuts up two logs at a time; the other two have fifteen saws each, and take but one log at a time. Immense numbers of saw logs are every year driven down from the head waters of the St. Francis, sawed up in this establishment, and prepared for market in the shape of boards of various widths and thickness; clap-boards, sugar boxes, shingles, laths, barrel staves, heads, &c.; most of which are taken on the cars direct to Portland, and thence shipped to South America or other foreign part. There is also a planing machine here.

The village of Brompton Falls consists mostly of laborers' cottages, with however, some few dwellings of more convenient size; a Roman Catholic chapel; a post office and railway station; and in the absence of any Protestant house of worship, a large and convenient school house supplies the want, where ministers of the different denominations hold occcasional or stated services.

This township contains assessable property valued at $108,629; also 106 voters; and has five elementary schools. For the year 1866, the sum of $831,82 in all, was levied for school purposes; the government grant for that year being $81,74. A post office has also been opened on lot 18 third range. The population including the gore, is given as 1,168.

CLEVELAND.

The township of Shipton was erected and granted December 4th, 1801. It originally included fifteen ranges; but the seven ranges lying nearest the St. Francis river were set off and erected into a distinct township named Cleveland, in 1855. (For account of early settlement, quality of land, &c., see Shipton.)

The only considerable body of water in Cleveland is Spooner pond, so called from a settler in the near vicinity. It is situated in the most northerly part of the township, on the height of land between the St. Francis and Nicolet rivers; is oval in shape; one mile in length by about one-fourth of a mile in width; and is fed wholly by springs. It lies higher than the surrounding country, as springs issuing from the ground 250 yards from its banks, flow in other directions. The water is shallow near its shores, but gradually deepens toward the centre. It discharges through a small stream into the St. Francis at Kingsey. Excellent fish are abundant in this pond, and as its surroundings are pleasant, it has became a favorite resort for the disciples of Walton.

The St. Francis copper mine has been worked here to some extent and with partial success, but operations on it are now suspended.

The assessable property in Cleveland is valued at $185,000. For 1866, the sum of $1,615,20 in all, was levied for schools; the governement grant for the year being $216,60.

Richmond is the only village in its limits. It was incorporated in 1862; its present assessable property is valued at $92,000. Here are located the railway buildings at the junction of the Quebec and Portland lines. This station is 76 miles from Montreal, 96 miles from Quebec city, and 221 miles from Portland. The Court House and public offices for Richmond county are also located here, and beside a post office at the upper section of the village, is another near the station some distance down the river. There are six or more principal stores; a printing office whence issues a weekly paper; an iron foundry; four public houses; many small trading and mechanics' shops; and some 86 private dwellings.

The bridge across the St. Francis river connecting the townships of Shipton and Melbourne, was built in 1841 at a cost of about $20,000; and has been a means of facilitating intercourse between the two sections, as well as a great convenience to the public at large.

Of the churches in Richmond, St. Anne's, (English) was the first erected. Previous to the year 1830, there had been no resident clergyman in Shipton, but the Right Rev. Dr. Stewart, Archdeacon Mountain, and others occasionally visited and instructed the people, at which times service was held in the school house. The church edifice was consecrated in 1830, when the Rev. C. B. Fleming took charge of the mission. He remained 17 years, and was succeeded by the Rev.

Dr. Falloon who held the incumbency till his death in 1862; since which, the Rev. Messrs. Gay, and Roe, have in turn succeeded to the charge ; the latter of whom remains to the present. The congregation worshipping here, assemble from both sides of the river.

A Roman Catholic church building, situated near the railway station, was the second built in the village, and has now a large congregation, as many of the inhabitants are of that faith.

The third belonged to the Free Scotch (or Chalmers) church, the congregation of which was formed shortly after the disruption of the Presbyterian church of Scotland. It has at present 105 communicants, eight of whom are elders, an order peculiar to that body ; being a number of lay-men possessing a sort of balancing power between the clergy and people. In connection with this congregation are three stations where service is held periodically for the benefit of the scattered inhabitants. The church building in Richmond stands on an elevation near the Court House. The present minister is the Rev. J. McKay.

St. Francis college is also located here. The charter for this institution was obtained in 1855, when a preparatory school was opened. The buildings were finished in 1856, since which time the college has been in successful operation. It is unsectarian in religion, though evangelical in its influence. It is designed to prepare young men for the higher departments of teaching and the learned professions; while the preparatory department is training the young in the earlier stages of their education. The favorableness of its location, and the efficient character of the instruction given, commend it to the approval and patronage of the public. The population of Cleveland is given as 1,450 souls.

MELBOURNE.

A tract of land lying within the district of Three Rivers, bounded north-east by the St. Francis river, south-east by Brompton, south-west by Brompton Gore and Ely, and north-west by Durham, was erected into a township named Melbourne, April 3rd, 1805, and granted to Henry Caldwell and John Davidson the elder, and their associates, viz., Edward Bowen, Geo. Hamilton, John Caldwell, Jane Caldwell, Martin Cannon, John Davidson, John Hennesy, Matthew Lamon, Thomas Adolphus Simpson, Henry Donaldson, James Donaldson, Peter Donaldson, John Donaldson the younger, Hugh Donaldson, David Donaldson, John Ellison, George Gallup, John Gibson the elder, John Gibson the younger, Peter Hunt, Augustin Hibbert, Willard Hill, Thomas Lancaster, John Miller, Archibald Miller, Daniel Miller, Daniel Mudget, Oliver M. Pearce, Andrew Patterson the younger, Jonathan Stickney, John Stickney, John Stimpson, Daniel Stimpson, Ephraim Stimpson, Joseph Stimpson and James Stimpson.

The first locations were made in Melbourne in 1799

and the few succeeding years, and were attended with the usual difficulties and reverses. The early people here, however, enjoyed one advantage over those in the interior sections, in having the river to serve as a highway to and from the older settlements, while yet there were no roads passable through the wilderness.

About the year 1816, a Union Church building was erected in Melbourne by the united efforts of the scattered inhabitants. It was located on the main line of road leading toward Montreal, at a point intersected by other lines, and was the only house of worship in the township till 1838.

The land in Melbourne is mostly high and rolling, much of it having been originally covered with hard wood. The largest stream of water is the creek which flows north from Brompton lake, beside which there are others sufficiently large to carry mills.

The amount of taxable property is $200,000. In 1866, $1,163,68 in all, were levied for schools, the government grant for the year being $233,56. There are nineteen school districts.

Three slate quarries have been opened in different sections of the township, the most important of which is the Melbourne quarry, located some five miles above the St. Francis bridge, and about one mile back from the river. A large number of hands are employed upon these works. The slate is pronounced by competent judges to be of excellent quality, and a ready market is found for all that can be made. The Rockland and Albert quarries which have been more recently opened, are situated in other sections of the township. Many of the workmen in these quarries are from Wales.

There is abundant proof of the existence of mineral deposits in the earth within the limits of Melbourne, not only in surface indications, but in the fact that surveyors have found the operations of the compass seriously interfered with from this cause. Colored marbles, serpentines, Asbestos, &c., have also been found here.

Melbourne Lower Village, so called from being situated on the river below the bridge, was incorporated in 1861. It extends over 600 acres of land, and has assessable property valued at $44,000; also two churches, a post office, three stores, a public house, mechanics' shops and some sixty dwellings.

Melbourne Upper Village, so called from being located above the bridge, is not incorporated. It has two church buildings, stores, offices, a public house, and some twenty-five or thirty dwellings.

The people in this locality were mostly Presbyterians by preference, and in 1839, the Rev. J. McMoran was sent by the Presbytery of Quebec, to reside in the place. Soon after this, a church building was commenced, but not finished till 1842. Mr. McMoran remained till the disruption of the Scotch Church, which extended to Canada. The Rev. Messrs. McFarland, Clarihue, and a student of Queen's College,

Kingston, have successively filled the pulpit, but only for a short time each. The next was the Rev. J. Sieveright, who remained five years and extended his labors to Windsor and Brompton gore. In June 1861, the Rev. T. G. Smith came to preside over this church, and not only officiated regularly in the above named places, but had a fourth service at a locality near Rockland slate quarry where a small house of worship has been built. Sabbath schools are also held in these places to gather in the young.

The Congregational Church at Melbourne was organized about the year 1837, and a place of worship built in the lower village soon after. Their pulpit has been successively filled by the Rev. Messrs. Dunkerly, Anderson, Bayne, and Frink.

The congregations worshipping in these churches assemble from both sides of the river. A house of worship belonging to the Wesleyan Methodists stands on a prominent point a short distance above the bridge.

The Adventists have also a place of worship at the lower village.

Companies of volunteer infantry are under organization both in Melbourne and Richmond.

There are many pleasant locations on the bank of the St. Francis in this township. After leaving the river, the stage road to Waterloo leads over what appears a continuously rising ground to Melbourne ridge, where in a well settled farming section, are a Wesleyan Methodist chapel, a store and post office. It then enters Brompton gore where stands a small house of worship belonging to a congregation of the Presbyterian Church of Canada in connection with the Church of Scotland, and a little further on is another, belonging to the Canada Presbyterian or Free Church. This locality bears indication of having been but recently settled.

Taken altogether, it is evident that the Scotch element greatly predominates among the inhabitants of this immediate vicinity. The population of Melbourne is given as 1,621.

SHIPTON.

A tract of land lying within the district of Three Rivers, bounded north-east by Tingwick, south-east by Windsor, south-west by the St. Francis river which separated it from Melbourne, and north-west by Kingsey, was erected into a township named Shipton, and granted December 4th, 1801, to Elmer Cushing and his associates, viz, George Barnard, Elijah Hastings, Henry Barnard, Job Wetherel, Stephen Barnard, Lot Wetherel, Job Cushing, John Lester, Joseph Hicks, John Hicks, John Brockus, James Doying, Daniel Doying, John P. Cushing, James Barnard, Nathaniel Fessenden, J. B. LaBonté, Amherst Steward, Jonathan Steele, William Dustin, Benjamin Leet, Ephraim Magoun, Charles Clarke, Thomas Hill, Joseph Keyser, Ephraim Magoun the younger, John Robinson, Theodore Barnard, Thomas Ellison, Benjamin Moulton, Joseph Perkins, David Leviston, Abner Rice, William Rumlet, Jonathan Smith, Timothy Chamberlin, Daniel Blunt, Robert Green, Ephraim Blunt the younger, Amos Cutting, John Martin, Joseph Gamelin, John McLure, John Oakes, James Tobyne, and Baptiste McLure.

The first parties who entered the tract to survey and explore it were George Barnard, Prentice Cushing, John Brockus, Joseph Kilburn, and a company of workmen, who all came in on foot through the pathless wilds, bringing axes and surveying instruments, guns, ammunition, and provisions. They traced the outlines and made such divisions as were necessary to give the associates opportunity for location, which partial survey took place in 1797.

Elmer Cushing, the agent, settled on lot 16 in the fourteenth range, May 24th, 1798; and within the few succeeding years, many others chose locations in the vicinity, most of whom were from the New England States. At that time there were no roads or settlements for fifty miles to the north, and the nearest on the south, was one just commencing at Ascot about thirty miles distant.

The first road leading through Shipton was a line from the Little Forks in Ascot, to the French settlements, which was opened in 1802. The next was from the present site of Richmond to that of Danville, as settlements extended in that direction. The first mills were built by Elmer Cushing in 1802; part of the necessary irons for which were brought through Lake Champlain, down the Richelieu and St. Lawrence, and up the St. Francis; the remainder being obtained from a distant township, and brought to Shipton on a hand sleigh.

The surface of Shipton is somewhat hilly; the most prominent elevation being the Pinnacle, said to rise 300 feet above the surrounding country. The soil is favorable for agricultural purposes, grain and vegetables growing well, though it is said to be best adapted to grazing. The Nicolet river which runs through the north-east part is the largest stream of water, though there are others of sufficient size to carry mills.

The present township of Shipton, comprises only the first eight ranges originally belonging to it. The first mills built within its present limits, were near the site of Danville, and in 1812, a mill was built in that place.

The amount of taxable property in Shipton is $267,687; the number of legal voters 363. In 1866, the sum of $2,806,45 in all, including the village of Danville, was levied for school purposes; the government grant for the same period being $302,06. There are twenty school districts within the township and village. There are also three grist mills, ten saw mills, an iron foundry, tannery, two carding and clothing shops in the township, and some three miles east of Danville, a slate quarry has been opened where school and roofing slates are prepared for market. There are indications of the existence of mineral deposits in various localities of the township; yet no efficient efforts have as yet been made to bring them into notice. The British American Land Company have lands for sale here.

At Castlebar, 2½ miles north-east of Danville, a post office and store have been opened; and also a post office at Dennison's mills, six miles in a south-westerly direction. The Grand Trunk railway leading to Quebec, passes entirely through this township, and has a station at Danville.

The village of Danville which was incorporated in 1860, is just one mile square, and contains assessable property to the amount of $70,355; and has seventy-six legal voters. There are five churches, one academy, nine general stores, two public houses, a tin shop and hardware store, mills, tannery, iron foundry, furniture and carriage shops, and other mechanical works, beside a large collection of dwellings. The stream of water which furnishes moving power for these industrial works is rather small, but has a reservoir formed by an artificial embankment, which contains a reserve in case of need.

Occasional services had been held in the north-eastern part of Shipton by clergymen of the Church of England, before the arrival here of the Rev. Mr. Lonsdell in 1843; and after his departure in 1847, the Rev. Messrs. Fleming and Lloyd at times visited and instructed the destitute people. In 1857, the Rev. M. M. Fothergill who was employed as travelling missionary in that part of the Eastern Townships included within the Diocese of Quebec, visited Danville at intervals, and did much toward awakening an interest in behalf of the church in the place. Steps were taken which resulted in the permanent establishment of a mission and the erection of a church edifice here; of which mission Mr. Fothergill was appointed to the charge. He remained five years, and was succeeded by the Rev. G. J. McGill, and two years later, by the Rev. H. J. Petry.

There is also a congregational church here, which body was first organized in 1832, and a meeting house subsequently erected. The Rev. A. J. Parker is pastor. The Wesleyan Methodists and Adventists have each houses of worship here also; beside which, there is one belonging to the Roman Catholics.

The population of Shipton is given as 2,132.

STOKE.

This tract which originally lay within the district of Three Rivers, is bounded north-east by Dudswell, south-east by part of Dudswell and Westbury, south-west by Ascot and the St. Francis river which separates it from Brompton, and north-west by Windsor. It contains 70,984 acres of land, and was erected into a township named Stoke, Feb. 13th, 1802; and in part granted to Jane Cowan and her associates, viz., James Cowan, George Cowan, Gideon Alexander, William Woodworth, William Woodworth the younger, Gershom

Woodworth, Lot Woodworth, Samuel Lathrop, Jonathan Wood, Edmund Honsinger, John Campbell, Elijah Smead, Henry Welch, John Dewar, James Taylor, and twenty-six others.

Notwithstanding this grant, no permanent settlements were effected in Stoke till a much later date, and even at the present time, it is but sparsely inhabited.

An elevated range or ridge of hills called Stoke mountains runs nearly through the township in a north-easterly and south-westerly course, rendering those parts rather rough; though in other sections the land is said to be of excellent quality and well adapted to farming purposes. A considerable body of water called Stoke pond lies within its limits, the outlet of which is one of the principal streams in the township, and helps to form the head waters of Windsor Brook which has its extreme source in the tract. The other streams in Stoke are but insignificant, and either fall directly into Stoke pond, or the St. Francis river.

Considerable improvement has been made within this township during the few later years, as five elementary schools are now in operation here. The population is given by the census of 1861, as less than one hundred; but must have increased rapidly since that period.

WINDSOR.

A tract of land lying within the district of Three Rivers, bounded north-east by Wotton, south-east by

Stoke, south-west by the St. Francis river which separates it from Brompton, and north-west by Shipton and Cleveland, was erected into a township named Windsor, July 14th 1802. Certain parts of this township were subsequently granted to officers and privates of Canadian militia, and to the widows and orphans of such as were deceased. These grantees were 130 in number.

The township was originally divided into fifteen ranges; but as the grantees were altogether French, the first six of these ranges were set off for their use, and now form a separate municipality, the inhabitants of which, have a church, post office, and schools of their own, and manage their internal affairs. This part of the township is called " St. George de Windsor," and is more compactly settled than the other section. In 1866, $423 were levied here for schools; the government grant for that year being $70,10.

In English Windsor, the first settlements were made by a few emigrants from the New England states who located themselves along the course of the St. Francis for convenience. The first who settled here permanently was Capt. Josiah Brown who came in about the year 1800, and located on lot 12 in the twelfth range.

Soon after Capt. Brown, came Peter Frye, Nathaniel Webster, John Thomas, Nathaniel Caswell, Moses Baily, Ebenezer Moore, and others. The first mills here were built in 1803.

On one occasion Capt. Brown in company with a

party of Indians had gone out hunting for the purpose of supplying his family with Moose meat, a very common article of diet in those days. After some success, and the failure of their stock of bread, the company separated, and he started on his return home, drawing an Indian sled loaded with the fruits of his expedition. It was intensely cold; considerable snow lay upon the ground, and in stepping upon ice he thought firm, he broke through and became partially wet, which added greatly to his discomfort. His strength gave way so that he was obliged to abandon his load and hurry forward lest it should fail him entirely, when on coming to a deserted cabin he attempted to open the door, but his stiffened fingers were unable to undo the fastening and he was obliged to go on. Crossing the river, he approached his own house; yet was too thoroughly chilled to utter a sound, and as it was dusk, was not recognized by a person who had seen him approach, and thought that his walk and look indicated bewilderment and hesitation. The outer door was unlatched so that he entered without effort, but no one was there and he remained standing without power to lift the latch of the inner door or make an audible sound, till the person who had seen him approach, and wondering why he did not come in, opened the door and recognized him. It was fast growing dark, and the stupor stealing over both mental and physical powers, had so changed the man that his own wife had not known him. His mouth was open, and ice had formed upon his face; and though a long confinement to a sick room part of which time he was delirious followed this exposure, by proper care and good nursing, both hands and feet were preserved, the nails only coming off.

Though the surface of the land here is somewhat broken and rough in sections, there are no very high hills, and aside from some few swampy districts, it is generally suitable for clearing and cultivation. The wild land is mostly owned by individual non-residents; yet since it was found that the best quality of soil lies back from the St. Francis, many Scotch emigrants have located in the interior.

The only stream of any magnitude is the " Brook," one branch of which comes from Stoke, the other being the outlet of a pond in St. George de Windsor. These two branches uniting, form the stream or brook on which, for more than a mile up from its mouth, there are numerous mill sites, some of which have been improved. Some few years since, works were erected here for reducing wood to a pulp used in the manufacture of paper, which was to supply the paper mill at Sherbrooke.

The amount of assessable property in English Windsor is about $85,000; the number of voters including non-residents owning property here, 144. In 1866, the sum of $658,20 in all, was levied for school purposes; the government grant for the same period being $61,84. There are five elementary schools in operation. A public school of higher grade is much desired, which want has hitherto been supplied by select private schools.

There are five or six stores in Windsor; a post office, railway station, and several mills. A house of worship belonging to the Presbyterians is located about two and a half miles below Windsor mills, where a' clergyman from Melbourne holds service once in two weeks, and religious meetings are held in a school house near that point, each intervening Sabbath. The Methodist missionaries on Melbourne circuit hold meetings in school houses near the mills and on the opposite side of the river, each Sabbath alternately; and it is in contemplation to build a church edifice at the mills.

About one mile back from where Windsor Brook falls into the St. Francis, powder mills have been built and are in successful operation. The powder made here is in general use for mining purposes, and the works will probably be enlarged in time.

But far the most important of the industrial works erected here, is the new paper mill, which forms a manufactory complete in itself. As the pulp mill above mentioned was designed to supply the paper mill at Sherbrooke, another of the same kind is included in the new establishment. One of the principal buildings is 175 feet in length by about 88 in width, and is three stories high; another is 128 feet in length, by 60 in width; one is 90 by 60 feet; another 60 by 40; and others still of smaller dimensions. One of the tall chimneys is about 90 feet in height; the other about 70 feet. These buildings are of brick, and are so connected as to form one complete establishment worked by steam. A large number of hands find employment here.

This is the only place in Canada where pulp is made of wood, to be used in the manufacture of paper. The kinds of wood most in use, are basswood and poplar. The pulp thus made is mixed with about one fifth of rags or other fibrous material, and manufactured into excellent paper. That made in Sherbrooke is already used extensively in the newspaper establishments of our country.

Isolated as Windsor had long been before the construction of the railway, frequent and familiar intercourse had been kept up with the settlement opposite, till from habit and constant association the people of both sections had come to consider themselves members of the same community.

It is now in contemplation to unite the two localities by a bridge over the St. Francis, which will serve as an additional bond of union.

For some distance above the mills, along the course of the St. Francis there are a series of rapids, known as the "Little Brompton Falls," which offer sites for the erection of mills to a great extent. Taken altogether this situation is said to be unrivalled in the Eastern Townships for manufacturing purposes. The rocky banks of the river afford a firm foundation; there is sufficient fall; the flats along the margin are high enough to be safe from harm by inundation, and the contemplated bridge between Brompton and Windsor, would bring such works near the railway station at the latter place.

About the year 1848, considerable excitement was caused by the disappearance of a young woman about 16 years of age, named Sarah Campbell, belonging here. She had been out with a party of others on a fishing excursion up the " Brook." Logs lay over the branches at different points, on one of which the party crossed on their way to the fishing ground. As night approached, they started on their return home, when instead of keeping with the others, this girl took as she thought a shorter way to the high road, intending to reach it before them. On their arriving at the point, not finding her there, they very naturally supposed that she would soon overtake them, and kept on their way. Having often been over the ground, she fancied herself familiar with the various windings and crossings of the brook, and supposed she took the right path ; but either in her haste to get soonest to the highroad, or that she was too confident of being in the right way and neglected proper examination of the ground, she got bewildered and went far astray. The falling darkness overtook her thus wandering farther and farther from the right course ; but having the dog with her, she felt a sort of assurance of protection, and composedly prepared herself a couch of hemlock boughs on which to sleep. As it was in the month of September, and the nights were chilly, she had rather an uncomfortable lodging.

In the meantime, her companions of the previous afternoon had gone to their homes without suspecting that anything was wrong, and it was not till her own family found that night failed of bringing her home that any alarm was felt. But when she was missed, it was already dark. A party was sent out and repaired to the point where she was last seen, when they made the usual demonstrations but to no purpose, and after a prolonged search, returned unsuccessful. A much larger party took to the woods next day, regularly prepared to penetrate the forest fastnesses, and furnished with organized signals; but the day wore on in fruitless efforts, and night compelled their return, only bringing with them tidings of their want of success. Each day the effort was renewed but with the same results; still there was the one sad answer to all inquiries; all the while the interest and excitement becoming deeper and more intense.

On the 18th day, the dog came home, when the last hope of finding its young mistress alive, died in the minds of her friends; and consequently the search was given up as hopeless.

But on the 21st day, to the astonishment of all, she found her way out of the labyrinth, in which a bewildered imagination had involved her, and arrived at the house of a neighbor in so reduced and miserable a state, as to be unable to reach her home. During all this time her living had been principally wild fruits. Those in search of her had been looking too far away, as it was thought, she could not at any time have wandered more than ten miles from the point where she went astray. The population of Windsor is given altogether as 1,167.

CHAPTER VII.

STANSTEAD COUNTY.—BARNSTON.—BARFORD.—HATLEY.—MAGOG.
—STANSTEAD.

THIS County comprises the townships of Barnston, Barford, Hatley, Magog, and Stanstead. Its *chef-lieu* is Stanstead Plain. The circuit court for Stanstead county is held at Stanstead Plain, from the 1st to the 4th of the months of February, June, September and December. The agricultural shows are also held at Stanstead Plain.

BARNSTON.

January 1st, 1801, a warrant was issued by Robert Shore Milnes, Esquire, Lieutenant-governor, &c., for the survey of a tract of land lying within the district of Montreal, bounded north by Hatley and Compton, east by Barford, south by the Province line, and west by Stanstead. The tract containing 64,500 acres of land, was erected into a township named Barnston, and in part granted to Robert Lester and Robert Morrogh, and their associates, viz., James Shepherd, Joseph Bartlett, Joseph Bartlett the younger, Clement Drew, Elihu Buttolph, William Kent, Abraham Cocklin,

DD

Isaac Hellican, Edward Hogan, Stephen Lampman, John McCarty, Abraham Kelliker, Jacob Mantle, Joseph Dolph, Matthew Morehouse, Asahel Porter, Jonathan Hart, and Jacob Brown.

Prominent among the early settlers of Barnston, are the names of men not found in the recorded list of associates, viz, those of Baldwin, Wheeler, Cleveland, Cameron, Billows, Cutting, Hollister, Mosher, Hill, and Norton, beside many others.

Sections of this township are hilly and rough, the highest elevation being Barnston Pinnacle in the south; beside which, is a range of hills called Barnston mountains.

The largest body of water in its limits is Baldwin's pond, lying between the mountains in the southern part, and the most considerable stream flowing any distance in Barnston, is the outlet of that pond, called Negro river or Burroughs' stream; which, though by no means a river in magnitude, is yet sufficiently large to carry mills at several points in its course through the township into Stanstead. The Coaticook river enters the north-east corner, whence it passes into Compton.

The Grand Trunk railway enters Barnston from Compton, and has a station at Coaticook. It crosses the Province line near the division between Barnston and Barford, and has another station at the Boundary.

Much of the land in Barnston is of excllent quality for agricultural purposes. Most of the timber originally standing was hard, and a great deal of maple sugar is made here. Particular localities in this township have borne their share of the obloquy usually falling to the lot of frontier settlements; but here, as elsewhere, pursuits which were dishonorable in themselves and demoralizing in their tendencies, and which found encouragement in cupidity or indolence, are no longer tolerated but frowned down by an improved public feeling.

Coaticook. This village is located in the north-east corner of Barnston on the Coaticook river which at that point affords numerous sites for the erection of industrial works. These constitute the principal business importance of the place, and have been the great stimulant to its rapid advancement, as it has been mostly the growth of the last twelve or fourteen years. This place has daily communication with Montreal by the Grand Trunk, and with Stanstead and other points by stage; beside which excellent roads connect it with the different localities around. It is 122 miles by railway from Montreal. It was incorporated in the year 1863; and has a population of about 1,200 souls; is a port of entry; has four church buildings; a parochial school in connection with the Church of England, and two elementary schools. In 1866, the sum of $334,80 in all, was levied for educational purposes, the government grant for the same year being $79,24. It has also seven stores; a post office; a town hall and lock-up house; three public houses; mills; extensive works for the manufacture of a great variety of agricultural implements and for the making of various articles of domestic utility; also an iron foundry; two carriage shops; a carding mill, &c. A volunteer infantry company is under organization here.

The village of Barnston Corners is about four miles from Coaticook on the stage road leading to Stanstead. It contains a Calvinist Baptist church; one belonging to the Wesleyan Methodists; a post office; town house, an academy, stores, public house, a variety of mechanics' shops, and some twenty-five or thirty dwellings. *Baldwin's Mills* are five miles south from Barnston Corners. Here are mills and a variety of mechanical works. At *Way's Mills*, four and a half miles west of the Corners, are two stores, a post office, tannery, carding mill, furniture and blacksmiths' shops; and at Libbee's mills, six miles west of the Corners, are a grist and saw mill each, a store and mechanics' shops.

A Baptist church was organized in Barnston as early as 1810; but was disbanded after some years, and the body at present under organization was formed in 1833. Their ministers have been successively the Rev. Messrs. Powell, Mitchel, Baldwin, House, Green, Campbell, Ferguson, and the Rev. R. Nott, present pastor. Their house of worship is at Barnston Corners.

Freewill Baptist ministers visited this section as early as 1806; but the church now in existence was not organized till 1830. The Rev. Messrs. Moulton,

Harvey, and T. P. Moulton, have been their ministers successively. Their house of worship is at Coaticook.

Till within a very few years, Barnston has been connected with other townships in a circuit belonging to the Wesleyan Methodist conference ; but at present, only the Corners and Coaticook are connected ; in each of which places is a house of worship. The minister resides at Coaticook.

No Episcopal clergyman had resided in this vicinity till 1862, when the Rev. John Foster was sent to Coaticook. As the result of his labors, a convenient church edifice has been erected in that village, and also a school house built of brick, for the school designed to train the young in the principles of the church.

The population of Barnston is given altogether as 3,098 souls.

BARFORD.

A tract of land lying in the district of Montreal, bounded north by Compton and Clifton, east by Hereford, south by the Province line, and west by Barnston, was erected into a township named Barford, April 15th 1802, and granted to a company of 52 individuals.

The first permanent settlements in this township were made along the course of the Coaticook river, mostly by families who had emigrated from the New England states, among whom were those named Lyman, Hollister, Drew, Childs, and Straw.

The land in this township is of uniform good quality, though back from the Coaticook it becomes somewhat rough and hilly. Its agricultural properties and products are similar to those of the neighboring townships.

Two small streams which are the outlets of ponds south of the line, unite within this township to form Coaticook river, which runs north nearly through it, when it diverges a little to the west and enters the corner of Barnston, passing thence into Compton. In several places along its course before reaching Coaticook village, the channel of the stream is broken by rocky obstructions; but after passing the deep gorge below that place, it gradually loses the characteristics of a rapid stream.

The amount of taxable property in Barford, is $156.-538; the rate payers 196 in number. There are six elementary schools under the control of the commissioners; in one of which, the French language is taught. In 1866, the sum of $636,00 in all, was levied for schools; the government grant for that year being $79,14. There is also help from the supplementary aid fund, to the amount of $30 yearly.

There are two Baptist church organizations in Barford, the first of which was formed in 1837, the second in 1863. The Rev. Joseph Chandler is pastor of the former, and the Rev. Alvin Parker, of the latter. As yet, they meet for worship in school houses. There is also a society of Freewill Baptists in another part of the township. It has been in contemplation to build a house of worship for such of the scattered inhabitants as prefer the doctrines and mode of worship of the Church of England.

HATLEY.

The tract lying within the district of Montreal, bounded north by Ascot, east by Compton, south by Barnston and Stanstead, and west by Magog and the little Magog lake and river of that name, containing 348 lots, was erected into a township named Hatley, and in part granted March 25th, 1803, to Henry Cull and Ebenezer Hovey and their associates, viz, Job Chadsey, Joseph Fish, Samuel Fish, William Taylor, Joseph Ives, Emos Mix, Samuel Rexford, Benjamin Rexford, Isaac Rexford, Joel Hall Ives, Chester Hovey, Abiel Abbott the elder, Stephen Burch, Chauncy Haycock, Jonas Martin, Reuben Martin, Daniel Green, Peter D. Blanchard, Abiel Abbott the younger, Reuben Simmons, Paul Hitchcock, Jesse Wadleigh, Asa Daggett, Amasa Merriman, David Chamberlain, John Abbott, Providence Williams, Martin Adams, Harvey Clarke, Joseph Davies, Edmund Boyden, Japhet Le Barron, and Eli Ives.

Captain Ebenezer Hovey settled in the western part of the tract in 1793, and was soon after followed by other pioneers. Lake Massawippi was first discovered by Captain Hovey, as with a party of explorers, he was out examining that section of the tract. Thus engaged they came suddenly upon the opening in the forest where is situated this fine body of water. It is nine miles in length, with a varying breadth, and extends mainly north and south, though the northern end diverges to the east, while the southern end turns to the west, giving the lake something of the form of the letter S. Varieties of excellent fish abound here. The largest streams are the Tomfobia which comes from the south and enters the lake at the south-east, and the Massawippi river through which the surplus waters are taken in a north-east course into Ascot where it is joined by the Coaticook, then by the Salmon, all contributing to swell the volume of water which enters the St. Francis at Lennoxville.

Lake Massawippi presents a natural obstacle to intercommunication between the two sections of the township. The part lying east of the lake is generally level or undulating, while that on the west is hilly and even mountainous. In the immediate vicinity of the lake is a range called the Massawippi hills rising boldly from the water; and in the south-west corner of the township, are the Bunker hills extending from Stanstead. Seven of the original western ranges of Hatley were set off toward forming the township of Magog. The population of the western section is still sparse; but the several localities east of the lake, are more thickly settled. The land in this section is excellent for farming purposes, and evidences of the prosperity of its inhabitants, are abundant.

The stage road from Waterloo to Stanstead leads

around the south-western end of Lake Massawippi, where the ledge of mountains approaches so near the water as not to leave room for a carriage way between them; and for about one mile, it winds through a pass which has been mostly blasted from the over-reaching rock, or built out from the stoney base, in a foundation of the necessary width.

The surveyed route of the "Massawippi valley railroad" runs north from the Province line till it strikes the Tomfobia river in Stanstead; then follows that stream till near its entrance into the lake; when passing up the east side to the outlet, it follows down the Massawippi river, and connects with the Grand Trunk at some point near Lennoxville.

For the year 1866, the assessed value of property in Hatley was $456,234; the number of qualified voters 432; the assessment for municipal purposes $599; and for the poor $320. For the same year $1,361,50 in all, were levied for school purposes; the government grant being $257,08. There are fourteen school districts in the township.

Charleston or East Hatley contains two church buildings, an academy, post office, three stores, a public house, a variety of mechanical works, and some thirty or forty dwellings. It is an exceedingly pleasant village, situated in the midst of a fine farming section.

Massawippi Village is also east of the lake but much nearer it than Charleston. It contains one house of worship, a post office, three stores, a public house, mills, and mechanical works, with twenty-five or thirty inhabited houses.

North Hatley at the outlet of the lake, has a post office, store, and small collection of dwellings. Such Indian relics as hatchets, arrow points, &c., found in recent excavations in this vicinity, give evidence that the place was frequented by the Indians before the advent of the whites. This settlement was not commenced till about the year 1820.

The first religious body organized in Hatley was a small society of Freewill Baptists.

Many of the early settlers had been connected with this people at their former homes, and were visited by some of their preachers at an early day. They are now numerous here. Their ministers have been successively, the Rev. Messrs. Boody, Smith, Moulton, Tyler, Abiel Moulton, Parks, Young and Hurd; the two latter of whom still reside in the township. The house of worship at Massawippi is occupied alternately by the Freewill Baptists and Wesleyan Methodists; and another on Hatley *East road*, by Freewill Baptists and Adventists.

At a very early period Hatley was visited by the American Methodist preachers; but in 1821, the societies were transferred to the charge of Wesleyan missionaries, and for years it was included with other townships in a circuit. Recently, however, it has become a separate station.

About the year 1817, a mission of the Church of

England was established here, chiefly through the instrumentality of the Rev. Dr. Stewart. The clergy men here have been successively the Rev. Messrs. Johnson, Jackson, and Burrage; the last named being present incumbent.

The population of Hatley is given as 2,274.

MAGOG.

This township is bounded north by Orford, east by Hatley, south by Stanstead, and west by Bolton and Lake Memphremagog. It was formed of the seven western ranges of the original township of Hatley, united to the nine eastern ranges of the township of Bolton as at first constituted; and thus the early history of Magog is simply that of those parts of the townships of which it was formed.

Capt. Ebenezer Hovey, one of the agents and grantees of the township of Hatley, first located on the east side of the outlet, near the point of its issue from the lake.

Lake Memphremagog is about thirty miles in length, one-third of which is south of the Province line. Three rivers each about thirty miles long, are its chief tributaries; viz., the Clyde, Black and Barton rivers, all of which enter the lake on the Vermont side. The principal place contiguous to it south of the boundary, is Newport at the head of Steamboat navigation; which is a port of entry and derives added importance from being situated on the extension of the Connecticut and

Passumpsic river railroad. Taken altogether, these advantages render it a sort of centre for commercial intercourse between the countries. Four townships, viz., Stanstead, Magog, Bolton and Potton, lie along the border of the lake in Canada.

The Mountain House, situated by the lake side at the foot of Owl's Head mountain, is about twelve miles below Newport, and five miles above the ferry between Georgeville in Stanstead, and Knolton's landing in Potton. Steamboats plying up and down this lake, land regularly at this point for the convenience of arriving and departing guests; and a post office has been opened here, as the house is much frequented during the season of summer travel, and has became a favourite resort for lovers of quiet, parties fond of boating, or those wishing to ascend the mountain, from the top of which is a view much admired by lovers of natural scenery.

The northern end of this lake is entirely within the township of Magog. The outlet takes a north-east course, its channel somewhat obstructed by rapids, till at a distance of about four miles from its source, it expands into the little Magog lake which is about five miles in length. The river again contracts at a point about midway between its source and mouth, and flows in the same course with only an occasional rapid suitable for a mill site, till it reaches the Upper Town in Sherbrooke.

The surface of the land in Magog is somewhat rough,

and seems to promise when more fully cleared, better for the general purposes of grazing than for the production of the finer grains. The village situated at the point where the river issues from the lake, contains a Roman Catholic church, a Union Protestant church building, a post office which was opened at an early day, several stores, two public houses, a variety of mechanical and manufacturing works, and some thirty or forty private dwellings. A company of volunteer infantry are also under organization here.

The place is principally important as the terminus of steamboat navigation on the lake, and is also on the direct stage route between Stanstead and Waterloo; and while the steamboat makes its regular trips, is connected by daily stage with Sherbrooke and Waterloo. Lines of public road from various directions centre here.

The assessable property in the township is valued at $177,930. For the year 1866, the sum of $1,147,20 in all, was levied for educational purposes; the government grant being $119,72. One grist mill and three saw mills are in operation here. Population given as 1,059 souls.

STANSTEAD.

A tract of land lying within the district of Montreal, bounded north by Hatley and Magog, east by Barnston, south by the Province line, and west by lake Memphremagog, containing 77,870 superficial acres, was erected into a township named Stanstead, September 27th, 1800, and in part granted to Isaac Ogden and his associates, viz., George Hogle, Abraham Friolt the younger, Amos Hawley, Benoni Grant, Ebenezer Clarke, John Hogle, Samuel Filer, Philip Derrick, Johnson Taplin, Israel Wood, Thomas Filer, Joseph Friolt, Charles Kilborne, Andrew Patterson, Abraham Friolt the elder, John Curtis, Lyman Brunson, Henry Emerick, Abraham Salls, Ephraim Hawley, Alexander Ferguson, Crosby Towner, Andrew Young and Conrad Derrick.

The first permanent location in Stanstead was made by Johnson Taplin who settled at the Plains in March 1796, soon after which, Captain Moses Copp settled at Copp's ferry, now known as Georgeville. Among those prominent in the early days of Stanstead were persons named Lee, Morrill, Hubbard, Nash, Hibbard, Mansur, Rogers, Young, Ruiter, Bodwell, Magovor, Peaslee, and many others whose names do not appear in the list of recorded associates. Dr. Isaac Whicher also came here to reside at an early period.

The land in this township is of a superior quality for agricultural purposes; farming in its various branches being the ruling interest of the people. Much of the surface lies in elevated plains, there being apparently little waste land. In the north-west is a range called Bunker hills, extending into Hatley and Magog.

The largest stream of water is the Tomfobia, which comes from Holland, Vermont, but an insignificant stream; yet by constant additions from small rivulets, accumulates sufficient water to carry mills. It at first runs in a western course, then turns south to the Province line at Rock Island, thence flows west nearly to Bebee Plain, when it turns to the north and finds its way into Massawippi lake in Hatley. Its largest tributary is Negro or Burroughs' Stream, which comes from Barnston and passes through the north-east corner of Stanstead into Hatley. Near the line between these two townships, a very remarkable fall, or rather succession of falls occur on this stream, the small volume of water carried over the precipice alone preventing its being classed with cataracts of the first magnitude.

In the north-west of Stanstead is Lovering Pond, which reaches into Magog. This discharges into Fitch Bay, an arm of lake Memphremagog, which extends some distance in a north-easterly direction into the interior. At places it is so narrow as to appear a mere stream, or rather its general appearance is that of a succession of small ponds connected by small streams. Above these narrows it is called Fitch Bay, but below them, is known as East Bay.

Stanstead is very generally settled, a perfect net work of roads which intersect at numerous points connecting the different localities. Mineral indications exist in parts, and a valuable granite quarry has been opened and worked to some extent. In 1866, the nominal valuation of property was $884,100; the number of legal voters 715 ; the assessment for municipal purposes $1,400 ; and $4,278 in all, were levied for educational purposes, the government grant being $579,69. There are in all ten church buildings, thirty-two school districts, six grist mills, twelve saw mills, one woollen factory and a great variety of manufacturing and mechanical works in the township. A cheese factory has recently gone into operation here.

Stanstead Plain was incorporated as a village in the year 1857, and contains five church buildings, eight or ten stores, a distributing post office which was opened about the year 1817, a custom house, an academy and district school, three public houses, a great many mechanics' shops, and some eighty private dwellings. The county business is done here. A branch of the Eastern Townships bank is also in operation here. The county agricultural fair grounds, and Crystal lake cemetery grounds are in the vicinity, and within the corporation are the usual numbers of offices belonging to gentlemen of the different professions. A volunteer infantry company is also under organization here.

Daily stages connect the village with the terminus of the Passumpsic Railroad, with the Grand Trunk at Coaticook, and with other points ; beside which are two lines of tri-weekly stages arriving and departing. It is also expected that when constructed, the Massawippi Valley road will approach within a short distance of the village.

In some respects, Stanstead Plain is unrivalled, as it is without doubt the most regularly laid out of any village in the Eastern Townships. Its location is both healthful and pleasant, in the midst of a rich agricultural section. It has but one principal street extending in a direction nearly north and south, not so compactly built but that ample room is left for gardens and ornamental grounds on a small scale. Many of the dwellings more recently erected, combine elegance with convenience.

Rock Island. This village is situated one mile south of Stanstead Plain, and contains six general stores, two family groceries, a post office, public house, one flouring mill, an iron foundry, two boot and shoe factories, a chair factory, a printing office whence issues a weekly newspaper, planing machines, and other mechanical works. The locality is separated from Derby line in Vermont, only by the stream which is crossed by bridges at different points.

Georgeville, twelve miles north-west of Stanstead Plain, is on the eastern shore of lake Memphremagog, and contains two church buildings, a post office, academy, three stores, a custom house, two public houses and a collection of some thirty or more dwellings.

Fitch Bay, situated at the head of the bay of that name, seven miles north-west of Stanstead Plain, has one church building, a post office, two stores, a grist and saw mill each, a cabinet shop and other mechanical works, and a collection of houses.

Bebee Plain, two miles south-east from Stanstead Plain, has one church building, a post office, two stores, a custom house and small collection of dwellings.

Griffin's Corners, four miles west of Stanstead Plain, has one church building, a public house and a town hall for meetings of local council, school commissioners, &c.

At *Cassville*, six miles north of Stanstead Plain, is a house of worship, an academy, and some few private dwellings.

The fact that the early settlers of the township came from different sections, and were unlike in their religious views and training, accounts to some extent for the number and variety of religious sects among them.

The Roman Catholic church edifice occupies a prominent location in the village of Stanstead Plain.

The early American Methodist preachers were the first to penetrate these wilds in their visits to the settlers. In 1821, they were superseded by the Wesleyan Methodist missionaries, and at present the Canada conference controls the interests of this body. The house of worship in use for many years by the congregation of Methodists in Stanstead, has been found too small and inconvenient, and a new edifice has been built, exceeding in convenience of arrangement, taste and finish, anything of the kind in the place.

Congregationalists.—The pioneer minister of this order was the Rev. James Hobart. The first society was organized in 1816. Among the early ministers were the Rev. Messrs. Osgood and Rankin. The church building now in use was erected about the year 1830, during the pastorate of the Rev. Mr. Rankin, who has been succeeded in turn by the Rev. Messrs. Gibb, Hall, Sabin, Hay, McDonald, and Rogers, the last of whom is present pastor.

The first clergyman of the Church of England sent to this settlement, was the Rev. Richard Knagg who remained three years. The next attempt to revive the interests of the Church here, was made by the Rev. H. Burrage of Hatley, who visited the place in 1840. A small church was organized, who met for worship in a place temporarily provided, and soon after, the colonial missionary society sent the Rev. W. L. Thompson to Stanstead. Through his efforts aided by friends of the enterprise, a convenient church edifice was erected, and the church has become a permanent institution. Mr. Thompson has been succeeded in turn by the Rev. H. Darnell and the Rev. A. A. Allen, present incumbent.

The sect called Adventists were introduced here in 1838, by the Rev. W. Miller who has been succeeded at different periods by the Messrs. Litch, Himes, Greene, Hutchinson and Orrock.

The house of worship at Fitch Bay belongs to the Congregational Church and society. It was dedicated October 21st, 1866; the Rev. L. P. Adams, pastor. Of the two church edifices in Georgeville, one belongs to the Church of England, the Rev. J. Thornloe, incumbent;

the other to the Wesleyan Methodists. Union houses have been built in other localities, that at Cassville being occupied by the Methodists and Freewill Baptists alternately.

Population of Stanstead given as 4,847 souls.

CHAPTER VIII.

WOLFE COUNTY.—DUDSWELL.—HAM.—SOUTH HAM.—STRATFORD
AND GARTHBY.—ST. CAMILLE.—WEEDON.—WOTTON.—
WOLFSTOWN.

THIS county contains the townships of Dudswell, Ham, South Ham, Stratford and Garthby, St. Camille, Weedon, Wotton and Wolfstown. The *chef-lieu* is South Ham. At present it is connected with Richmond county for electoral purposes.

DUDSWELL.

A tract of land lying within the district of Three Rivers, bounded north-east by Weedon, scuth-east by Bury, south-west by Stoke, and north-west by St. Camille, was erected into a township named Dudswell, May 13th, 1805. One-fourth of this was granted to the heirs of John Bishop, Napthali Bishop, Barnabas Barnum, Ebenezer Barnum, Jehiel Barnum, Stephen Barnum, Richard Barnum, Thomas Farlan, David Ferriss and Champion Smith.

John Bishop who had enlisted in the American revolutionary army, was taken prisoner by the British, and as such carried to Quebec. It appears that during this lengthened captivity, his uniform good conduct and obliging behavior, so far won upon the good will of those in charge of the prison, that as a mark of approbation and particular favor, he was granted access to books, and was likewise assisted in the study of mathematics for which he had a decided taste. Naturally gifted with quick perceptions and a retentive memory, and being withal of an observant and inquiring nature, he readily saw that in patiently resigning himself to the necessities of his situation, and improving his powers and opportunities to the utmost of his ability, he was fitting himself to meet any emergency that might arise.

By these means he acquired a knowledge of the science of surveying, which after his return home, was turned to practical account. He followed this profession several years in Vermont, during which time he married and settled in life, but at length decided on a removal to Canada.

Having formed valuable acquaintances with parties in Quebec during his compulsory sojourn in that city, he visited it again, this time voluntarily, and was highly favored in meeting with friends who were able and willing to forward his wishes and plans. He therefore took the preliminary steps toward obtaining for himself and associates the grant of a township of land. Next, he visited the tract designated, made some necessary preparation for a removal thither, and returned to Vermont. In October 1800, he brought his wife and seven children —the latter all under fifteen years of age—to the new home provided for them in the wilderness of Dudswell.

A widowed sister named Chaffee, and her son, accompanied the family, these being the first permanent residents of the tract. Owing to the wretched state of the roads, their waggon was left at Derby, Vermont, and the remainder of the journey made on horseback through ways almost impassable from the mud, till they reached the Little Forks. Here there were a few log dwellings, and from this point, the line was indicated by marked trees alone. Their progress was necessarily slow, eight or ten miles being considered a day's journey of this manner of travelling. Several families of associates came on to the ground soon after this.

Business connected with the settlement of which he was the head and founder, required Mr. Bishop to be frequently from home; during which journeys he was often a sufferer from fatigue and exposure. On one of them made in the month of March, he was taken sick and lay ill at the house of a friend about 14 miles from home, till the following June, when, anxious as he said, to reach his home to die, he was carefully conveyed to the river St. Francis, and brought in an Indian bark canoe to within a short distance of the home to which he was with difficulty removed, and from which he never again ventured, though he lived till August.

This distressing calamity fell with overwhelming

force upon the helpless family he left behind; and the sad event had the unhappy effect of deranging the entire plans for the settlement so auspiciously begun. Much of Mr. Bishop's success in obtaining the required number of associates, had been owing to his personal popularity as a man of energy, ability, and integrity, qualities that gave him great influence. Unfortunately his death took place at a time when the stability of the settlement was by no means assured; just at the critical period that required the assistance of his soundness of judgment and decision of character.

The conditions by which the charter of the township was to be obtained, had not to any great extent been complied with, yet several families had moved on to the premises in good faith, and many others had pledged themselves to do the same. But now that the leader in whom all confided, was gone, the latter declined further action in the matter.

In this doubtful state of the business, Napthali Bishop, a brother of the deceased, came forward to assume charge of his late relative's affairs; and after much embarrassment and delay, succeeded in obtaining a grant of one quarter of the township, by which means, titles to the lands that had been settled upon, were confirmed to the occupants.

In some portions of Dudswell, the land seems gently undulating and quite free from stones, while other sections are rough and hilly. To the north-west commence those elevated grounds, which after a gradual rise backward from the St. Francis, terminate in the Stoke mountains. Bishop's pond, west of the centre of the township, is something over a mile in length, by less than half that width. It is fed mostly by springs as only a few small rivulets find their way into it. Willard pond, farther to the north-east, is nearly of the same size, their outlets uniting to form a stream sufficiently large to carry mills. The St. Francis river flows directly through Dudswell, and is crossed by ferries at different points.

For the year 1866, the sum of $697,11, in all, was levied for school purposes; the government grant for the year being $82,18. There are an academy and nine elementary schools in the township.

Marbleton, a small village north of the centre of Dudswell, contains an English Church; two stores; a post office, public house, mills, and a variety of mechanical works; beside a collection of dwellings. Within a short distance are other mills. The place received its name from the quantities of marble that abound in its vicinity. Several varieties are found here; some white, some nearly black, but the greater part of a greyish hue, or veined and clouded with different shades of the same color. Some effort has been made toward opening and working a quarry in the village; but like many other enterprizes undertaken without adequate means or encouragent, it fell through. An excellent quality of lime is manufactured here, for which material is abundant.

FF

At a point where the stage road from Sherbrooke is intersected by the line coming from the ferry at East Dudswell, another post office called "Dudswell Corners" is located. The academy is in the same vicinity, also a public house; the section around being a rather thickly settled farming locality. The Methodist chapel, a neatly painted wooden structure, stands on the opposite side of Bishop's pond.

On the south-east side of the St. Francis is a settlement now known as East Dudswell, though formerly called Pequod, yet with what propriety, the imagination must conceive. There are still considerable tracts of unsettled land in the township.

The population is given as 669 English speaking inhabitants and 65 French Canadians.

HAM.

A tract of land lying within the district of Three Rivers, bounded north-east by Wolfestown, south-east by South Ham, south-west by Wotton, and north-west by Tingwick, was erected into a township named Ham, July 29, 1807. It appears, however, that little if anything had been done toward its settlement till a later date, as the census of 1861 gives it a population of only 606 French Canadians, and four English speaking inhabitants. It is a distinct municipality, and for the year 1866, the sum of $360,80, was levied for schools; the government grant being $68,96. Mineral indications exist within its limits, and mines have been worked to some extent. The nearest approach to a village in the township, is a small settlement containing a Roman Catholic chapel, a store, post office, and mills. A weekly mail arrives from Arthabaska station, 21 miles distant.

SOUTH HAM.

For many years this tract was known as the *augmentation* of Ham; during which period it was but a dreary solitude, broken upon only by the sound of the hunter's gun or the laborer's voice, as the line known as "Craig's road" was being constructed directly through it, connecting the townships south, with Quebec. In 1830, Israel Rice settled on this road within the augmentation, where for many years his house was a resort for all descriptions of travelers.

Later, however, other English speaking families have located here, and in November 1857, the tract was erected into a township named South Ham, which is not only a distinct municipality containing 114 English speaking, and 109 French Canadian inhabitants, but is also the *chef-lieu* for Wolfe County. In the year 1866, the sum of $154,00 was levied here for schools ; the government grant being $25,22. A mine of antimony has been opened in this township.

STRATFORD AND GARTHBY.

A tract in the district of St. Francis, bounded northeast by Price, south-east by Winslow, south-west by

Lingwick and Weedon, and north-west by Lake Aylmer and the river St. Francis which separate it from Garthby, containing 51,000 acres of land, was erected into a township named Stratford, April 3rd, 1856.

Another tract in the same district, bounded north-east by Coleraine, south-east by Lake Aylmer and the St. Francis river which separate it from Stratford, south-west by Weedon and South Ham, and north-west by Wolfestown, containing 46,000 acres of land, was erected a township named Garthby, May 25th, 1855.

These two townships are situated in a rough and hilly section of country, and are as yet but sparsely settled. They are united in one municipality; and for the year 1866 the sum of $63,00 was levied for schools; the government grant being $31,08. The population of Stratford is given as 413 souls; that of Garthby as 275.

ST. CAMILLE.

This is a small municipality formed from part of the original township of Wotton. It contains a Roman Catholic church, a post office and two stores, and weekly mails arrive here. For 1866, the sum of $139,00 was levied for schools; the government grant being $54,94. Its population is given as 479 French, and 7 English speaking inhabitants.

WEEDON.

A tract lying within the district of Three Rivers, bounded north-east by Garthby and Stratford, south-east by Lingwick, south-west by Dudswell and north-west by South Ham, containing 64,032 acres of land, was erected into a township named Weedon, February 28th, 1822; and granted to Louis Gugy, Augustin Gagnon, Michel St. Pierre, Joseph Germain, John Monroe, Margaret widow of Francois Lemaihe, Esq., Elizabeth and Margaret daughters of Francois Lemaihe, Mary Algers, and Charles Patterson.

The St. Francis river enters this township from lake Aylmer, and flowing some distance, expands into lake Louise. Again contracting, it receives the waters of Salmon river, and passes into Dudswell. Many other small streams and outlets of ponds also enter the St. Francis in Weedon. The inhabitants are almost exclusively French Canadians, and have a church, post office and schools. The sum levied for their support in 1866, was $934,46, the government grant being $91, 46. The stage road from Sherbrooke through Dudswell and Weedon, is continued on to the north-east. The census of 1861, gives it a population of 809 inhabitants.

WOTTON.

A tract lying in the district of St. Francis, bounded north-east by Ham, south-east by St. Camille, south-west by St. George de Windsor, and north-west by Shipton and Tingwick, containing 47,500 acres of land, was erected into a township named Wotton, June 2nd, 1849. This is an independent municipality, with a population of 1,504 French Canadians and 29 English speaking inhabitants.

For the year 1866, the sum of $561,92 was levied for schools; $173,32 being received from government. There are here a Roman Catholic church; also stores, mills, and a post office where a mail is received twice per week. Wotton is about ten miles east of Danville in Shipton, and 27 miles north from Sherbrooke.

WOLFESTOWN.

The tract in the district of Three Rivers, bounded north-east by Ireland, south-east by Garthby, south-west by Ham, and north-west by Chester and Halifax, was erected into a township named Wolfestown, and in part granted August 14th, 1802, to Nicholas Montour and his associates, viz., William Walsh, John Murphy, Luke Gaul, Pierce Kief, Mathew Reagan, Dennis Daly, Michael Broderick, and Timothy Lynch.

This township is the most northern in Wolfe County, or in the district of St. Francis. The nearest railway station is at Somerset on the Quebec road, twenty-two miles distant; from which, a weekly mail is brought here. A French church, stores, mills, &c., go to make up the settlement. In 1866, the sum of $597,21, was levied for schools; the government grant being $140,18.

Parts of this township are said to contain excellent agricultural land. It is an independent municipality as regards the management of its internal affairs, with

EASTERN TOWNSHIPS. 471

the exception that for local municipal convenience, the tenth and eleventh ranges are united with Ham.

The last census gives it a population of 354 English speaking, and 1,118 French Canadian inhabitants.

CONCLUSION.

In the foregoing pages we have considered these townships as when covered by primitive forests and the deep silence of nature was unbroken save by the hunter's gun or his victim's death-cry: have noted the earliest efforts made to plant the standard of civilization in these wilds, and marked the gradual disappearance of the forest beneath the vigorous arm of the settler: have recounted the labors, perils, and privations through which our forefathers struggled to gain subsistence and build up homes for themselves and families here; and have reviewed the well earned success that has finally crowned their efforts.

It has already been seen that most of our early settlers were men of limited means. In far off sections we hear of villages and towns springing into sudden wealth and prosperity from the influx of foreign capital; but here, unless in very exceptional cases, the people have been forced to depend on their own exertions. Before an enterprize requiring capital could be entered upon, the capital itself was to be created; and before this could be effected, it was often necessary to overcome many counteracting influences of which our people know full well.

Justice to ourselves requires that we take into account the fact that our own section is younger than some parts of the country, or than many porticns of the adjacent republic; and that till a very recent period of years, its condition has been unfavorable to progress in such pursuits as tend to advance and enrich a people speedily. Commerce was long confined to the cities; manufactures were in their infancy if in existence at all; and our agricultral products were limited in kind and quantity.

Now, however, affairs wear a changed aspect. The work of improvement has been slow to our impatient wishes, but in comparing the present of to-day, with the past of thirty and forty years, the change is surprising. Both material interests and educational improvements have made rapid advancement, and we have now arrived at the point which promises well for our future if we but prove true to our best and highest interests, and the moral improvement of our people keeps pace with their intellectual culture and material prosperity.

Our greatest danger in this age of progression—of becoming quickly rich—of unparallelled vicissitude, is that during the bustle in which we necessarily "move and have our being," we become so absorbed in the strife that our moral perceptions are obscured, and in prospect of immediate present acquirement and enjoyment, we lose sight of the legitimate ends and aims of life.

A people may become highly civilized, may advance in wealth, learning, and the arts; may possess cultivated and refined tastes, and even pay an exacting attention to the conventionalities of life, and yet be sadly wanting in that moral element which has its foundation only in Christian principle, and which in fact, is more conducive to the permanent prosperity of a nation, than would be all the wealth of the Indies or the learning of the schools.

Not by any means would we be misapprehended as under-valuing wealth; on the contrary, its possession is greatly to be desired as conferring legitimate advantages and opening numberless sources of enjoyment, beside giving power to benefit others; but as in the present age and existing state of society, it is in itself considered the passport to honor and power, and by so many is thought the *only* avenue open to distinction, its legitimate value should be understood as a *means* rather than an *end*.

Neither is learning to be lightly esteemed, for the day is long past when ignorance could be deemed the " Mother of devotion," and education is universally acknowledged an essential to the welfare and progress of a people.

But wealth, learning and refinement, may exist without that controlling moral principle which is necessary to restrain the passions and regulate the affections; and which, in connection with those advantages in individual cases of rare mental endowment, unite to produce the highest type of human character. The cultivation of this ennobling quality tends greatly to the elevation of a people in the scale of nations.

They have read history to little purpose, who have not seen that as a people become rich and self-inflated, and the over-mastering passions of human nature are allowed to rage unrestrainedly, divisions and distractions arise to undermine and weaken the body politic ; fearful changes are impending ; anarchy ensues ; and by degrees the people sink back to the level of a greatly lowered standard of national character.

We may profitably look back to the nations of antiquity, and in the history of their departed greatness, read the impressive truth that all prosperity is delusive which is founded on immorality and wrong ; and further, may rest assured that the most truly enlightened policy that can obtain in the councils of a people, is the earnest and consistent purpose to uphold the right. No time serving and double faced expediency ; no truckling and sycophantic subserviency ; no vascillating compromises between right and wrong, can be of lasting good.

Several of those early nations were far advanced in wealth, learning, and the arts, and in some respects are said to have even surpassed the efforts of modern genius ! " But where is all their glory gone ?"

When the inhabitants of our own " Mother Isle" were still barbarians, China was at the summit of her grandeur ; yet the oceans that separate Britain from the " Celestial Empire," are not wider in space, than is the moral difference now existing between the national characteristics and social systems of these two peoples.

THE END.

www.ingramcontent.com/pod-product-compliance
Lightning Source LLC
Chambersburg PA
CBHW051900300426
44117CB00006B/471